Praise for *Your First Year as a Nurse*, 2nd Edition

"Should be required reading for all new nurses, those who are recent grads, and those reentering the workforce. It is the most honest, practical, comprehensive, and straight-talking book available for nurses."

> —*LeAnn Thieman, coauthor of* Chicken Soup for the Nurse's Soul *and* Chicken Soup for the Nurse's Soul, Second Dose

"A must-read for all new graduates. Keep it under your pillow . . . and read it again and again. Think of it as your go-to best friend and guide to begin—and nourish—your career. It will help you fall and stay in love with the most wonderful career imaginable."

> —*Donna C. Maheady, EdD, ARNP; founder of ExceptionalNurse.com*

"Gives the reader an education on what can't necessarily be gleaned from school in a 'real life' format."

> —*Arlene Koch, RN; new hire support and retention coordinator, CES, Methodist Medical Center, Peoria, Illinois*

"The tips and information provided will make a positive difference in getting a job, surviving the first two years, and getting ahead in the nursing profession. It is informative and exciting to read."

> —*Leo-Felix M. Jurado, MA, RN, NE-BC; APN professor and chairperson, Department of Nursing, County College of Morris*

"Speaks to some of the most contemporary issues facing a new nurse: the anxieties of taking responsibility for patient-care decisions, the challenges of working with multidisciplinary teams, communicating and collaborating with physicians, and 'finding yourself' as a professional within a fast-paced, not always 'welcoming' environment. I recommend this read for any new nurse struggling to see the 'whole picture' and wanting to make their mark on the profession."

> —*Dr. Judy Boychuk Duchscher, RN, BScN, MN, PhD; assistant professor, Nursing University of Calgary*

Also Available in the Your First Year Series

Your First Year as an Elementary School Teacher
Your First Year as a High School Teacher
Your First Year in Sales
Your First Year in Real Estate

YOUR FIRST YEAR AS A

NURSE

2ND EDITION

MAKING THE TRANSITION FROM TOTAL NOVICE TO SUCCESSFUL PROFESSIONAL

DONNA WILK CARDILLO, RN

Best Wishes —
Donna
Cardillo

THREE RIVERS PRESS · NEW YORK

Copyright © 2001, 2010 by Three Rivers Press, a division of Random House, Inc.

Published in the United States by Three Rivers Press, an imprint of the
Crown Publishing Group, a division of Random House, Inc., New York.
www.crownpublishing.com

Three Rivers Press and the Tugboat design are registered trademarks of
Random House, Inc.

A previous edition of this work was published in the United States by Prima Publishing,
Roseville, California, and by Three Rivers Press, an imprint of the Crown Publishing Group,
a division of Random House, Inc., New York, in 2001.

Library of Congress Cataloging-in-Publication Data
Cardillo, Donna Wilk.
    Your first year as a nurse: making the transition from total novice to successful professional/
Donna Wilk Cardillo.—2nd ed.
        p. cm.
    Includes bibliographical references and index.
1. Nursing—Vocational guidance.   2. Nursing—Philosophy.   I. Title.
    [DNLM: 1. Nursing   2. Nurse's Role.   3. Professional Competence.
    4. Vocational Guidance.
    WY 16 C2707ya 2010]
    RT42.C32 2010
    610.7306'9—dc22   2010015562

ISBN 978-0-307-59174-6

Printed in the United States of America

10 9 8 7 6 5 4 3 2 1

Second Edition

To my husband,

Joseph,

who makes all things possible in my life.

CONTENTS

Graduation and pinning are joyful events: filled with anticipation—and uncertainty. You worked hard to get through nursing school and to pass the licensure examination. Your job interviews are scheduled, and, after reading this book, you will feel confident to meet with recruiters to discuss your first RN position. The day finally comes—orientation begins and reality strikes a chord of uncertainty as you receive your first assignment. As you come to realize that every nurse has started out in similar circumstances and made it through the novice stage of his or her career, you begin to settle in to your new environment.

There will be times, however, when uncertainty extends beyond the actions that you can control. Take, for example, the fact that economic conditions and other factors can cause the job market for new graduates to fluctuate. If you live in an area of the country where new graduate positions are scarce, you will find yourself questioning all that you have read and been told about the nursing shortage. You may have student loans to repay and perhaps a family to care for in addition to supporting yourself.

Chapters 10 and 11 will help you navigate the new health services landscape, especially if you are having difficulty finding your first RN position. In chapter 10, "Professional Practice Issues," pay close attention to the details on how to protect the most important credential you will ever possess—your nursing license. Chapter 11, "Career Conundrums," addresses how new nurses entering the workforce are affected by the complex relationship between economics and the nursing workforce, the anticipated loss of RNs to retirement, and the aging population. Other chapters cover vital information to get your career off to the best possible start. Read this book from cover to cover to optimize the value of its many nurses' stories and journeys. Make notes. Abundant lessons are contained throughout.

At any point in a nurse's career, he or she may be faced with an unanticipated challenge. It is important to remain positive and seek solutions; when one door closes, many new doors open, and behind every door is another opportunity. One aspect of the nursing profession that will never change is the vast array of work settings and specialties to explore. When I first joined the nursing workforce as a new graduate, there was an oversupply of RNs. As a diploma school graduate, I chose to go immediately on for a BSN. I worked part time while in school, which gave me some leverage when I completed the degree and went searching for a full-time job. With only one job offer, I had to relocate and work nights on a unit I did not feel ready for (ICU). To my surprise, I found that I loved working nights and that the ICU was a good fit for me! What's more, relocating gave me the opportunity to explore new experiences and friendships that I still cherish today.

Whether you are facing uncertainty about your ability as an RN or about landing your first RN position, approach the future with an open mind and explore every option available to you. Maintaining self-confidence and a positive attitude are essential. Strive to be the best nurse possible and you will not fail!

Congratulations and best wishes for a successful nursing career.

Diane J. Mancino, EdD, RN, CAE
Executive Director
National Student Nurses' Association, Inc.

ACKNOWLEDGMENTS

No one ever succeeds alone, and I am no exception. There are so many people to thank who have helped in immeasurable ways to make this second edition, as well as the original version, a reality.

Diane Mancino, for writing the preface. A very special thanks, for I appreciate your interest and enthusiasm in this project, along with your help and support, more than you know.

Laura Gasparis Vonfrolio, my friend, mentor, and role model, who is always looking to support and encourage nurses, including myself, to reach new heights. The original version of this book would not have happened without you.

Jeanne Beaugard and Rosemary Farrell, who are my friends and colleagues and two of the best nurses I know, for your support, input, feedback, proofreading, ideas, and enthusiasm about this project. You are both very special people.

To all the nurses in the United States and Canada who either shared stories and information or helped in some way, your generosity of spirit and commitment to nursing are outstanding. You are all a tribute to this profession and I admire each and every one of you: Donna Angelucci, Sue Ruck, Joan Orseck, Barbara Paragoris, Cheryl Szenasi, Ann Heiss, Carol Paterson, Jennifer Cooper, Sarah Perry, Rob Girotti, Linda Toth, Cathy Gallo, Lori Radcliffe-Allen, Claire Ocampo, Pat Bemis, Joni Boyd, Kelly Kay, Paula Murphy, Grant Tomlinson,

Sue Bookey-Bassett, Bob Giusti, Michele Helias-Willem, Charlene Barbour, Lois Regan, Bob Smith, Paula Schneider, Vickie Gustafson, Leo-Felix Jurado, Donna Maheady, Patti Rager, Lucille Joel, Scott DeBoer, Shannon Sanford, Kevin Hawkins, Rich Cipollino, Sanna Henzi, Bill Getman, Pennie Coleman, Norma Rodgers-Hunter, Victoria Hunter, Barry Harris, Kevin King, Justine Mize, Honey Beddingfield, Scott Eddy, Tom Alicandri, Barbara Gleba, Cary Cook, Rebecca Caswell, Wendie Howland, Mary Stone, and Stacy E. Wahl and the North Shore University Hospital novice nurse night-shift support group.

My husband, Joe; my parents, Helen and Stanley Wilk; my sister and brother, Barbara Bastian and Ed Wilk; all of whom I can always count on for words of wisdom, encouragement, and support. Thanks for always believing in me.

My wonderful son and daughters, David, Pia, and Justyna Cardillo; my precious grandsons, Joao "Junior" Miguel and Sebastian Alexander; my mother-in-law, Rose; my brothers- and sisters-in-law and nieces and nephews: Barry, Nancy, Eugene, Linda, Paul, Pam, Mimi, Anna, Andrew, Matthew, Lily Belle, Max, and Jasper, thanks for your support, enthusiasm, and interest. You all add so much to my life.

INTRODUCTION

To say that the nursing profession has changed over the last few decades would be the understatement of the century. Today's nurse is more educated and skillful, uses more critical thinking skills, is more autonomous, makes more decisions, and has more responsibility than ever before. We've come a long way in the recent past and continue to move forward.

And that's not all that has changed. Traditionally, nursing students were almost exclusively women right out of high school. Today, there are more men entering the profession all the time. In addition, many men and women are coming into nursing as a second, third, or fourth career—many in midlife and some even later in life. I often hear, "I always wanted to be a nurse and now I am finally doing it," or, "I never considered nursing as an option until now." Of course, there are still plenty of young men and women who come to nursing directly out of high school.

What hasn't changed, in my opinion, is that nursing is still the greatest profession. In spite of all the changes, it still offers rich and diverse opportunities. Where else can you use both your heart and your head, be challenged every day, and make an enormous impact in the lives of others?

Some of the major challenges facing nurses today are short staffing, sicker patients, shorter hospital stays, and limited financial resources. Everyone is expected to do more with less, and that is not just in health care. Ask anyone in any profession today. We're all working differently than in the past.

Many negative stories about the nursing profession seem to be circulating recently, either in the news or from unhappy nurses. But I have some good news for you: In the course of researching and writing this book, I interviewed scores of new and recent graduates, and 99 percent told me the most wonderful and heartwarming stories about the help and support they get from their coworkers and superiors, the joy of helping others, and how they are thriving and moving forward in spite of the challenges. I also interviewed experienced nurses who spoke of a profession that offers them great rewards as well as endless opportunities for professional and personal growth. Unfortunately, the positive stories don't seem to get much airtime, while the negative stories get told over and over again. In this book, I share with you many of the wonderful stories I heard and my own experiences.

After speaking with so many new and recent graduates, I am inspired and encouraged by your strength, dedication, and intelligence. I have great faith in you all and renewed faith in the future of this profession. I am counting on you to carry on the fine traditions of nursing. I can't wait to see what you all do next and where you take this profession in the future. I know you will be great.

Once you enter this profession, you will never be the same. Your life will be forever changed. You will develop an appreciation for life and a respect for death beyond that of the average person. You will see the best and the worst of the human spirit, and you will become a better, more compassionate person because of this. You will walk the path of the healer and illuminate the darkness for those you help. Your life and your work will have meaning and sacredness. You will come to understand the meaning of life and death.

Not for one minute have I regretted becoming a nurse. Nor have the great majority of my colleagues. It has been my privilege and my pleasure to be a part of this wonderful profession for well over twenty years, and it is my conclusion that there is no more noble profession on the planet. I have never once been bored or been at a loss for something new and different to do, and I have always felt that I was making a difference and contributing to the world in a big way.

I want to personally welcome you into my beloved profession—nursing. I look forward to calling you "colleague."

YOUR FIRST YEAR AS A NURSE

2ND EDITION

CHAPTER 1

YOUR NEW CAREER

It's your first day as a nurse and, boy, are you nervous. Did you make the right decision? Is this the right career for you? Can you handle the responsibility? The nervousness, anxiety, and indecision are normal. When the reality of your chosen profession becomes evident, it can be overwhelming. But never lose sight of the reason you chose to enter this glorious profession—to help others, make a difference, and make the world a better place to be. That's what it's all about.

Most of us start out scared, nervous, and perhaps even feeling inadequate. Remember that after the end of your first day on the new job, you'll be more experienced than you were that morning. After each day, you will be further along than you were the day before. Before you know it, days will turn into weeks, weeks into months, and finally you'll find yourself with a full year of experience under your belt!

It's important, in this early phase of your career, to set small, realistic goals for yourself. Set an initial goal to get through orientation. Then set a goal to get through your first three months, then six months, and then one year. Most experienced nurses agree that it takes about a year before you feel comfortable with most common situations. It will probably take two years to be completely comfortable with all situations. So be patient and just persevere.

In many ways, your education is just beginning. I used to say, jokingly, that I never learned anything until I got out of nursing school. Although that isn't completely accurate, when I was finally working on my own as a nurse and was out of the student mode and no longer in the safe confines of my instructor's wing, it sometimes felt like as if I were starting from scratch. For certain, I'll never forget how overwhelmed and scared I felt the first time I was handed the narcotics keys to hold on to through my shift. I wanted to say, "Oh, you've made a mistake. I'm not responsible enough to carry these keys." I suddenly realized the responsibility I had. I wondered if I could meet everyone's expectations.

Nursing in North America

While there are some minor differences, such as in credentials and terminology, nursing in the United States and nursing in Canada are very similar. The biggest difference is that Canadian nurses work within a national health-care system and nurses in the United States work in a largely private system. This does not, however, translate into a significant difference in day-to-day practice.

Nurses in the United States are licensed by the state(s) in which they practice, and Canadian nurses are likewise licensed by the appropriate province or territory. Nurses in the United States who are involved in clinical practice should obtain their own malpractice insurance in addition to the coverage they may or may not have from their employer. With the exception of advanced practice nurses, this is a much less common practice in Canada, where the legal climate is very different. In Canada, employers often cover nurses for liability, though most have additional coverage through their provincial and national nursing associations. However, the Canadian legal climate is changing. More and more nurses are being named in lawsuits. Potential litigation is a concern for every nurse to take seriously.

Both Canada and the United States utilize nurse practitioners (NPs) and clinical nurse specialists (CNSs). Both countries also utilize practical nurses, although their titles may vary depending on which part of the continent they are practicing. You will find licensed practical nurses (LPNs) and licensed vocational nurses (LVNs) in the United States. In Canada, there are registered practical nurses (RPNs), LPNs, as well as several other titles, though the trend is to use only the title LPN across the country. When nurses are licensed in Canadian provinces other than Quebec and Ontario, where membership is left to individual choice, they automatically become members of their provincial and national nurses association, the Canadian Nurses Association (CNA). In the United States, professional association memberships are completely up to each nurse.

Despite such minor differences, nurses in Canada and the United States have the same challenges, rewards, goals, frustrations, and joys.

I also remember how I would gaze at more-experienced nurses with awe. They seemed so confident, so in control, so calm in a crisis, and so all-knowing. I couldn't imagine that I would ever reach that level of practice.

But an amazing thing happened along the way. Not only did I continue to learn and grow in my new career, but here I am, more than twenty years later, loving every minute of this wonderful profession and giving advice to other nurses. I've come a long way from being a scared, self-conscious rookie nurse who thought that the person who gave me the narcotics keys was not thinking clearly. You, too, will someday look back and see how far you have come.

Externship Versus Internship

An externship differs from an internship. While an externship or "summer nursing associate program" is usually available to student nurses, an internship or nurse residency program is usually offered to a new RN as intensified training during his or her first year of employment and/or in preparation for working in specialty areas such as the intensive care unit (ICU), the operating room (OR), and labor and delivery (L&D).

Many externs continue to work part time at that facility until they graduate. Not only does an externship give them significant clinical and leadership skills, but the experience looks great on their resume and gives them a foot in the door for possible hire after graduation.

Internships for new RNs vary in type and scope and are different from general employee orientation. Some have been developed by the individual hospital or

health system, and others are part of a nationally developed curriculum. Characteristics of internship/residency programs may include the following:

- Classroom and skills lab instruction
- Online learning opportunities
- Unit-based clinical experience with preceptor
- Mentors
- Support/self-care groups
- "Looping" to other related units in the facility

It is in your best interest to find the longest and most comprehensive new
graduate orientation/internship program available. A one-year program is ideal and
very desirable. However, not every facility offers this.

In fact, you've already come a long way. Phase one of your nursing education and training was your formal schooling. Consider your first job as a nurse
to be phase two.

Don't be too hard on yourself in the beginning. You're not expected to
know everything as a new graduate. In fact, no one—not even the most experienced nurse, doctor, or other practitioner—knows everything. For each of us,
myself included, learning is an ongoing process. If you're not learning, you're
stagnating.

So now it is time to begin phase two of your learning process: your first job.
Where do you start? What do you need to know? The key to getting the job you
want is to have a plan, prepare, and dive in!

PREPARING TO LAND YOUR FIRST JOB AS A NURSE

How can you enhance your education and experiences and thus improve your
chances of getting the job you want from the start? There are many ways.

While you're still a student look for hospitals that offer externship programs.
Often run during the summer months, these are programs specifically for stu-

dent nurses. You will work in the clinical area with a preceptor—an experienced nurse who is assigned to work closely with you, show you the ropes, assist you in performing procedures, and make sure you learn what you need to know.

In addition, most health-care facilities offer tech positions, such as emergency department (ED) tech and electrocardiograph (ECG) tech. Many nursing students also work as nurse's aides or as patient care assistants (PCAs). As a student nurse with some additional training, you may qualify to become a licensed or certified nursing assistant (CNA). If long-term care is in your future, working as a physical therapy aide can be a great experience. Check with the nurse recruiter or human resources department in several local facilities to see what your options are.

Consider any part-time job in the health-care field that will enhance your experience, particularly if it will increase your familiarity with a facility where you might want to work after graduation. By working part time, you will increase your contacts at that facility and have the opportunity to display your skills and demonstrate your work ethic. These types of positions will help you develop that critical sense of autonomy that you need to be successful as you work independently, rather than as a student nurse.

> *"Don't worry if you're not offered every job you apply for. I was rejected at two hospitals when I first got out of school. That's okay, because I eventually found a great place to work, with a manager who is totally supportive."*
>
> —Bill, new grad

Learn everything you can—every day. Apply yourself. Show up for class and clinicals. Stay for pre- and post-clinical conferences. Listen to and learn from your fellow students and their patients' experiences. This *is* your future. Prepare, prepare, prepare. Take advantage of every learning opportunity that comes your way.

Look for opportunities to enhance your credentials and experience. Obtain cardiopulmonary resuscitation (CPR) or advanced cardiac life support (ACLS) certification from the American Heart Association or its Canadian equivalent, the Heart and Stroke Foundation of Canada. Although any acute care hospital will certify you in CPR, having it before you are hired gives you a competitive edge, and with it, you will feel more secure in the clinical arena. Finally, enhancing your computer skills is a good foundation for any job.

Be sure to become active in the National Student Nurses Association (NSNA) or the Canadian Nursing Students' Association (CNSA). Each offers nursing students leadership and career development opportunities as well as tangible benefits such as malpractice and health insurance.

Attend both the state student nurse and state chapter of the American Nurses Association's (ANA) annual conventions. Be sure to dress your professional best—in a business suit or other business attire. You'll find exhibitors from various health-care facilities—prospective employers—and representatives from educational institutions, professional associations, and companies that have products and services of interest to nurses.

These professional gatherings are a great place to find out which facilities are offering externship or internship programs, what their graduate orientation program entails, what specialty areas are available at each facility, and however else they may be suited to you. You can start planning for your future at these events. It's never too soon to start making contacts and gathering information for your future. Networking—making personal contacts and connections—at events like these is the best way to land the job of your choice.

What Is the Right First Job for You?

If jobs are plentiful in your area, you can be somewhat selective about your first job. The job market is predicted to be good for nurses for the foreseeable future, but the nursing job market fluctuates just like the stock market. There will always be excesses and shortages. If jobs are scarce in your area, you may have to be less picky, but you should still evaluate carefully every job offer presented to you. (See chapter 11 for tips on finding a position in a tight job market.) It is ideal to choose a facility that offers a strong orientation program and has good educational support services in place (such as unit educators, ongoing in-service, internships, and so on). You will be building a foundation at your first job, and your first year in practice is critical.

Educate Yourself

The following are some questions you should ask any potential employer:

- What specialties are available to new graduates?
- Do you have internship programs?
- What does your new-graduate orientation program consist of?
- Do you allow time off for seminars and continuing education?
- What type of ongoing, in-house, in-service training is available?
- Do you have unit-based educators?
- Are the educators available on all shifts?
- How long will I work with a preceptor?

What's Really Important?

While money is important, it should never be your primary consideration. When all is said and done, all the money in the world won't make up for a bad work environment or lack of support.

Benefits are also important and may be more valuable to you than the base salary. Consider what, if anything, you will have to contribute to these. Aside from the usual benefits of health and life insurance, ask about tuition reimbursement. Continuing your formal education is an important part of your professional development and ongoing career management, and considering the cost of higher education, tuition reimbursement is a precious commodity. While retirement is a long way off for some, scrutinize retirement plans, especially plans in which the employer contributes. Most facilities have printed material listing all the benefits for your position, so be sure to compare the benefits from one employer to another.

What You Need to Know About Any Job

Know exactly what you are getting into before you get into it. Always carefully read a copy of the job description, and ask the following questions:

- Will I be required to work on weekends and holidays?
- Will I have to take call?
- How are performance evaluations done and how often?
- Will I be required to float—do shift work?

Find out the answers to these important questions *before* you start.

You should also ask around and find out which facilities have the best reputation for nursing in your area. Ask your nursing instructors, physicians you know, and especially other nurses. Listen to your gut, too. Is it a place where you would feel comfortable working?

HOW TO GET THE JOB YOU WANT

Networking is *always* your best way of finding the right job. Simply put, networking is making personal contacts and connections with people in your field of interest. It's talking to people whom you already know and letting them know what you're looking for. It's also meeting and making contact with new people at career fairs and career days, professional association meetings, conventions, and facility open houses.

Making direct contact with nurse recruiters in facilities you are interested in is also a good approach. Call them; write to them; e-mail them; connect with them on Twitter, LinkedIn, and Facebook; or present yourself in person.

It's All About You

Whenever you are making face-to-face contact with a potential employer, your appearance is critical. First impressions are made in as little as three seconds, and once they are in place, they are lasting. The first impression you make, good or bad, will influence the decision of whether or not to hire you.

For job fairs, interviews, professional organization meetings, and anything else career-related, always dress sharp. A business suit is your best bet for interviewing or making initial contacts at events such as job fairs or conventions. Stick to conservative and traditional styles and colors, and minimize accessories.

In addition to a professional appearance, nurse recruiters are looking for someone who makes good eye contact, smiles, extends a hand to shake, and engages in conversation. They are impressed by someone who acts in a professional manner, is courteous and polite, and is able to interact well. Nursing is a people-oriented job. Recruiters and prospective employers are looking just as much for a personality as they are for someone's credentials. *Never* get complacent or cocky about your credentials. You must still prove yourself.

> ## FROM THE FRONT LINE
>
> *"I recall a time that a nurse came in for an interview wearing two different earrings. I couldn't take my eyes off her earlobes! It was so distracting. Every time I looked at her, I found my attention drifting from one lobe to the other. I barely heard what she said. I don't even remember if I hired her. The only thing I can remember is that she was wearing two different earrings."*
>
> —Carol, nurse recruiter

If you have a specialty, unit, or shift preference, let the recruiter know, but your first priority is to express your willingness to get started in any area of nursing and your openness to other opportunities. Flexibility makes you very desirable in a recruiter's eyes.

Always send a thank-you note to the interviewer after an interview, regardless of your interest in the job. It's also a good idea to send one to any recruiters you meet at a job fair. Remember, networking is critical, and even if you don't need someone's assistance right now, you may in the future. Use a thank-you note to express what a pleasure it was to meet the person and thank him or her for taking the time to speak with you. Express your interest in the facility and the opportunities discussed, and convey that you look forward to hearing from him or her. This is a sure way to solidify yourself in a recruiter's mind. Make the best impression by sending a word-processed note on good-quality paper. Although this may sound old-fashioned, it will favorably impress even the most technology-dependent person. A quick e-mail immediately after the interview is great, but follow it with a formal hard-copy note.

Ideally, your professional appearance and approach will pay off, and you will get the job you are seeking. Now it is time to prepare for your first day and beyond. Your new career is about to begin.

Where There's a Will, There's a Way

Jennifer always wanted to be an operating room (OR) nurse. She knew it wasn't always easy for new graduates to break into specialty areas, but that didn't deter her. While still a student, she was offered a chance to do an externship in a specialty of her choice at a nearby hospital. Jennifer naturally chose the OR. She spent three weeks in a concentrated program at a special-surgery hospital.

Jennifer's next step was to participate in a community college's externship being offered to RNs. The college was a considerable distance from Jennifer's home, and because she was only a student and not an RN, she was able to attend the classroom portion of this program but not the clinical portion. Because she felt this experience would bring her one step closer to her goal, she didn't mind the travel or the limitations.

After graduation, Jennifer increased her experience and credentials by joining the Association of periOperative Registered Nurses (AORN) and pursuing advanced cardiac life support (ACLS) certification—before she had a job as an RN. "I was willing to do anything that would spark some conversation during an interview. Also, these things gave me something extra to offer—something to put on my resume."

Jennifer later accepted a position in a plastic surgeon's office that had an OR on site. Six months after that, Jennifer landed the job of her dreams. Today, three and a half years after graduating, she remains in that dream job in the pediatric transplant OR of a prestigious hospital, where she works with some world-renowned surgeons. She loves what she does and knows she is making a difference.

Like Jennifer, you will find obstacles—some big, some trivial—at each step toward your goal. Overcome them. Persistence and determination will always win out in the end!

EVERYTHING YOU NEED TO DO BEFORE YOUR FIRST DAY

So you have landed your first nursing job in what hopefully will be a long, fulfilling, and rewarding career in nursing. All those long nights of studying and the hard work have paid off. You're ready to be a nurse, right? Not quite. There are several things that you must address before you actually begin your first job as a nurse.

Get a Copy of Your Job Description and Read It!

Every job has a job description. A job description outlines the requirements and responsibilities of your specific position. To do your job correctly and excel at it, you must know what is expected of you and what you need to do to meet and exceed those expectations.

While taking time to read your job description and understand your responsibilities may sound fundamental, most people don't do it. As a result, they have little idea what their job really entails before they clock in for that all-important first day. They aren't clear on what they should or shouldn't be doing, which is critical in any type of patient-care environment. Start your nursing career off right by reading and understanding your job description and knowing your responsibilities.

Read and Understand Your Nurse Practice Act

This document, which should have come in the mail with your license, outlines exactly what your license permits you to do in the state in which you are licensed. You must practice only within the limits of this act. Obviously, it is critical that you understand *exactly* what you are permitted and not permitted to do. Read it and know it.

Obtain and Understand Your Employer's Organizational Chart

An organizational chart illustrates the structure and flow of every department at your new facility. It also illustrates how every employee fits into the facility. Understand the hierarchy of your organization and see where the nursing department and your unit fall in this structure. Learn what the exact chain of command is in your unit. This is a good start to learning who you need to go to for what, and it also serves as a way to "meet" your colleagues and superiors so you can recognize them as time goes on. You may not be able to get your hands on the organizational chart before you start, but most likely you can during orientation.

Learn as Much About the Facility as You Can

You should have some knowledge of the facility and organization from your interview preparation, but you need to learn as much as you can before your first day. Visiting a facility's or company's website is a great way to start. See who owns the facility, who the parent company is, what other hospitals and health-care facilities are members of the group, who the officers are, where the parent company's headquarters are, what major services the facility or corporation offers, and so on. Read any corporate literature you acquired during and before the interview process. Annual reports, brochures, the company's mission statement, as well as any other marketing materials are full of information you need to know.

The more you learn about the parent company and the individual facility, the better prepared and the more comfortable you'll be. Your knowledge will start to give you a sense of belonging and familiarity with your new employer and help you feel part of the family, even before your first day.

Join and Become Active in Professional Nursing Associations

Earlier, I mentioned the importance of student membership in professional organizations. Now it's time for the big leagues. Don't think about it and don't delay: Just do it. Join the American Nurses Association as well as your state chapter (go to www.nursingworld.org and click on "Constituent Member Associations"). Get out to meetings and special events. Network! Do it now, and you will always be grateful. Wait until later, and you will eventually wonder why you waited. Some associations have reduced dues for your first year out of school. Take advantage of them.

Get Professional Liability Insurance

Ask a colleague or your instructors or call your student or state nurses association for contact information. Even if a facility states that it covers you for liability, you should acquire this relatively inexpensive insurance on your own in addition to your employer's coverage. Consult an insurance agent and attorney to advise you further on this issue.

Questions to Ask the Recruiter or Human Resources Representative

- What time should I arrive on my first day?
- What is considered appropriate attire for my position?
- Is there a written dress code? How can I obtain a copy?
- What supplies or other items should I bring?
- When is orientation? Where will it be held? What does the first day of orientation consist of?
- Will the orientation be held only for recent nursing graduates or will new hires from other disciplines also be in attendance?

The more information you have about your first day and what to expect, the better prepared and less nervous you will be.

Buy a Pocket Drug Reference Book

Don't leave home without it. Carry it with you at all times while at work. Familiarize yourself with its layout, how it cross-references, and how you can best apply its information. And be sure you always have the most up-to-date version available. You might also use a non-phone PDA or pocket PC, but be absolutely sure to check your employer's policy on the use of any device, including cell phones, beforehand.

Personal Technology Warning

Several health-care professionals have been fired and disciplined in recent years after taking photos in the workplace and posting them on Facebook or other social media sites. Likewise, there are nurses who send tweets on Twitter and write posts on Facebook about patients and their workplace while on duty. Not only is this inappropriate, but it may violate confidentiality laws and policies as well as employer regulations about cell phone and Internet use while working.

YOUR NEW JOB

You've made it! You've acquired your first job as a nurse. Now what? Well, there is more to it than just showing up. You need to know the best ways to make a favorable impression on everyone you deal with—from patients to the countless colleagues and superiors you will meet. You also need to know how to get the most out of your orientation period and how to keep track and a record of the endless but useful information to which you will be exposed.

First-Day Checklist

What to bring:

- Notebook and pen
- Name badge (if given one)
- Parking and meal pass (if applicable)
- Your licenses and certifications
- Several copies of your resume

- Employee handbook
- Job description
- Corporate literature
- Any other documents and information you were given to read or review

Creating a Positive First Impression

I've already mentioned that first impressions are made in as little as three seconds. If that first impression is negative, it is very difficult to shake. First impressions are powerful, and people trust them. We all get a sense about other people when we first meet them, and that sense is based on the first impression. People make decisions, often on an unconscious basis, on whether to trust others, to listen to what they have to say, and to like or dislike them from first impressions. Your job is people-oriented. It should be clear why making a good first impression in every aspect of your professional life is important.

From the first time you meet a prospective employer at a career fair, convention, or open house, you will either be remembered or not. And, if you are remembered, it will either be in a positive, uncertain, or negative light. Your aim is to be remembered for good reasons—because you are professional, courteous, and knowledgeable.

What You See Is What You Get

Although you've already made an impression on the people who hired you, you will be meeting a lot of new people as you begin your new phase in life. Your overall appearance is one of the biggest factors contributing to first impressions. This includes your clothing, accessories, grooming, posture, facial expressions, gestures, and eye contact.

Many nurses think that their appearance doesn't matter. They believe how they tend to their patients is what really counts. And while it's true that your nursing care is the most important thing, taking care of your appearance is actually part of that care. People get a sense, based on your appearance, of whether you are a competent, credible person. Would you want someone unkempt and disheveled looking to change your dressing or hook up a new IV on your child?

FROM THE FRONT LINE

That First Job

"Take an active role in choosing your first hospital. Find a supportive environment to work in. Not just supportive coworkers, but a supportive orientation program. Find out the culture of each hospital. Talk to nurses who work there, ask your instructors, and ask previous graduates. Get referrals from the National Student Nurses Association members who worked there."

—Bill, new grad

"My first job is in the neonatal intensive care unit (NICU) in my home province in Canada. I have found that each hospital here has different expectations. In the province where I attended college, a new graduate could not get a job in a NICU—you had to have at least two years' pediatric experience. However, I was offered a job in both a pediatric emergency room (PER) and a pediatric intensive care unit (PICU) in the province where I went to college but couldn't get a position in either a PER or PICU in my home province even though I had done an externship in general pediatrics and in an adult ER as a student. It's all different."

—Victoria, new grad

"There was already a nursing shortage when I was getting ready to graduate. Before graduation, my friend and I attended a hospital open house. One of the nurses talked to us for ten minutes and hired us on the spot for an oncology unit. We readily accepted. Almost as an afterthought, she asked if we had a resume or something with our phone number on it. When I mentioned all of this to one of my instructors, she cautioned me about taking a job where there seemed to be almost a desperation to hire nurses. Boy was she ever right. I quickly discovered that almost all of the nurses on the floor were new graduates like myself. There really wasn't anyone to ask for help. Even my preceptor had been out of school less than a year."

—Shannon, new grad

No, and neither will your patients and their families. You've heard the expression "What you see is what you get." That's exactly how people react when they first encounter you. What they perceive about you from your appearance and demeanor is what they presume they will get in terms of care and treatment. To your colleagues, superiors, and patients, perception is reality. This means that regardless of who a person is or what he or she does, his or her perception of you will determine how you are treated and regarded.

How can you make the best possible first impression? Whether wearing a uniform, scrubs, or street attire, your clothes should be cleaned, pressed, and in good condition. Your shoes, whether pumps, oxfords, clogs, or other work-related footwear, should be polished and in good repair.

Always dress your best and be impeccably groomed. Being neat and clean is extremely important. Know the dress code of your employer and be certain to adhere to it. Even if others don't, it doesn't mean no one notices. People notice, especially supervisors. Your hair should be clean and off your face and shoulders. This is a matter of practicality as well. Fingernails should be trim and clean. Long and artificial nails can harbor bacteria. Be a healer, not a carrier.

You will be very close to many people in the clinical environment, both co-workers and patients. Out of courtesy and respect for them, keep yourself free of body odor, including offensive breath. It is best to avoid wearing perfumes and cologne in any health-care setting because many people are allergic to scents or just don't like them.

You should also maintain a conservative appearance. Keep your jewelry and accessories simple and tasteful. This is part of a professional appearance. It's hard to have confidence in someone who is wearing dangling earrings that clink and clank with every move or is wearing bright orange nail polish. Would you rather that patients and coworkers listen to what you have to say or be distracted by your outfit and accessories?

A Strong Impression

Years ago, I worked with a nurse who would come to work reeking of perfume. The scent was so strong that it was offensive. In fact, the overwhelming scent made me nauseous when I was close to her. Imagine how her patients must have felt, especially the ones who were already nauseous! A few people, including our supervisor, mentioned this concern to her, but my coworker didn't care.

To find her, we would look around, sniff the air, and joke, "I think she went that way." To make matters worse, she kept a bottle of this perfume in a communal locker shared by the nurses—and would redouse herself during her break.

Periodically, the bottle of perfume would "mysteriously" disappear from the locker. Of course, she would start asking around as to where her perfume was. And, of course, no one ever claimed to know what could possibly have happened to it. Unfortunately, she always brought another bottle soon after.

Obviously, this is an example of the type of impression and memory of yourself that you *do not* want to create.

Greet everyone you meet, when appropriate, with a full, firm handshake while making eye contact and smiling. Be friendly and enthusiastic. Show interest in other people. Sit up front for the orientation. Ask pertinent questions. Don't overpower, but get involved. Have lunch with people you don't know. Ask them about themselves. Be courteous and polite. Be respectful to everyone. The basic rules of decency and social etiquette go a long way in making the right impression.

First impressions are an ongoing issue in your professional life. You will meet new people more days than you don't in this line of work. You must project a professional image for yourself, your department, and your facility. Your image and the impressions you create will impact your relationship with your coworkers, physicians, supervisors, patients and their families, administrators, and everyone else. Keep in mind that you are a representative of the nursing profession. Whatever impression people have of you will translate into an impression they have of the whole profession. Learn the power of a positive image and make it work for you.

ORIENTATION

Many new nurses will start out working in an acute care hospital. Some will start out in long-term or sub-acute care or in other areas, including working in a physician's or nurse practitioner's office, clinic, or another alternate care setting.

Your orientation and work experience will vary in each of these settings, so we'll discuss each by category.

Acute Care Orientation

Most acute care hospitals offer three- to six-month orientation/internship programs for new graduates, although some offer year-long programs. This is a time to learn the ins and outs of the facility you'll be working for, meet some key people, and familiarize yourself with your unit and important hospital and nursing procedures. It is also a time to hone important clinical skills, gain experience under the watchful eye of a preceptor/educator, and get acclimated to your new environment.

Culture Shock

Claire practiced nursing for four years in her native Philippines before coming to the United States a year ago. She was looking for greater challenges in her professional life and wanted to experience "something different." She said half jokingly, half serious, "I think I got more than I bargained for in that regard."

She continues,

> I had to take all the exams for foreign graduated nurses in order to be eligible to sit for nursing boards (NCLEX-RN) in the United States. I prepared for those tests on my own by using review books. I also had to do all the paperwork for getting licensed here. When I finally became a licensed RN, I began working part time in a nursing home and part time in a hospital on a telemetry (heart monitor) unit.
>
> Nursing is very different in the United States than in the Philippines. Nurses here have much more responsibility. For example, back home, nurses don't start IVs. In the Philippines, most hospitals are teaching hospitals, so the residents and medical students do most of the procedures. There, the charge nurse was the one who had primary contact with the physicians. In the United States, nurses are

much more independent. Here, all nurses have regular contact with the doctors, start the IVs, use more critical thinking skills, and do *everything*. Nursing is also much more complicated here. In the Philippines, we were not so involved with families and discharge planning and case management. There are also much greater legal implications here. You have to be responsible for your own actions. So even though I have four years' experience working in the Philippines, I am starting as a new graduate here because I have so many new things to learn. Plus, I'm dealing with all the cultural differences.

In addition to all the new nursing skills I had to learn, I was also dealing with my new coworkers, who have different values from me. In the United States, you have to be direct and straightforward. You have to say what's on your mind. We're not so direct in the Philippines, so I have to adjust. I have to assert myself in terms of my job.

What advice would Claire give to other foreign-educated nurses from non-English-speaking countries?

Work on your English language skills. It will help you with your initial test taking as well as to assimilate into the new culture. Study a lot for your nursing boards. Be prepared for hard work, and hang in there. I see some new grads from the United States going through the same things as me, but they can adjust better because they don't have the cultural and language thing to deal with.

On the good side, I am inspired by my patients' attitudes toward me. When I do things for them, they tell me it is a great help. Many of the nursing home residents are helpless, and they really depend on me. It makes me feel so good to be able to help. They appreciate what I do for them. If I make them smile, my day is worthwhile.

During new employee orientation, you may be with new graduates only, with all newly hired nurses with varying lengths of experience, or with a mix of the two. In some cases, you may even start in a general orientation that includes new hires from many different disciplines. Remember that all new hires, whether they have no experience or ten years' experience, are in the same boat as you as far as being new to their jobs and the facility.

Get to know *all* the people in the group, no matter what shift, department, discipline, or title they hold. As time goes by, you will encounter these people again, and most likely again and again. You will remember them, and they will remember you as having extended yourself to know them. If you reach out to them, they will respond in kind.

Learn what they do and where they will be working (what shift, what unit), and find out when they will be starting their regular schedule (the departmentalized orientation schedules are different for each discipline). Force yourself to talk to other people. Everyone is feeling as you are (shy and nervous), and they will appreciate your initiating the conversation.

Acute Care Orientation: What to Expect

Your first day should be pure orientation. You are likely to get a tour of the hospital and meet some of the key players. Make eye contact with those you meet, smile, and, if the situation presents itself, shake their hand. It may be difficult to shake hands with everyone if you are part of a large group of orientees. But if you are one of a few or standing right next to the person you are being introduced to, extend your hand for a personal introduction.

Your orientation will be a mixture of classroom and clinical time. Over the next few weeks and months, depending on your orientation schedule, you are likely to go through training and certification in CPR, intravenous (IV) therapy, and medication administration. You'll be taught procedures for the use of various pumps and central lines and other related equipment. You'll review basic hospital policies and procedures. You will also be trained in documentation, including the use of computerized patient charting systems, which many facilities use. Depending on the extent to which computers are being used by the nursing department, you may have a more in-depth computer orientation.

If you are going into cardiac or critical care or other specialty areas, additional training will be required. Some facilities provide special internship programs for specialty areas that may last as long as three months. Your general orientation would be included in this program. Remember that every facility is different.

At some point, you will meet your preceptor and work with him or her in the clinical area. A preceptor is another nurse who has either volunteered or been chosen by the facility to work closely with a newly hired nurse for a designated period of time. We'll talk more about preceptors and your relationship with them in chapter 2.

When you get home each day, review your notes and the handouts that you received during orientation. If something is not clear or you have questions, make a written note and ask for clarification the following day. Use this time to learn all you can.

Your orientation period is your time to ask questions, learn, practice your clinical skills, and begin to feel comfortable in your new surroundings. When you are spending time on your assigned unit and have a few extra minutes, look in drawers, cabinets, and closets to learn where things are kept. Know where the fire extinguishers are and where the emergency crash or code cart is kept. The crash cart is usually accompanied by a checklist of supplies. Take some time to familiarize yourself with the content and the location of the contents. Crash carts are kept locked when not in use, so if you witness or participate in a "code," take a few minutes, after the code, to go through the drawers of the crash cart while it is still open.

If you were hired to work a shift other than days, your orientation period will likely be during the day shift. After that, you'll start your regular shift.

Long-Term Care

Long-term care (LTC) is somewhat different. Hopefully, you've had at least a brief rotation through LTC or the sub-acute setting and have been able to observe the differences in care, structure, and even terminology. LTC is a highly regulated environment, and you should familiarize yourself with those regulations to the greatest extent possible. Regulation books should be available at your facility. You should also be able to find them in your public library. Tell the librarian what you are looking for, and he or she should be able to help you find everything you need on the subject.

LTC Orientation: What to Expect

LTC facilities have shorter and less involved orientation. On average, it will run anywhere from two days to two weeks. Resources are different, too. If you go with a facility that is affiliated with an acute care hospital or is part of a large corporation, you will usually find a longer and more formalized orientation program and more support staff (educators and so on). Additionally, if you go with a facility that is affiliated with an acute care hospital, you may have a brief acute care orientation before your LTC orientation.

You may not have a preceptor in the LTC environment. After completing orientation, you need to look for role models—people you can look to for help and advice and model yourself after. We'll talk more about support staff and other resources in chapter 2.

Other Areas and Orientation

Little, if any, formal orientation is conducted in less acute areas, such as medical offices and clinics. Someone may show you the ropes for a day or two, but you will be largely on your own to learn after that. Again, find a friendly person to buddy up with and look for role models.

Smile!

Nursing can be tough. Dealing with patients, staff—all those people! Here are some tips to help you keep your positive attitude and get through the day:

- Don't take yourself too seriously as a new grad. A good sense of humor is vital.
- At times, you will feel overwhelmed. Try to relax and look at your situation in a positive way. Roll with the punches and celebrate each and every accomplishment—even a small one.
- During your first year, you need a lot of perseverance. Hang in there. It will be worth it in the long run.
- Nursing is hard work. Be prepared for that. But the work isn't the issue; it's the difference you make.
- Keep your expectations realistic. Do the best you can and ask for help when you need it.

- Be patient with yourself. You have a wealth of knowledge—knowledge that will be constantly built on. The old saying that learning never stops certainly applies to nursing and health care.
- Be kind to yourself. You've accomplished a great deal already. You deserve a pat on the back.

Wherever you wind up working, now or in the future, you will find that every company and facility has its own culture. Get a feel for the facility and see how you fit in. Observe how people do things, why they do them, and how they handle themselves in every situation.

HOW TO STAY ORGANIZED FROM DAY ONE

You'll be receiving a lot of paperwork before you start your job and even more after you're hired. You'll receive copies of policies and procedures, tip sheets, and other educational material. Keep all of this information organized and accessible. A three-ring binder or pocket folder works well for this.

Creating and Maintaining a Professional Portfolio

It's never too early to start tracking your on-the-job experiences, continuing education classes, certifications, and any other relevant training or learning. This is important. You can't possibly rely solely on your memory when you want or need to cite such things. Keep this information separate from the educational materials you accumulate.

Get a second pocket notebook or three-ring binder for this purpose. What you are doing here is creating a professional portfolio. Start by getting clear plastic insert sheets, within which you should store your licenses, diplomas, and other certificates. Then, simply add to this portfolio as necessary. As time goes by, a thorough and up-to-date portfolio can make a huge difference in your career opportunities and success.

Keep a log of your own experiences (e.g., procedures done, etc.) and any in-service or continuing education classes you attended. Your preceptor or unit

educator may be keeping such a list, but you need to do this for your own records. Documentation of clinical competence is becoming more of an issue in
the clinical area. That means it is important to have a record of your experiences
in writing if you are ever called on or questioned about them. You can't possibly
recall from memory everything you've ever done.

Ask for copies of your evaluations and progress reports throughout your
orientation and future employment. Review these from time to time, and keep
them as a part of your portfolio. Particularly good evaluations can be used as
a type of reference when looking for a transfer or promotion, even if you are
changing employers.

Creating and maintaining a professional portfolio will also help you track
your progress, give you easy and quick access to important papers, and keep
your credentials and experiences organized from day one. As your career develops, keeping an up-to-date portfolio will make your life easier and will ensure
that you are ready to present yourself on short notice should an opportunity
unexpectedly present itself.

CHAPTER 2
SUPERVISORS, PRECEPTORS, AND GETTING HELP

Wherever you work, you will have an immediate supervisor, the person you report to directly. If you work in a health-care facility on the day shift, this person will probably be the nurse manager for your unit. If you work evenings or nights, you may report directly to the designated charge nurse on your shift, but the nurse manager is ultimately in charge. Titles may vary from facility to facility, so be clear as to whom you are directly accountable. If you're not sure, ask.

The nurse manager (or equivalent) is the person who has overall responsibility for your unit, and what a big responsibility that is. Imagine being held accountable for all the personnel, all the patients, and all the paperwork and administrative duties. Then imagine managing a budget for your unit, twenty-four hours a day, seven days a week. It is a daunting task, which not everyone is cut out for.

"Be certain to get as long a preceptorship as you possibly can."

—Rich, new grad

Your supervisor has risen to his or her position because he or she exhibited some strong leadership traits, such as good vision and forethought, commitment, organizational skills, the ability to inspire others, excellent clinical skills, solid communications skills—and that's just the beginning. Your supervisor has a great responsibility, but he or she cannot do the job at hand alone. That's where you come in. You are a part of the team. Think of your supervisor as the team leader, or as the captain of the ship—at least of your section of the ship.

Get a copy (or look in your employee handbook) of the organizational chart and understand the chain of command or leadership of your organization. There is a definite reporting structure in every company. Be sure you know what your facility's structure is.

WHAT YOUR SUPERVISOR WILL EXPECT FROM YOU

Ask your supervisor what is expected from you and what he or she considers to be an ideal employee. This is important information for you to obtain, and your supervisor will appreciate your asking. Clear expectations on both of your parts is key to a successful working relationship. Find out what the expectations are, and then meet them and exceed them.

Of course, each specific type of job and facility has its own requirements and expectations, but there are several things you can definitely count on your supervisor to expect from you.

Be on Time for Work

In fact, you should come in early so you have time to put your things away, use the restroom, get coffee if you want, and be ready *before* your scheduled work time. Starting work at 7 A.M. doesn't mean you dash in just in time to have your time card read "7 A.M." Rather, it means that you are present in your unit and ready to start work at 7 A.M. Lateness is irritating and disruptive to the workday, and it shows disregard for your coworkers, particularly toward the person you are relieving who must wait for you to be ready and on-shift before leaving for the day. People who are chronically late can forget about ever getting promoted.

Show Up When You Are Scheduled to Work

Calling in sick on a regular basis will not do much for your career, either. It puts extra work and strain on your coworkers and throws off the day's scheduling and staffing ratios because it is often not possible to get a replacement for you at the last minute. It is one of the most common complaints that supervisors have about staff members. Chronically calling in sick is also a quick way to alienate your co-workers. And you can forget about future promotions or recommendations.

Be a Team Player

Although this term is used in just about every profession, it is one of the most important qualities that supervisors look for in an ideal employee. A team player is someone who understands that the whole is greater than the sum of its parts. That is, although each person has his or her own job to do, the department, or team, has an even bigger job to do. This is especially true in nursing, where there are often many separate individuals involved in the care of one patient and where effective communication and teamwork is a must in order to provide effective and appropriate care. Everyone on a team pools their resources, supports one another, and works together. There is no *I* in *team.*

Helpful Hints for Figuring Out Your New Job

- Make the most of your orientation period.
- Learn about workplace protocols.
- Familiarize yourself with your new environment.
- Master all equipment.
- Take time to read and learn policies and procedures.
- Observe those who know what they're doing.
- Align yourself with someone who has been around for a while and ask that person to "show you the ropes."
- Once you get the hang of things, show the ropes to someone new.
- Ask questions of those in the know.

Do Your Job

As fundamental as this sounds, it is not always done. You have a job to do for your employer and your unit each day. Take pride in your performance, and when you are given an assignment, it is your responsibility to get that job done. Stay focused on the task at hand and be diligent about performing each task to the best of your ability.

Ask Questions When You Need Help

Supervisors understand that you don't know everything. They will expect you to ask questions and ask for help when you need it. At some point, every supervisor was new on the job, just as you are now, and undoubtedly benefited from seeking and receiving answers and advice. Communicate your needs to your preceptor and/or to your supervisors, depending on the circumstances and existing reporting structure.

Always Be Honest

Be honest about yourself and your abilities. Be honest when reporting things to your supervisor, even if you are reporting a mistake you made. Be honest about your accounting of time and resources. As time goes by, you will have the opportunities to acquire more and more responsibility, and whether your coworkers and superiors feel they can trust you will go a long way in determining just how much additional responsibility you will be granted. Be honest and ethical in everything you do.

Don't Waste Time

Time is a precious commodity in our lives and especially in our work. All of us are required today to do more in less time. You can't afford to squander time by coming back from a break late, lingering too long at the water cooler, doing tasks yourself that should be delegated, and the like. Your time—and that of everyone who works with you and depends on your services—is too valuable to waste.

Use Resources Appropriately

Everything has a cost, and money that your employer has to spend to cover avoidable losses translates into less funds for raises or bonuses. With that in mind, don't waste supplies; don't steal; don't abuse the telephone, access to the Internet, or the copy machine; and don't waste time. Each of these has either a direct or an indirect negative impact on your facility's bottom line. Likewise, don't ask personnel to do personal favors for you.

Come to Work with a Good Attitude and Be Ready to Work

Attitude is everything, and a good attitude makes all the difference. A positive attitude will perk up your patients, coworkers, superiors, and anyone else you come across. Work is work, but it is also a big part of our lives. Learn to enjoy it. Roll up your sleeves and be ready for action—every day. It's that simple.

It Goes with the Territory

Once you are a nurse, consumers will expect you to always have answers, even when they give you third-hand information or inaccurate information about what they think their doctor told them, what procedure they think they had done, or what medication they think they are taking.

After I had just been accepted to nursing school, a relative called me and said, "I just got back from my doctor's office and he gave me a shot. What do you think it was?" This was all the information I was given, yet I was expected to somehow know what the drug was. Keep in mind that I hadn't even started nursing school yet—I had only been accepted! I proceeded to ask some questions and was able to ascertain that this relative had apparently been given an injectable equivalent of a water pill for high blood pressure. I felt so smug.

You will also have to figure out what people are talking about when they give you their medical history and completely mispronounce their diagnosis, surgeries, tests, or medications. You will have to keep a straight face when someone tells you that they had a "head scam" instead of a "head scan" or when they say they have "fibrovagina" when they mean "fibromyalgia."

You'll have to be patient when people tell you that they had major abdominal surgery but they don't know what was done or if anything was taken out. Likewise, they don't know what remains in. Ditto when they come in with a household object embedded in a body cavity and have no idea how it got there.

You'll have to revert to the use of phonics when people write on their medical history form that they had a "tubala gation" instead of a "tubal ligation." Or, you may find that a person has listed his or her father as having "old-timer's disease" instead of "Alzheimer's disease." You'll also learn to figure out that "immaculate generation" really means "macular degeneration," a condition of the eye.

Investigative work, careful listening, learning to ask the right questions, and reading between the lines are as much a part of nursing as taking blood pressures and giving out medications.

Practice Clear and Regular Communication

One of the most important things you can do is develop open lines of communication with your supervisor. Learn to express yourself in a clear, concise way. Understand that there are good and bad times to bring certain things up, and be sensitive to that. Learn to read other people's moods, and respect that another time might be better to approach certain subjects with someone. When you do talk with coworkers, learn to listen. The more you listen, the more you learn.

WHAT TO EXPECT FROM YOUR SUPERVISOR

Think of your supervisor not only as your boss, but as a mentor and as a source of far-reaching knowledge. You should also expect support as needed, opportunities to learn and grow, regular feedback on your progress and abilities, evaluations that are fair and objective, and suggestions to make you a better employee.

During your orientation, ask your supervisor how often you will be meeting with him or her to evaluate your progress and to discuss how things are going. Express your sincere desire for constructive feedback and your openness to suggestions and constructive criticism.

A good deal of what you get from your supervisor will depend on you. If you have a great attitude, show a willingness to work hard and to learn, and are supportive of your supervisor and the department, it is likely that you will be considered a valued employee. If you are enthusiastic, interested, and respectful, it will be reciprocated.

Getting Along with Your Supervisor

One of the first things you should do when you start your job is thank each and every one of your superiors for the opportunity to work in their department. Let them know that you are open to any new work and learning opportunities that may become available and that you are a team player.

Every supervisor has a different personality and management style. Each has a unique way of doing things and idiosyncrasies. Get to know each supervisor as an individual. Learn what is important to him or her and how he or she likes things done. Observe and ask appropriate questions to learn why, as well as how, things are done.

Hopefully, you will be fortunate to work for people who are competent, caring, and enthusiastic about their work. You will like some of your supervisors better than others. Occasionally, you may even have a supervisor whom you don't like. That's okay because you don't *have* to like everyone you work with, and it's unlikely that you will. At the very least, maintain respect for your supervisor's position. Just because you don't like certain supervisors doesn't mean they don't have some valuable lessons to teach you or that they're not good managers.

Sometimes supervisors' reputations precede them. That is, you may hear, before you ever meet them, that they are tough, difficult to get along with, or some other negatives. Reserve judgment and go in with an open mind. Develop your own relationship and form your own opinions. I have gotten along great with some supervisors who were reputed to be "a bear to work with."

FROM THE FRONT LINE

Lovin' Life

"When I was a senior in high school, I had no idea that men could even be nurses! Two of my aunts were nurses, but I didn't talk to them about it. I never saw a man as a nurse, either. So when I went to my guidance counselor, I said I wanted to do something in health care, like becoming a physician's assistant or 'taking care of people' because I was good in biology and science. She said, 'Sounds like you want to be a nurse!' Thank God she had that insight! Can you imagine getting paid for what you love to do?"

—Rob, nurse

All this being said, if you are lucky enough to get good supervisors whom you like, respect, and can learn from, cherish them. In all cases, supervisors deserve your cooperation to complete the job at hand.

Don't develop or buy into an us versus them mentality in regard to staff and management. Some staff people see themselves in a different camp from management and view members of management as the enemy. This attitude is nonproductive, fosters hard feelings, and erodes team spirit. Instead, respect each person's role, including your own, and go from there.

Diamond in the Rough

One of my first supervisors was a tough old broad. Miss Roberts (not her real name) was the director of the ER in which I worked during the early part of my career, and she ruled with an iron fist. Most people, including the doctors, were very intimidated by her. However, Miss Roberts was very dedicated to her department, her chosen profession, and the hospital we worked for. She was devoted to her staff and would stick up for any one of us in a pinch.

At the time, I thought she was a little too harsh, had unreasonably high standards, had paranoiac tendencies, and insisted that everything be done just so. She was fanatical about documentation and legal issues. She was quick to criticize and stingy with compliments.

Along the way, though, I learned many valuable lessons from her, one of which was never to burn my bridges. I can still hear her saying, "Miss Wilk [my maiden name], always leave a job or professional relationship on good terms. You never know when or where you'll run into that person again and want or need something from them." Sage advice that I heeded—and preach today.

Miss Roberts also taught me the importance of good documentation in nursing to cover myself, and my employer, from potential legal liability. Once, when a psychiatric patient was admitted to our ER, I noticed she had old bruises, scabbed-over scratches, and other old injuries on her body. Remembering Miss Roberts's lectures on good documentation, I took extra time to meticulously document all the old injuries I observed. When the patient came back a few weeks later and claimed that the ER staff had physically abused her and caused her injuries, Miss Roberts got out the ER chart and showed her my notes. The woman left deflated and disappointed. We never heard from her again.

When I resigned from that job, Miss Roberts told me that I was a "diamond in the rough." After I left, I heard that she continuously referred to me in a positive way, making statements such as "If Miss Wilk were here, she'd be able to get that done." Could it be that she actually missed me and had thought well of me?

I see now that she expected a lot of me and just took it for granted when I did a great job. She was sometimes critical because she expected so much from me. After some time had passed, I began to realize what a positive influence she had been in my life in many ways. She taught me much and gave me many wonderful opportunities to challenge myself and expand my experiences. These opportunities helped me to build my confidence as a nurse, develop an impressive resume, and become a better person as a whole.

Managers and administrators have an awesome responsibility, even though at times it may seem that all they do is go to meetings or sit in their offices doing paperwork. If you haven't walked in their shoes, it's hard to imagine what they actually do. Respect their position and take steps to learn more about them. Ask them how they got to where they are and what advice they have for you to be successful. Find out what their hobbies are. You may have something in common with them.

Take time to compliment supervisors on what they do well. When attending a seminar or continuing education class, get an extra set of handouts for your supervisors. They will appreciate that. There is a big difference between being a brown-nose or a kiss-up and offering an occasional, sincere compliment to your supervisor. Everyone appreciates positive feedback, although supervisors rarely get it from their staff. Give your supervisor some occasional feedback about what you find helpful.

ABOUT YOUR PRECEPTOR

As we discussed earlier, your preceptor has either volunteered or been chosen to work with new hires. Your preceptor is there to show you the ropes, see that you get basic clinical experiences, and ensure that you perform them at a satisfactory level. Your preceptor is also there to help out with questions and problems.

Understand that preceptors have their own job to do and are not available exclusively to help you. In fact, there will be times when your preceptor may seem too busy to help you or is having a bad day. In that case, you have many other resources available to you, which we'll discuss in a moment.

Getting the Most Out of Your Preceptor

You will work closely with your preceptor for anywhere from a few weeks to a few months. Make the most of this unique and short-lived situation to learn all you can. Find out what your preceptor expects from you. Ask questions, observe, and look for new experiences. Not everyone likes their preceptor, but appreciate his or her knowledge and what he or she has to offer. Appreciate the help your preceptor gives you and offer thanks each time.

During orientation, you will most likely have regularly scheduled meetings with your preceptor and nurse manager or preceptor and staff educator to assess your progress. These meetings will help determine if you are in the best unit for your skills and abilities and how much longer you need to work with your preceptor. If these meetings are not a regularly scheduled part of your training, ask your preceptor to sit down with you at intervals and discuss your progress. Determine what you still need to work on, and ask any questions you have at that time.

GETTING THE HELP YOU NEED

There will be many times in the course of your first year that you will need help and guidance. Many people are reluctant to ask for help, but you will *need* help. Many resources are available to you—learn to utilize all of them. Don't just rely on your preceptor or any other one person.

Where to Go and Whom to Ask for Help

Obviously, when you have a question or need help, your preceptor is your logical first source. However, your preceptor will not always be available. Your

---

FROM THE FRONT LINE

Get What You Need

Remember Shannon, who found herself on a unit with all new graduates, including her preceptor? Here is a continuation of her story:

"Not only was my preceptor a relatively new graduate herself, but she received her one-year employee evaluation while precepting me, and it was not a good one. After that, she became very disgruntled and angry. She started bad-mouthing the hospital to me all the time. It was a bad situation. I went to my supervisor and told her I needed a new preceptor. I got a new preceptor, and things improved. But there were other new grads who didn't speak up. You have to speak up for yourself and say, 'This is what I need.' "

—Shannon, new grad

"My preceptor had a reputation that preceded her. I heard that she was a difficult person. Her personality ran hot and cold, but generally she was good with me. There were some things she did well and others she didn't. For example, she was good at documentation and at getting things done, but she was not good at personal care. So I learned what I could from her and was careful not to pick up any of her bad habits. I also learned that everyone has their own style."

—Pennie, new grad

---

colleagues and any other experienced workers are excellent sources of information. While your supervisor is there to help you, consider your other resources, too. They are everywhere you look.

Ask your preceptor and your supervisor whom you should go to when you need help or have a question. Most health-care facilities have staff educators, while some large hospitals have an educator just for a particular unit, especially in critical care and specialty units. In many cases, there are a few educators who cover the entire facility, with each assigned to particular units. Find out who the educator is for your unit, and seek that person out if you need help or have a question.

And ask questions—lots of questions. Acknowledge what you don't know. Be clear on what you need answered. When I was younger, I was very intimidated by asking questions. I thought questions showed my ignorance. I have since found that most people are happy to teach you something when you show genuine interest. So, show some enthusiasm for your learning. It makes others want to put more time in with you and to help you more. People are always more inclined to help you when they feel their time is well spent.

Be assertive with your needs, but always make sure you have read up on the subject and are familiar with the procedure before you ask for help. If you do need help, and you will at times, simply say, "I haven't done this before, and I need assistance." Or call the unit educator, explain your situation, and ask, "Can you show me how to do this?" Use unit educators and other resources when appropriate because this can take the burden off staff people, who are busy and focused on their own assignments.

Helping Yourself

Show some initiative. Be an active participant in your training. Don't wait for others to tell you to observe a procedure or perform one. When you hear that

---

FROM THE FRONT LINE

Making an Adjustment to Your New Job

There are many new things to do at your new job beyond perfecting your clinical skills. You'll encounter new people, new places, and new ways of doing things. It can all be a bit daunting.

"Aside from all the clinical skills new grads have to deal with, there is all the equipment, the machines, the computers, and even the phone system to learn."

—Rosemary, nurse

"When I graduated a few years ago, my greatest challenge was adjusting to a new job. There was so much to learn: the paperwork, the protocols, how they wanted things done, and how they didn't want things done. It was all very overwhelming. I also had to get to know the doctors and how each preferred things done.

"I asked a lot of questions—a lot of questions. I was never afraid of asking questions, and all the nurses were very helpful to me. If I found one who wasn't willing to answer my questions, I just didn't ask that nurse again. There was so much to learn. It was like doing homework each night."

—Michele, nurse

an interesting procedure is being done on the unit, *ask* if you can participate or at least observe. Volunteer to perform procedures that you need to gain experience in. Show a willingness to learn. This will impress those around you—not to mention accelerate your learning and experience.

Remember that everyone has a fear of doing something for the first time. But you only have to do things for the first time once. After that, they start to become familiar. It's called learning.

Know where reference materials are on your unit and use them. You should be referring to the Policy & Procedure (P&P) and Standards of Care manuals on a regular basis. Before performing a procedure for the first time, look it up in the P&P manual. This will not only be helpful to you in performing the procedure, but it will ensure that you practice within established guidelines. Make copies of these as necessary and learn them. Continue to refer to P&P manuals as you learn. Great efforts have gone into developing them, and they are there for a reason. Familiarize yourself with them.

Grace Under Fire!

When I first got out of school, I took a job in a county psychiatric hospital. Six months later, I heard of a higher-paying job that had opened in the ER where I had worked as a student, so I switched jobs. I was told I'd be starting out with orientation for two weeks, working the night shift, and working with an experienced nurse.

My second night on the job, I came in and discovered that it was the night nurse's day off and I would be working alone! I was very nervous, to say the least, but I was assured by the unit clerk that because this was a small community hospital and it didn't usually see much trauma, weeknights were generally pretty quiet. Though that should have tipped me off, I instead simply convinced myself I'd survive! At about 2 A.M., a man burst through the ER doors shouting, "I've been stabbed!" He ran past me into the treatment room and threw himself on a stretcher.

When I finally caught up with him, he had sprawled himself facedown on a stretcher, and I could see that his back was a mass of clotted blood. The unit clerk located the ER physician, and I began to take the patient's clothes off and take his vital signs. When the ER doctor came in, we sprang into action, getting an intravenous line started and cleaning the wounds to assess the seriousness of the situation. Suddenly, the man began to have difficulty breathing.

The ER doctor ordered that the on-call thoracic (chest) surgeon be summoned. This only added to my unease, as the surgeon on call that night was a big shot in every sense of the word—a very talented surgeon, but generally unfriendly, intimidating, and a no-nonsense kind of guy.

The surgeon quickly took over, and the ER physician stepped out before I could explain I was new on the job and wished he would stay. The surgeon asked me for a (gasp!) thorocotomy tray and directed me to set up the underwater drainage bottles, which at that time were used instead of suction to produce negative pressure for chest tubes. This was all new to me. I got out the tray and called the night supervisor to locate the drainage equipment.

When the equipment arrived, the surgeon asked me to set it up. Horrors! I had no idea what to do. Although I was a wreck inside, I very calmly—at least on the surface—looked at him and said, "I've never set one of these up before. You'll have to tell me what to do." I'll never forget the surgeon's eyes as he looked up at me over the half glasses perched on the end of his nose, relaying a look of "You're kidding, right?" He proceeded to walk me through the procedure.

Somehow, I held it all together and made it through that experience and the night. Both the patient and I survived, and I learned more that night than I could have ever expected I would.

Your pocket drug reference book should be with you at all times, but there should also be a drug reference guide available on your unit.

If you are given a checklist of procedures that you need to demonstrate proficiency in during orientation, you may have to dig around to be exposed to all the things listed. Some of these procedures may not be done with any regularity on your unit. Ask the nurse educator to arrange for you to perform or observe the procedure on another unit, if possible. Take an active role in your training.

Utilize any other available resources. For example, the pharmacist, physical therapists, and social workers are available to you, and they all see situations in a different light than you, so their input will be helpful. Don't hesitate to talk with these people when you see them. Call them when you have questions related to their area of expertise. In fact, have lunch with these people so that you can learn more about what they do. Ask them to teach you something you want or need to learn. People will respond very favorably to you when they see you are eager to learn and are going out of your way to do so.

Look to friendly, competent people on your unit for help—and do not limit yourself to seeking out those who have the same job title as you do. I was recently speaking with an RN who told me that when she first started out, an experienced LPN took her under her wing and taught her everything she knows today. Help is all around if you avail yourself of it. Don't take anyone's help for granted, and always thank those who help you. Also, stay in touch with your instructors from nursing school. Obviously, they are experts in the areas they teach, and they can offer many insights and helpful tips once you get out into the real world.

Focus on your own learning. When you go home at the end of the day, do research on cases you had that day and will have the next day. Use the Internet and refer to your textbooks, drug reference books, and procedural guidelines. You are still very much in the learning process, so you will still have homework to do, even though you are out of school! Your workplace is now your classroom.

HOW ARE YOU DOING?

With all this learning going on, it is important to keep track of your progress and see what others think of your performance. You must seek feedback. Feedback is very valuable, and you should ask for it on a regular basis. Ed Koch, former mayor of New York City, used to ask the media and his constituents, "How'm I doin'?" He was, wisely, always looking for feedback. Some people are afraid of feedback because they are afraid of hearing something negative. But feedback can be both positive and negative, and what's negative can be worked on. Ask what you're doing well and what needs improvement, and don't take constructive criticism personally. People will generally respect you for asking, and be grateful if your supervisor takes the time to give you feedback about your performance. This way, you'll know exactly where you stand and what you need to work on.

The experience in the box titled "Grace Under Fire!" taught me a great lesson. Even in a situation where you are certain that you can't function, there is always a way. As long as you keep your faculties together, stay calm, use logic,

"Be open to the way your colleagues do things. Don't say or get hung up on, 'This is the way we did things in nursing school.' When in Rome, do as the Romans do."

—Shannon, new grad

think on your feet, and ask for the help you need, you will succeed. In a way, I feel I was being tested that night. Baptism by fire, perhaps. I later realized that if I could get through that situation, I could probably get through other seemingly impossible and terrifying situations, too!

I had many other less-than-desirable experiences, especially with doctors (which I'll talk about later), that made me feel stupid, incompetent, unprepared, and otherwise inept. But I lived through them all and kept moving forward, and here I am today telling the stories. You will do the same thing.

UNDERSTAND WORKPLACE PROTOCOLS

There are many unwritten rules that must be followed in the workplace. These rules are a code of conduct, of sorts, about what is and is not okay to do. Knowing and following these unwritten rules will go a long way to helping you fit in and make a smooth transition into your new job.

Understand the Chain of Command

Your department has an established chain of command, and you should never go over anyone's head. If there is something that concerns you or that you are having a problem with in your department, including a coworker or superior, talk to your nurse manager about it first. You need to make an attempt to resolve issues with your nurse manager before going any further. If you still do not feel you have resolution after this attempt, check your employee handbook to see how to proceed from there. Every facility has an established grievance procedure. Resort to this only if all else fails. Starting a formal grievance procedure should not be taken lightly.

Don't Criticize in Public

This goes for doctors, coworkers, supervisors, your department, and facilities—don't criticize them in public, and that includes posting messages on social media sites. It is completely inappropriate and unprofessional and reflects poorly on you. If there is something you need to discuss with your supervisor, do so in private.

Don't Introduce Surprises

When attending a meeting, don't bring up any surprises for your supervisor. This is not the time or place. If the lines of communication between you and your superiors are open all the time, take advantage of this and discuss any "surprises" when they occur.

Solutions Only, Please

Karen was concerned with the rate at which nurses were resigning from her unit. The hospital was making every effort to recruit new nurses, but she felt that issues of retention were being ignored. She angrily approached an administrator in the hallway one day and asked what members of management were doing about retention. Needless to say, her negative approach was not well taken.

Her nurse manager called her in later that day to discuss the incident, which had been brought to her attention. Karen didn't understand what the fuss was all about. But after that day, she began to feel that her nurse manager and administrators regarded her in a negative light.

What could she have done differently? First, if she had concerns about retention, she should have talked to her nurse manager. She should have been prepared with some specific issues in writing that she thought should be addressed, and she then should have offered some solutions. If her hospital had a recruitment and retention committee, she could have volunteered to sit on that committee. She could also have offered her help and support to the nurse manager in working on issues of retention for their department by asking, How can we improve this situation? How can we make it better?

You can act as a change agent if you develop good communication skills, follow workplace protocols, use humor and tact, and offer solutions instead of simply pointing out problems.

Don't Be a Know-It-All

Even though you may have had significant work experience prior to becoming a nurse, you are still the new kid on the block at this point, and you must resist the temptation to tell others what to do or how to do it. Make observations before offering comments and suggestions about the way things are done in your unit. Avoid saying, "We did it this way at the other hospital I worked at." Don't be a know-it-all. Take some time to learn how your department works and become familiar with its personnel and how and why they do things. Over time, as you become established, your experience, observations, and suggestions will be welcome.

There Are No "Problems"

When reporting something that you think needs to be changed or addressed, avoid the word *problem*. It makes people cringe. A colleague often calls me and says, "We have a problem." This statement immediately puts me on the defensive and makes my stomach go into a knot. Often, what she is reporting is not a problem at all but simply something that needs clarification. I've asked her to use different phrasing in the future.

Offer Solutions

Don't present an issue or a concern without presenting a solution. If you have suggestions to make, do so constructively. No one responds well to outright criticism. If something needs to be accomplished, use language such as "How can we get this done?" rather than "What are you going to do about it?" If you don't understand a certain procedure or protocol, rather than criticize it right off the bat, ask, "Why is it done this way?"

SUREFIRE WAYS TO BE PROMOTABLE FROM THE START

Even though you're just starting out, it's never too soon to prepare for your future. The earlier you begin planning for your future and positioning yourself to move above and beyond your current level, the more success and satisfaction you will obtain from your career. If you present yourself in the best possible light and position yourself as a future leader from day one, advancement will follow. Here's how you can do that.

It's all about attitude. Attitude is everything. Much of your current and future success will depend on your attitude. If you are positive, upbeat, and willing to learn, you will get the attention of your superiors. If you are someone whom others want to be around, someone who enjoys what you do and lets it show by the way you carry yourself and by your enthusiasm, you will go far.

Pay attention to your physical appearance and body language. Keep your appearance impeccable and professional. Rather than being a shrinking violet, walk tall, keep your head upright, and make good eye contact with people, regardless of how you're feeling. Create a professional image to match the professional person you are. You are at work to learn, help, and succeed. Your demeanor should express that.

Show some serious initiative. Seek out challenges and opportunities. Make things happen for yourself. Take charge of your career from the start. Have confidence in yourself from day one and always *let yourself learn.* Don't wait for someone to tell you what to do. Take the initiative and do it on your own.

Develop and maintain outstanding work habits. Arrive to work early. Don't call in sick excessively. Adhere to established guidelines. Do your job and do it well. Exceed expectations—your own and those of your coworkers and superiors. Anywhere you go where people are working, you will see one person who obviously has it together and is a 100 percent leader. Be that person.

Be a role model. Be helpful, considerate, and respectful to all. Be the type of person to whom others look up and know they can trust. It is a great feeling to know that people value your advice, input, and assistance.

Be a work in progress. Continually work on your personal and professional development. Read, take classes, study, observe others, and dive headfirst into new situations. Always look for new opportunities and ways to make yourself better.

Don't Sweat the Clinical Stuff

Many new nurses are in a panic because they have had very little, if any, opportunity to perform various procedures, such as bladder catheterization, NG tube insertion, tracheostomy care, and so on. They also fear that experienced nurses will turn their noses up at them for not having that proficiency or even exposure. But the truth is that those "tasks" can be learned by anyone with some due diligence. Wendie, an experienced nurse educator, puts it all in perspective.

When I taught nursing students, we would have this talk about what I called "stuff"—the check-off list, like a birder's life list or a stamp collector's inventory. That's all it is. We teach lay people "stuff" all the time. Think of the parent with a child on a home ventilator who knows how to change a trach tube and suction. Or the middle-aged woman who does her husband's home dialysis (hemo or peritoneal). They can do tasks well—in some cases, better than licensed persons. But are they *nurses*?

The fact is that *nobody* gets to do all that stuff in school. You don't have to. What you need to learn is the difference between what nurses do and what nurses are. You need to learn principles of sterile technique, assessment, anatomy and physiology, pharmacology, psychology, and, above all, asking questions and developing the habit of lifelong learning. Your schooling doesn't stop at graduation or at one year after that or when you get your first professional certification. It goes on forever.

You will have plenty of time to do your first NG tube insertion, IV start, Foley insertion, IM injection, suctioning, wound packing, or any of a thousand other pieces of "stuff." One of my students, a young woman with a long work history as a nursing aide, came to nursing school for the credential because, as she said, she could already do what nurses did, but she needed to have the license to administer medications.

One morning, I found her in the nursing station about 9 A.M. reading a nursing magazine. I said, "What are you doing out here? Why aren't you with your patient?" She said, "He's all done up." That is nursing aide–speak for the bath/linen change/feed—the tasks of the early morning. As an experienced aide, she was much better at this than most of her classmates, who were new to patient care and who would still be making beds at 11:30. I told her to get back in there and stay with her patient, be with him, a man in his sixties who had recently been diagnosed with cancer that would probably kill him within a year. Even if there was no conversation and he didn't need anything, she should stay with him. She shot me a look and heaved herself out of the chair.

The next time I saw her was around noontime, when she came out for noon meds. She was almost in tears. After spending about fifteen minutes in silence with her patient, he started talking, and talking, and talking . . . He spoke of his family, his fears, his joys, his sense of being overwhelmed, and more. He had been on this excellent oncology unit for a week, but nobody had sat down and just listened. I said, "Now you know the difference between what a nurse does and what a nurse is." I got cards from her for years.

CHAPTER 3

BECOMING A TEAM MEMBER

From the first day on your new job, you are part of several teams: You are a member of a team in your unit, a member of the nursing department team, and a member of the company and facility team. Every person on the team has a different role to fill and job to do. Each team member is equally important. So how will you fit in?

TEAMWORK

Starting any new job, whether you're experienced or a novice, makes you feel like a fish out of water. Overcome that feeling by getting to know your coworkers. But don't leave that to chance. You are the new kid on the block, and it's up to you to make this happen for yourself.

Begin by introducing yourself to everyone on the unit. Extend your hand to shake and tell them your name and title. Ask them about themselves and make a note of their names. Go out of your way to meet the people on the incoming and the outgoing shifts, too. Greet them and introduce yourself. You never know when you might work with them or you will need their help. Plus, it makes you feel more a part of the whole team.

When you first get into a new unit, take some time to get to know the people—the "players." Take a backseat and observe. Do a lot of listening and watching. Who is strong clinically? Whom would you like to model yourself after? What is each person's real function? Whom do others seem to migrate toward? Sometimes, the friendliest people are the biggest gossips and the quietest people may be your greatest allies.

The more people you get along with at work, the happier and more successful you will be. You don't have to like everyone you work with, and it's unlikely that you will. But it is still possible to get along with people in spite of that. A lot of dissension comes simply from not getting to know other people and judging them too quickly. You wouldn't want other people to make quick judgments about you, so don't do it to them. Getting to know people better is key to understanding and respecting them.

Understand that you are dealing with a multitude of personalities. Everyone is different, comes from a different background, and has a different approach to things. If there is someone you don't like, try to get to know that person better. Have lunch, talk on a break, or visit at a social function. Chances are, you each will discover something that breeds respect and helps you to see each other in a different light. Try to find something about everyone that you like or respect. One of your coworkers may not be your favorite person, but perhaps he or she has a good sense of humor. Your supervisor may be a little brusque, but perhaps he or she is great with patients, and that is something you can admire.

Getting to Know You

I remember a coworker whom I didn't like at all. She did, however, have a great sense of humor, and I could appreciate that. Although we would never go out of our way to be in each other's company, we were able to share an occasional good laugh, and that made all the difference. I also had the opportunity to meet her son, and I was impressed with what a polite, personable young man he was. I remember thinking, "She couldn't be all bad to raise such a nice son."

So, before you rush to judgment, get to know the people with whom you are working and what each person is really all about. Everybody has strengths. Discover and focus on other people's strengths, not their weaknesses.

Finding Your Place

When you're getting started, don't be intimidated by more-experienced nurses. You worked just as hard for your license as they did. Remember that every nurse started out exactly where you are today. Without new graduates like you, the profession would soon fizzle out. You are an important part of the cycle. You are the future of nursing. Don't ever forget that. Also, you have every right to be where you are. And you have every right to learn and develop like your predecessors have done.

Specific Tips for Starting Out on the Right Foot with Your Coworkers

Each and every day, you can do a number of things to strengthen the bond between you and your coworkers as well as enhance the cohesiveness of your team. So take time to learn and be aware of these specific ways to help not only your situation, but your team's as well. The better you get along with and understand one another, the easier and more fulfilling everyone's time at work will be.

FROM THE FRONT LINE

Be Nice!

"In terms of assimilating into the culture of your new unit, my experience was that friendly, friendly, friendly *works best! I began as a casual (per diem) in the neonatal intensive care unit (NICU), and because I didn't work with one group of people all the time, I got to know many of the 150 NICU nurses very quickly. I highly recommend forcing yourself to talk a lot—to everyone. Ask questions about the unit, their families, how long they have worked there—anything to get whomever you're working with talking. Even if you feel really shy and out of place, you will be accepted a lot more quickly if you force yourself to be outgoing.*

Since you need to become part of a team, you must integrate quickly. Go out of your way to be helpful to others because they will remember and they will help you when you need it. Now I'm full time and already am good friends with the group I'm working with. If you have good relationships with your coworkers, it will be easier to seek out new opportunities within your workplace and network for the future."

—Victoria, new grad

Be supportive of your supervisor, coworkers, unit, and facility. Everyone has a job to do and is part of your team. Everyone is working toward the same goal. You don't have to like everyone you work with, but at least respect them for the job they do. Don't bad-mouth your coworkers, including your supervisor. Be a positive representative of your unit and facility at all times. If you have a complaint or an issue, go directly to the person who can help you with a solution.

Find something to like or respect about everyone you work with. If nothing else, consider the fact that you both work in health care. Try to have lunch or coffee with as many staff members as possible in the beginning. The sooner you break the ice with your new team members, the easier it will be to iron out any eventual problems. Plus, you will be more comfortable spending your time around people you have met and know.

Be a positive influence. Be a role model. Stay upbeat and positive. Do your job and do it well. Develop a professional image. Look for ways to get things done and to improve things. Watch the masters of your trade and learn from them. Remember, everyone started out in the same place you are now in. With attentiveness, hard work, and initiative, you can end up on top, too.

Don't get caught up in gossip. Avoid the rumor mill. Don't listen to gossip and don't spread it. If you partake, expect to be gossiped about, too. Gossip is a waste of time and energy. It is counterproductive, and it exerts a negative influence on you, your department, and your coworkers. Being labeled "a gossip" is something to avoid.

Avoid negative and mean people. They will drag you down. If someone tries to pick a fight with you, ignore that person and do your job. There is an expression that goes, "Win the battle, but lose the war." An individual battle against another is counterproductive to the challenge you are facing, which is to become a valued commodity to your team and facility. If you have a problem, talk to the appropriate personnel.

Always look for ways to help your coworkers. Help others whenever the opportunity arises. If you adopt a "me only" attitude, you will soon be alone. Be a team player. One hand washes the other. If you notice other team members who are having a bad day, offer to help them or relieve them for a few minutes. Believe me, you will have your share of lousy days, and a helpful hand will be very welcome. It is everyone's job to take care of one another.

Scratch, Scratch

A nurse told me of a colleague who was always available to change shifts when someone asked her. She did it happily and with a smile on her face. So on the occasions when she needed coverage, other nurses were more than willing to help her out. "In fact, we would go out of our way to help her because she was always helping us. You scratch my back, and I'll scratch yours. That's what it's all about."

Learn to manage conflict. Remember, it's a fact of life that you will always have conflicts with people. If not resolved immediately, conflicts have a tendency to escalate. Learn to talk things out, seek clarification, and reach a middle ground. It's often easier than you think when you remain open to the possibility of resolution.

Build camaraderie. Learn to enjoy the company of your coworkers. Use humor appropriately, spend breaks together, and look for opportunities to get to know one another better. Don't simply focus on integrating yourself within the team—you should also pay attention to the team's mood and the relationships among its members. Without stepping on toes or butting into other people's business, do what you can to promote team well-being. As you become more experienced and accepted, you will be more comfortable with this and take on a greater role.

SOCIALIZE WITH YOUR COWORKERS

Aside from making a living and having a career, one of the most fulfilling parts of any job is the relationship you build with your coworkers. These people often become a second family for you. You spend a great deal of time with them, go through some rough times together, may laugh and cry together, and, in this profession, will likely grieve together. Make the most of this. It can enrich your life in unexpected ways. I'm not suggesting that you get overly friendly with your coworkers, but all the ingredients are there for you to develop and nurture these relationships.

Socializing with your coworkers, during and after work, is as important as working together. Any good relationship in your life is built on respect, shared experiences, and common goals. But the good, fun times often help get you through the tough times and the bad days. Socializing also helps you develop a sense of being connected to your department.

Get Out There!

Attend holiday parties, awards dinners, and company picnics when you can. It shows that you're a team player; that you support your department, your employer, and your coworkers; and that you enjoy being in their company. Besides, attending company-wide events has some career benefits, too. At holiday parties and company picnics, for example, you often have the opportunity to rub elbows with administrators and higher-ups whom you would not normally have access to. Be sure to introduce yourself to these people, and include a handshake. Say something such as "Hi. My name is Janet Gorden. I'm a registered nurse in the ICU."

"Always offer to help somebody—even if you don't know what you're doing. You just might learn something in the process."
—Kevin K., new grad

Reciprocate in your department. If others periodically bring in food and you partake, bring in some yourself. Don't get the reputation of being a mooch. This is all part of being a team player. If your department is having a baby shower for a coworker, be a part of it. If you take the last cup of coffee, brew a new pot.

Everyone has limited time to get out to social events, so have fun while you're working, too. While staying focused on your job, find things to laugh about, discover silly (yet appropriate) things to do in the course of the day, and utilize ways to break the tension. One nurse told me that she and her coworkers sometimes pick a song for the day and everyone sings that all day. "It just gets very funny when you hear someone else singing the same dumb song. It helps to ease the tension and keep things light."

Tips for Workplace Social Events

- Even though you are at a party or picnic, you are still "at work." That means you have to maintain a certain sense of decorum throughout. You should enjoy yourself—that is the purpose of the event. But don't go overboard.
- If alcohol is involved, stick to one drink.
- Although you may be dressing in your party or informal attire (for a picnic), don't wear anything too revealing or provocative. In fact, the higher your position within the organization, the less skin you should show!
- Don't be the last to leave.
- Be sure to greet your supervisor and treat him or her with respect, courtesy, and friendliness. If you bring your spouse or a date, be sure to introduce your companion to your boss.

THE GOOD, THE BAD, AND THE UGLY ABOUT NURSING

Every profession has its own unique, quirky pettiness and prejudices. No matter what you do or where you are, you won't be able to escape them. However, you certainly can control how much time and thought you put into such things. The following are some potential issues that you likely will encounter in nursing.

I'm Better Than You Are!

There is an eternal debate among nurses about who the better nurse is. It can be in the form of who has the better education, which specialties are "smarter," and everything in between. Unfortunately, there aren't many working environments that remain unexposed to such silly arguments. So let's take a look at them and perhaps answer some questions and perhaps prevent a conflict.

Who's Smarter?

The diploma school graduate, the associate degree nurse, or the baccalaureate-prepared nurse? While this debate keeps coming up like a bad penny, it is a fruitless discussion because every nurse passed the same rigorous exam to be licensed and practices under the same guidelines. Your best bet is to avoid this discussion altogether because it is a non-issue and you can't win, even if you try. Participants in this debate are usually very passionate about their viewpoint and often get defensive and angry, and the discussion goes round and round, making everyone dizzy. The reality is that, although each educational program may have a slightly different focus (each with its own advantages and disadvantages), once licensed, a nurse is a nurse is a nurse.

Fitting In

Carolyn considered herself a very shy person. She believed that doing her work was the most important thing. For the most part, she kept to herself, reading a book during lunch, avoiding department holiday parties and social events, and steering clear of hospital-wide gatherings. When the department had a holiday party and everyone brought in food, Carolyn didn't bother because she didn't eat any of the food the others brought in anyway.

One day, when traveling to a seminar with a colleague, she was shocked when the colleague told her she had a reputation for being a "snob." The coworker explained that because Carolyn essentially avoided everyone and their activities, her coworkers assumed that Carolyn thought she was better than them.

Carolyn was devastated, but she realized her coworkers were right, even though they had misinterpreted her behavior. She had never really felt as if she fit in anywhere she worked. Was it possible that she was the cause of her feelings of being an outcast? She mustered up some courage and decided to try to change. She started by going to lunch with her coworkers, rather than sitting alone, and getting to know them. She saw an immediate change in their behavior toward her. When the department had its annual holiday party, Carolyn showed up with a batch of cookies.

Carolyn reflected on what she had learned.

I always thought I just didn't fit in. I never realized that it was my own behavior that was making me an outcast. I'm thankful to the coworker who confronted me with my reputation. It made me realize that my own behavior was responsible for my sense of always being on the outside looking in. It was my responsibility to get myself in, and I should not have expected others to do it for me. I still don't always find it comfortable to socialize at company picnics and similar events, but I force myself to go. I am much happier at work. My coworkers seem more willing to help me, too.

So Special

There is a perception by some nurses that certain specialties think they are better than others. Whether you will witness any of these particular examples, I don't know, but you certainly will at some point be caught in between such a debate. When I worked in the emergency department (ED) years ago, there was an ongoing feud between my department and the ICU. I'm not even sure what it was about, but it had been going on as long as the Hatfield and McCoy thing.

I have heard ICU nurses referred to as snobbish or that they "think they are so smart." Emergency department and post-anesthesia care unit (PACU) nurses are sometimes accused of having disregard for the floor nurses because the ED and PACU nurses just want to "dump their patients on them."

Psychiatric nurses are commonly accused of always trying to psychoanalyze everyone, including their nursing cohorts, and are often thought of as a bit different from others. (Just for the record, I did a little psych nursing early in my career. You can draw your own conclusions.) Frankly, psychiatry has always been intimidating to those who don't work there. We often criticize what we don't understand.

Nurses who advance into administration are often referred to as traitors who abandoned those in the front lines. Reality: Who better to manage, supervise, and administrate than another nurse? Imagine a health-care system where nurses were in charge of everything. Nirvana, no? Professional advancement should be applauded, not criticized.

Nurses who go into nontraditional specialties, like case management or quality improvement, are often said not to be "real" nurses. In truth, being a nurse is about who you are, not about where you work. Nurses are multitalented and versatile. There are many ways and places to have a positive impact on health care. We are vital at the bedside, and we are just as vital in every other aspect of the health-care arena.

The reality is that every nurse is equal but different, no matter what the specialty or department. Each nurse has an important job to do. We do not op-erate independently of one another. Instead, we are all spokes in the same wheel.

Survival of the Fittest

I would be remiss if I did not bring up an often-repeated mantra in nursing: *Nurses eat their young.* This is meant to indicate that experienced nurses do not always support their new counterparts and have been known on occasion even to be downright mean to students and new graduates. Unfortunately, this vile expression is perpetuated by some nurses who need to focus on their own nega-tive perspective.

Jewels of Nursing

I recently spoke with a new graduate who told me how wonderful his first manager was to him—how she welcomed him with open arms, showed him the ropes, and always made sure he had good preceptors. "I really owe her a debt of gratitude," he told me.

Another new graduate told me that because he worked nights, he had several different preceptors during his orientation. He developed a particularly close rela-tionship with one of his preceptors, who continued to help him and be available to him after she was no longer his official perceptor. "I could call her at 2 A.M. if I needed to, and there were a few times that I did. She always took my call and was happy to help me. I don't know what I would have done without her."

Good people await you. Now go find them.

I take issue with this statement for several reasons. First, it is a generaliza-tion, and no generalization is ever true of an entire population. Second, for every negative experience any nurse wishes to relate to me about a time that an-other nurse was inconsiderate or discourteous, I can give you five stories about nurses who were professional and giving and regularly went out of their way to help a new graduate.

Whenever I hear a nurse say, "Nurses eat their young," I respond by saying, "I don't do that. Do you?" He or she always replies that they don't either, but they know others who do. I have yet to meet a nurse who admits to doing this, yet many nurses insist it is the norm rather than the exception. Reality: It is a well-guarded secret that most nurses support other nurses.

Say It Isn't So

It isn't so. If ever another nurse gives you a hard time, look at that individual and the circumstances rather than assuming the behavior is indicative of the entire profession. You will always encounter some people in the workplace who are less than pleasant and helpful. That describes the human race, not just the nursing profession.

As one in the next generation of nurses, you have an opportunity to shatter the stereotypes, put an end to the feuds, dispel the myths, and start spreading some positive expressions about nursing. Start a positive chain reaction in your professional life. When someone says something negative, counter it with a positive. You can continue a negative cycle, or you can break it. It's all up to you. You have the power to effect change.

Remember Where You Came From

When I was a new graduate, I heard from several student nurses that a fellow new graduate was giving student nurses a hard time on her unit. My friend and I confronted her and said, "What is this we're hearing about you giving students a hard time? Have you already forgotten what it was like to be a student? Are you trying to make yourself feel superior in some way by busting them?" She looked a little embarrassed and got defensive. She said something to the effect that she had to make sure they (the students) knew what they were doing. We told her that we were surprised and disappointed to hear of her behavior and that we hoped we wouldn't hear any similar stories about her in the future. We told her to treat the students with respect. Apparently our "intervention" had an impact because we heard things improved considerably after that.

ALL ABOUT RESPECT

First and foremost in getting along with your coworkers is to have the utmost respect for them and who they are and what they do. Respect breeds respect. And when people believe you respect them, they will do anything for you. Respect is not something you can fake. You are either sincere or you are not, and people will be able to determine which is the case.

You will work with a lot of different people with varying levels of responsibility and training. Each is a valuable member of the team. If you think for one minute that you can do your job without your coworkers, you are wrong. Show appreciation for those who work with you—at every level. Here are a few ways to demonstrate your regard and appreciation for your coworkers.

Thank people when they help you. Don't take their help for granted. The words "thank you," when used sincerely, go a long way to breed respect. If people believe you appreciate their help, they will give it freely.

Show that you'll chip in and help them. A helpful deed now and then will go a long way toward showing and gaining respect. Don't be above helping ancillary people. If you work in an environment where aides give much of the physical care, don't be above giving care as needed. Word will get around that you are a helper, so others will be willing to help you. Always remember you are part of a team.

Arrive on time to work. The fact that I am mentioning this again emphasizes its importance. An on-time arrival reflects on your character, your work ethic, and your level of respect toward your team members. Arriving on time gives consideration to the prior shift. The last thing a night nurse with two kids waiting at home wants to do is sit around waiting to give you a report while you take your sweet time showing up for your shift. Do this, and you will quickly alienate people. And don't think that people on another shift can't harm your reputation. If people don't like or don't respect you, word gets around fast.

Understand each person's job. Read and know the content of the job descriptions of those you interact with. It is very important to know this so that you will not be asking someone to do something outside of his or her responsibilities. Know what you're permitted to do in terms of delegation, and embrace your delegating privileges. Efficiently delegating responsibilities to the *appropriate* personnel is a sign of a well-oiled team.

Sincerely compliment people when they do a good job. Praise often and be specific. For example, rather than just saying, "You did a good job," say something such as "I admire the way you spoke with that patient. You were able to calm her down and explain what needed to be done." The more specific you are, the more likely that particular behavior will be repeated, imitated, and passed along.

Greet your coworkers each day with a hello and a smile. Learn people's names and use them often. If you don't know or remember someone's name, just ask. People appreciate having their presence acknowledged. Learning about a person's family or outside interests and inquiring about them from time to time also goes a long way in establishing goodwill.

Respect their knowledge. Some people in positions with a lower level of responsibility than yours have been there a long time and can teach you a lot. They have insights and perspectives on how things work. Don't hesitate to ask for their help and advice.

You don't own anyone. Don't refer to your team members or other ancillary staff as "my CNA" or "my unit clerk." It implies ownership. Rather, say, "My coworker, Janet, the unit clerk." It's okay to use the word *my* when referring to superiors, such as "my boss" or "my supervisor."

FROM THE FRONT LINE

Nice Guys Finish First

"When I started my current job, I made it a point to acknowledge everyone on my unit each day. I would greet them with a smile and address them by name. I went out of my way to say 'Good morning' and 'Good night' to them.

"Some of my fellow nurses noticed that the staff seemed to give me preferential treatment. I suggested that it was the fact that I acknowledged everyone on a regular basis and that the same thing might happen to them if they did the same. Some of the other nurses followed suit and noticed a difference in how the general staff regarded them."

—Barry, new grad

OFFICE POLITICS

The phrase "office politics" usually refers to the backbiting and undercutting that goes on in any workplace. Believe me, this is not unique to health care. No matter where you are, what your level or title, or what profession, there are always those in an organization who are looking to get ahead at other people's expense. This might involve trying to drag down those around them in an attempt to elevate themselves, using underhanded tactics to make themselves look good, or employing unscrupulous ways to get the attention of higher-ups and to knock out the competition.

Although the phrase usually has a negative connotation, some people would say that you can play either good or bad politics in the workplace. For example, if you go out of your way to have lunch with your boss so he or she will get to know you better, you might be said to be "politicking" in a positive way for your own advantage. However, if you were to overhear a colleague discussing an idea he or she wanted to present to the boss and you ran ahead and presented that idea to your boss as if it were your idea, you'd be practicing unfair politics. In any event, be on the alert for those practicing unfair politics and try not to get caught up in this game. Maintain professional relationships with those with whom you work. Even if you get very friendly with your boss, remember that this person is still your boss.

DEALING WITH CONFLICT

It is inevitable that some conflicts and sticky situations will arise from time to time with another coworker, your supervisor, or others. Learning to deal with conflict is an important skill in any work situation.

Back Pains

I remember when I was a department director in a hospital and a new director of human resources was hired. She was very bubbly and outgoing and was clearly very friendly with the vice president who had hired her. She would stop by my office frequently to chat, invite me to lunch, and tell me about all the wonderful things she had heard about me and how impressed she was with me. I was flattered.

One day over lunch, this new director asked me how I got along with my boss, a different vice president. I told her that I got along great with him and actually liked him a lot, but she persisted in uncovering something negative, and I finally said, "Well, I didn't like the way he responded to a problem situation with an employee in my department," and I proceeded to give her a few details. I also shared with her that I had once been told I was a possible candidate for future promotion to a vice presidency position.

Shortly thereafter, my boss called me into his office. He said he had heard that I was making derogatory comments about him and gossiping about things in our department. I knew immediately where the information had come from. What possibly could have been this woman's motivation for passing on this information and making other disparaging remarks about me to my own boss? I immediately confronted her, and she said that she and her boss—the vice president she was friendly with—felt I was getting a swelled head about my accomplishments and position and needed to have things put in perspective. I had been burned big time.

I told my boss that what he heard was taken out of context and had been blown out of proportion and that I had been relentlessly goaded for information. Fortunately, he knew me well enough and had enough faith in me to dismiss the incident.

Although I was initially devastated by this incident, I did not let it get the best of me. I simply continued to do my job as I always had. The incident left an indelible mark on me and taught me two very important lessons: keep my work relationships professional and bite my tongue more often than not. I never reveal information to someone I don't know well, especially information about others or myself that could come back to haunt me.

If you've done something wrong or inadvertently insulted someone or stepped on some toes, the first step is to acknowledge your blunder and subsequently apologize if warranted. People will respect you for sincerely apologizing, and that will often be the end of the incident.

Talk It Out

Talking things out, face to face, is always the preferable way to resolve conflict. You should never send an e-mail or a written note, if possible, when discussing sensitive issues. Any other way besides face to face—whether it be written correspondence or a telephone conversation—leaves considerable room for misinterpretation and misunderstanding. Even though it takes courage to face the person you are having a conflict with, it is the best way.

If you do need to speak to, say, your supervisor, make an appointment to stop by the office. By having a person set time aside for you, you will have the opportunity to discuss the situation thoughtfully rather than trying to resolve things in the hallway on the run.

Most conflict comes from miscommunication, and a big but often overlooked part of effective communication is good listening. Be sure you take time to listen attentively to the other party to gain his or her perspective. Good, attentive listening solves many problems and clears up many misunderstandings.

DEALING WITH DIFFICULT PEOPLE

Some people just seem to like to give others a hard time. Maybe it's because they are insecure or angry and unhappy with their own circumstances, or perhaps it's because others have given them a hard time and they feel they need to do the same to people to compensate. Whatever the reason, it is important to recognize these people and not take their behavior personally if directed toward you.

Bite Your Tongue

Yes, this can be painful, even in the figurative sense, but when a difficult person is giving you a hard time, bite your tongue and ignore it. However, if the situation starts to interfere with your work or reputation, you may have to confront that person. If you can help it, it is always better to try to resolve conflict with another directly rather than going to your supervisor.

When you do approach someone about a situation, be calm. Prepare yourself for what you want to say, and stay focused. Don't ever use degrading or insulting language. That serves no purpose. Remember that people who are seemingly difficult by nature can get defensive and intimidate you without much effort. Keep this in mind and say what you rehearsed.

Make sure the timing and the circumstances are right. Don't embarrass the other person by talking within earshot of others.

You *Can* Work It Out

When I was a freshman nursing student, there was an upperclassman who seemed to have it in for me. She was rather loud and bawdy and would make unkind comments about me. She would also try to confront me and provoke a fight on occasion when she encountered me in the dormitory.

Eventually, I felt that our situation couldn't continue as it was. I had to do something about it—but what? After talking the situation over with my friends, I decided I had to confront her. Finally, I mustered up all my courage and knocked on her door, prepared with what I wanted to say.

When she finally answered, to my utter horror I realized I had woken her up! What could possibly be worse? In a panic, I said, "We need to talk—whenever it is convenient for you." Mortified, I swiftly turned to walk away as fast as I could.

The next evening, I heard a knock on my door. There stood my nemesis. "You wanted to talk to me?" I said, "Yes, please sit for a minute." Once again, I mustered up my courage and said, "You and I don't seem to have hit it off for some reason. Maybe our personalities clash because we are alike in so many ways." This brought a smirk to her face. I couldn't believe she actually smiled, albeit just a smirk!

"I think maybe you're right," she said. With renewed courage, I said to her, "I'm hoping we can call a truce." She smirked again, and said, "Sure." I extended my hand to shake, which she accepted. I was partly relieved, partly stunned, and partly in disbelief as to what had just transpired.

By approaching her in a calm, reasonable, but firm manner, I said what I felt needed to be said, she listened, and we worked it out. After that day, she never bothered me again.

Learn to be a diplomat. People who are quick to criticize and are difficult in general are often in need of some attention themselves. Sometimes showing them respect and appreciation by giving them some praise and attention will calm them down and get them off your case.

If someone is giving you trouble and you know you should address the situation, take time to collect your wits and prepare what you want to say. In spite of any fear you may have about confronting this person, after you work up

FROM THE FRONT LINE

Reality

"I discovered some gossiping and backstabbing—people talking behind each other's back—on my unit. You have to learn whom to trust and don't put too much trust in any one person. You can still be a team player, though."

—Rich, new grad

"There was one coworker on my unit who was very friendly with me. I revealed to her that I was going to have to report another coworker for unprofessional conduct, and she went and told the person I was planning to report simply to pit one person against another. The whole situation blew up. Fortunately, my manager handled it well. She called in all the players, got the facts, and did what needed to be done. I learned a lesson: I won't reveal things like this in the future and will only talk to the appropriate people. Being forewarned is being forearmed."

—Bill, new grad

"When starting a new job, keep quiet and listen. Feel out who's who before getting too buddy-buddy with people."

—Pennie, new grad

"Be careful who you align yourself with. Some people are less credible than they appear."

—Kevin K., new grad

the courage to do so and talk to the person about your situation, you will experience a sense of empowerment. You will realize a bit more that you can control the situations around you and in your life. Your self-esteem will be boosted up a notch, and you will realize that sometimes facing things head-on is the only way to deal with them.

In reflecting on my situation described in the "You *Can* Work It Out" box, I realized that sometimes the only way to deal with a bully is to confront the bully. I don't know if she developed some level of respect for me for having the guts to confront her or if the fact that I compared myself to her gave her a different view of me. The reason doesn't really matter. I got the results I desired. If you stay rational and express your thoughts clearly, you will get the results you need, too.

Dating Coworkers

Many people will tell you that work and dating don't mix. While there may be some truth to that, the reality is that many people who work together do date, and some develop long-term relationships or even marry. This doesn't necessarily mean you should be on the lookout for a mate when you get a job, but stuff happens, right? However, keep in mind that it is best to keep personal issues separate from workplace issues to the greatest extent possible. Additionally, make sure you are clear on your facility's policy on such relationships before you dive on in. Many companies have some sort of policy, and you will be well served by knowing what your company's policy is *before* things get too hot and heavy.

For certain, dating someone you work with presents a unique set of challenges. For your part, it can be distracting, especially if you encounter this other person frequently during your workday, which would be inevitable if you both work in the same department. If you have a relationship with someone in a position higher than yours, people will always assume that you have a direct pipeline to confidential information or that you divulge department secrets to your lover. This is known as "pillow talk." If you get a promotion or special recognition for something, there will always be those who assume it is because of whom you are dating. True or not, this can be a difficult situation to deal with, and it might not only affect your job performance but also ruin an otherwise great relationship.

The Rules of Love

If you do get romantically involved with someone you work with, discretion is the key word. Here are a few tips to follow:

- Know your company's policy—both written and unwritten.
- Be sure to still have lunch with your coworkers on a regular basis rather than with your significant other all the time.
- Avoid pubic displays of affection such as hand-holding and kissing and playing footsies under the lunchroom or boardroom table.
- If possible, avoid traveling to and from work together. That is, maintain your separate identities. Of course, if you're married to each other, that's not a problem.
- Don't reveal intimate details to your coworkers about your mate or about romantic weekends together, and should the relationship dissolve, be the bigger person and simply do your job and keep silent about all things about your partner.

If you get a promotion while dating someone in authority, there will be those who never respect your position and create their own reasons for your climbing the company ladder. You may be a very competent person and very deserving of the promotion, but you may never be recognized for that.

If you hear, know, or suspect that one of your coworkers is dating or is otherwise involved with another coworker, discretion is key. If you happen to run into two coworkers at the mall or at a restaurant, mind your own business and don't make assumptions. Above all, don't spread rumors. Careers and reputations have been ruined by false rumors. Once rumors are out, the damage is done.

I recently asked another nurse what she thought about dating coworkers, and she revealed the following:

> Disaster, disaster, disaster. I worked on a unit where the manager was a male. At different times, he dated two of the female staff nurses. This created a competitive situation between the two women. They had to work together and take report from each other, and it made things very uncomfortable for everyone. Both of these relationships eventually ended, too, which created additional tension on the unit for the parties involved as well as for the rest of us. On the other hand, I have known some nurses who dated doctors, and a few of these couples eventually got married. They always maintained a professional relationship while on the units, calling each other by their surnames and the like.

I know several nurses who have had relationships with coworkers. Like all relationships, some have worked out well and some have not. The point is, consider how it will affect you at work. No matter what the case, proceed with caution and use the utmost discretion.

Dating Patients—Not!

Undoubtedly, you have spent a great deal of time in nursing school discussing the nurse-patient relationship. Presumably, you have also discussed the concept of "the therapeutic relationship." A therapeutic relationship between practitioner and patient, in simple terms, is one in which optimum results for the patient can be achieved.

This brings us to the subject of dating your patients or getting romantically involved with them. Although this is considered taboo in many cases, I know of a few nurses who have married former patients. Occasionally, you will even hear of a nurse who marries a patient currently in her or his care. While it may appear to have worked out well for a few, understand that you are treading on thin ice, and slippery legal ice, if you move in this direction. Some states in the United States have laws prohibiting sexual contact between caregivers and their charges. This is obviously very serious. If you are suspected of impropriety or accused of same, it can minimally result in disciplinary action by your employer and/or state board of nursing or other governing body. Many consider dating and sexual activity with patients, at the very least, unethical and unprofessional.

Here, we get into issues of professional boundaries. The intimate nature of nursing care, both physical and emotional, can lead to a misunderstanding of feelings and relationships. Also, there is an unequal balance of power in the relationship, with the nurse clearly having the upper hand. The patient is very vulnerable, the nurse has access to personal information about the patient, and the nurse has mastery of the environment.

Getting romantically involved with a patient—with or without sexual contact—compromises the professional association. There is a delicate balance required to maintain appropriate boundaries in the therapeutic relationship. Because you are first and foremost a patient advocate, consider the ramifications of crossing inappropriate professional boundaries with your patients. Although you will find varying opinions on the subject among your professional colleagues, it is a subject for you to consider seriously.

Of course, if you encounter a former patient outside of the therapeutic environment, that is slightly different. However, there still may be some ethical issues involved. In any event, proceed with extreme caution.

CHAPTER 4

PATIENTS, FAMILIES, AND DOCTORS

Patients, clients, or consumers of health care—whatever terminology you use, these are the people you serve. And these people are not just in hospitals, doctor's offices, and health-care facilities. They are your family, your neighbors, and the general public. Now that you're a nurse, people will rely on you and call on you for advice, information, and comfort. This is a great responsibility, but it is also an honor—one that you should be happy to have.

Of course, this doesn't mean that you should treat and diagnose all people. Rather, recognize your position as a role model, a referral source, an adviser, an educator, and a nurturer. Appreciate the position you hold in society. You can be a great help and comfort to family members and friends when someone in their family or their friend is ill or dying or trying to navigate his or her way through a confusing and complicated health-care system.

What they may not have told you in nursing school, but you may have already discovered, is that the public at large will now feel free to tell you about their ailments, their bodily functions, their injuries and illnesses, and their surgeries in great detail. They may tell you over dinner, at family gatherings, at social events, or at other inappropriate times. You will learn to smile, listen attentively, and nod. The point is, you are always a nurse, not just while in uniform or scrubs or officially on-duty. The general public considers nurses to be very approachable and very credible. In many cases, people feel much more comfortable talking with a nurse than they do with a physician. This is why they love to talk to you when they have the chance.

PATIENTS

That being said, let's talk about your patients, or clients, in a therapeutic environment. The therapeutic environment is one in which you are officially at work. Years ago, when health care became more business oriented and therefore competitive, the term *client* first surfaced as a way to refer to patients. The thinking was that, as health-care providers, we are providing a service, and our patients are therefore our clients. It was also believed that by thinking of patients as clients, we, the health-care providers, would be more customer-service oriented and have less of an "I know what's best for you, so don't question me" mentality.

Another perspective is that by calling those we serve *clients,* we put them in the driver's seat in terms of their care, whereas the term *patient* implies someone who is helpless and dependent.

When practiced to perfection, the customer-service orientation, including use of the word *client,* is a good one. It forces the whole system to focus on the patient—to make him or her the most important person. However, even with such good intentions, this is something we occasionally lose sight of.

There are some nurses who take exception to this and reject the word *client* and the customer-service concept. Some nurses believe health care is too business-oriented and therefore they reject any business-minded terminology. In reality, there is room for both *patient* and *client,* and in many circles, the two words are used interchangeably.

In addition, the term *business* in reference to health care is also an issue for some nurses for the same reasons they reject the term *client.* Health care has its roots in charity, where many providers did not get paid for their services or simply received a minimal wage. Everything was for the good of the people. However, today, we and other health-care providers want and need to get paid for our education, experience, and work. Health care *is* a business, like it or not. It is the business we work in. That does not detract from what we do.

The terminology, *client* versus *patient,* is not what really matters, so don't get caught up in it. Your predecessors have seen many changes in nursing and health care in the last few years and decades. And as with any change, there are those who resist and fight hard to maintain the old ways. You, on the other hand, come to nursing with a fresh start and have the ability to set precedents and create the rules as the new realities of nursing and health care evolve. Somewhere there is a balance. Find your reality between the extremes.

Remember Who You Are Dealing With

While your patients will rely on you for a variety of physical tasks and nursing duties, a smile, a touch, and a soft, comforting word go a long way. Focusing on caring in the purest sense will add to your own sense of gratification, too. Reflect on making a difference in a patient's existence rather than just hanging so many IV bags.

One of the most important things to remember is to never lose sight of the patients as people and to consider their personality, their modesty, and their dignity. Even if they come to you in an unconscious or a debilitated state, in reality they are just like you: vibrant and loved, with a family, friends, and a complete life. Imagine if your mother, father, or child were being treated by someone. You would want that individual to give your loved one a high level of attention, care, and respect. When you lose that focus, you become nothing more than a technician. Treat *everyone* as a person rather than as an illness or injury.

Most patients feel intimidated, powerless, afraid, and, often, confused. If you've ever been a patient yourself, you know the feeling of not having control, being vulnerable, and knowing you are out of your element. You should approach care with this in mind. Simply put, you are there to *help,* and you must remember that.

Understand and Be Patient

The most difficult patients can present the greatest challenge. Don't ever take it personally when a patient or family member lashes out at you. Look behind the anger and the frustration to see what is really happening. You are the caregiver. Remember your role and your responsibility. The great majority of your patients are decent people—focus on that.

When report is given and another nurse says, "That patient is very difficult" or something similar, reserve judgment and see for yourself. If you approach people with the attitude that they are difficult, you likely will find them to be so.

While your patients can indeed make your days a little longer, they are also what will get you through most days. Enjoy your patients for the time you have with them and appreciate the fact that you have an opportunity to enter their lives at a vulnerable time. You will have the privilege of escorting some into this life, seeing others out of this life, and witnessing every other imaginable scenario along the way.

You will learn a lot from your patients. They will teach you many things about yourself, your profession, and life in general. Some of them certainly will annoy you, some of them will touch your heart, and some of them will drain you one day and energize you the next. In the end, in one way or another, each one will have a permanent impact on your life and your soul, and you will be inalterably changed for having crossed paths with them. Through your patients, you will learn to value life, respect death, and see the strengths and weaknesses of the human spirit.

THE CONCEPT OF CARING

Fresh out of school, one is usually focused on learning the skills and procedures that go along with the profession. These things are, naturally, important. But even more important than your technical skills is your sense of caring for your patients and their families. Caring is first and foremost. You can start to care immediately—without orientation and without practice.

Utilize everything that drew you to nursing in the first place: your desire to help people, make a difference in other people's lives, ease pain and suffering, and contribute to the quality of life for your patients and their families. Convey your sense of caring for people, and they will be forgiving and patient with your lack of experience. When people believe you care for them, they will believe you did your best under the circumstances. It has even been shown that people are less likely to initiate lawsuits when they believe their caregivers care about them.

Carol, a nursing instructor at a community college, said, "We have an expression for students and new grads related to patients that says, 'They don't

care how much you know until they know how much you care.' That means
that a sense of caring can sometimes be more important to a patient than your
level of experience."

A deeper sense of caring is what separates nurses from other health-care
providers. This is what makes us unique. Nurses are there twenty-four hours a
day caring for patients. It is nurses who put the word *care* in *health care*. Focus
on patient-centered care, and you will always stay on track. The following are
some important ways to do that:

- *Put your patient first.* He or she is the focal point of your work, your
profession, and health care. Your patients are your world when you are
working. This is whom you should be thinking about when you start
your day. This is whom you should reflect on at the end of each day.
- *Be of service to your patients.* They are the most important part of the
equation. Nursing is a service business. Remember that.
- *Be mindful of the person.* As mentioned, each patient has a life, an
occupation, a family, an ethnic background, a religion—a *life*. This is
who they are, not simply the "patient in Room 402." And certainly
each is much more than part of your caseload for the day. Focus on
the person, not the illness or the diagnosis.
- *Treat your patients with dignity and respect.* This is much easier to
do when you look at each individual as a person and not as a patient.
Preserve their modesty. Speak to them respectfully. Treat them as you
would your own family.
- *Regard the patient's family with respect and dignity, too.* Put yourself in
the family members' position. They are an extension of the patient, so
involve them in the care. You need their help and support, and they
need your help and support, too.
- *Involve patients in their own care.* Talk to them, explain things to
them, and ask if they have any questions. This goes for a patient's family, too. If the patient feels involved with the care provided, you are
much more likely to get the information and help you need from the
patient.
- *Listen.* Listen with your ears and your eyes. Develop your intuitive nature to see what is really going on with the patient and his or

her family. Sometimes your ears are needed more to listen than your mouth to talk. Good listening is key to effective communication.

Language Barrier

When I was just a rookie and working in the emergency room, I needed to get a urine sample from a patient. I approached the man with a lab container and said, "We need to get a urinalysis. Could you please void in this specimen container?" The man looked at me with a blank expression on his face and said in a questioning tone, "What?" I decided to rephrase my request. "We need to run some tests. Would you please urinate into this container?" His expression did not change, and he said again, this time more emphatically, "What?" Feeling frustrated, I took a deep breath, thought for a moment, and decided to try one more time. "Please pee into the bottle," I said. His expression changed to one of understanding. He smiled and said, "Sure. Why didn't you say that in the first place?" I wondered the same thing.

• *Be aware of your language.* Speak to your patients in plain language—everyday English. Some nurses develop a bad habit of talking only in medical jargon. We lose the ability to explain things in a way our patients can understand. When we can't communicate clearly, we lose some of our effectiveness as a caregiver.

"I force myself to smile and act in a good mood with my patients even when I'm not. Interestingly, I find that by forcing myself to 'act' this way, it actually improves my mood."

—Barry, new grad

• *Empower your patients to help themselves.* Make sure their call light and other equipment are within reach when you leave them. Advise them what to do if they need help. Let them know when you'll be back and what will happen next. Explain your schedule, what they should expect, and when they should expect it.

• *Be pleasant.* Greet your patients with a smile (when appropriate) regardless of the kind of day you are having or the mood you are in. One nurse refers to this as "putting on my professional face before walking into the patient's room." Don't complain to your patients or tell them about what a bad day you are having or how overworked you are. It is certainly appropriate to tell them that you may not get back to them for a while because you have a full house today on the unit or something similar. Just remember that they want and deserve some of your attention regardless of your workload.

• *Set time limits with your patients.* Everyone is very busy and doesn't have enough time to teach and explain as they would like. When you go in to do diabetic teaching or something similar, you might say, "We have ten minutes together." Such a remark will help the patient understand what is about to happen. Further, the patient will not have unreasonable expectations of your time or feel shortchanged when you leave.

• *Don't make assumptions about your patients.* It is easy to get in the habit of relying on printed materials for patient education and discharge instructions. However, not every patient can read English, and some cannot read at all. You might say, "Are you able to read this?" or "Do you need any help with that?"

We often instruct patients to follow up with their family doctor, yet we rarely ask them if they have a family doctor, if they drive, or if they have someone who can take them to see the doctor. You might ask, "Do you have a doctor or nurse practitioner you see?" Maybe a patient needs a social service consult or simply some help arranging future transportation to a physician's office.

Speaking of nurse practitioners (NPs), get into the habit of always saying "physician or nurse practitioner" when you speak to people about their primary care providers. Remember that today physicians, NPs, and other advanced practice nurses provide primary health-care services. As nurses, we certainly must promote our own profession by using the correct lingo. You are promoting the fact that NPs are also primary health-care providers every time you ask, "Do you have a family physician or nurse practitioner?" It is also better to use the term *physician* rather than *doctor* when speaking to patients about their medical doctors. Many nurses have doctoral degrees and therefore also have the title "doctor." Though some do not choose to use the title *doctor,* using the term *physician* when referring to medical doctors is a step toward clarity.

HANDLING SPECIAL SITUATIONS

Your career as a nurse will be filled with unique situations and challenges. And it makes sense that your first encounters with these will be the most trying. Practice makes perfect. But hopefully, by giving some thought as to how you will handle some of the unique spots you will find yourself in, you can handle them thoughtfully.

Listening, Patience, and Effort

When I was a non-clinical department manager, I received a call from administration advising me that the adult son of one of our patients was irate about the fact that his mother was scheduled to be discharged. The man believed his mother was too sick to go home and was making accusations about the care she received.

When the man introduced himself to me on the phone, I could hear the anger and frustration in his voice. I asked him to explain his concerns and questions to me. Because he was so emotional and clearly distraught, I could do nothing but simply listen to him. There was no opportunity for me to say something, even if I had wanted to. The more I focused on listening to him, the more I could hear the frustration and sense of powerlessness in his voice.

After a moment of silence, he said, "Are you still there?" I replied, "Yes. I'm listening." With that, his voice immediately became calm, and he said in an even tone, "Thank you for listening to me. You are the first person who took the time to listen, and I appreciate that." I was able to ascertain that he primarily wanted to look at his mother's medical record, which he had not been allowed to do. Because many staff people didn't know if it was legal for him to look at his mother's chart, they kept putting him off, which only further infuriated him and made him think they were trying to hide something. He was demanding an immediate response and resolution to his request.

I posed the situation to my director, and she advised me that he could look at the record as long as his mother signed a release granting the hospital permission to show it to him. We got his mother's written permission. He came in the next day and reviewed the record and agreed to have his mother discharged. That was the last we ever heard of him. My listening, patience, and effort to help my *other* patient, the medical patient's son, paid off. The bottom line is that not only should you allow someone his or her say, but through concentrated listening, you will be able to really understand what is going on and come up with a solution to the problem.

Always try to find out about the real person behind the patient. If you are caring for a patient who is comatose or very debilitated, ask the patient's family to tell you about his or her personality and the things he or she enjoys. This will give you a better sense of the real person and show the family you care. I had a colleague who would ask the family of a comatose or debilitated patient to bring in a picture of the patient in his or her prime. She would tape it to the bed. This helped the staff get a sense of the personality behind the illness. It keeps the human factor alive.

If your patient happens to be a nurse, doctor, or other health-care practitioner, don't assume that he or she needs less care or instruction. A patient is a patient, and each is vulnerable, fearful, and perhaps experiencing a loss of control. Help your patients get through their situations.

If a patient's family member is a doctor or a nurse, don't feel threatened. Treat that family member as a professional colleague and respect the knowledge that goes with the territory. But always treat each family member of someone who is ill or injured as an individual who needs assistance and compassion.

"I had to really learn to listen to my patients. Sometimes the textbook said one thing, but they were telling me another. Many patients know their own illness better than anyone else. They can tell you a lot about what is going on with them if you only listen."

—Barry, new grad

INSTILLING A SENSE OF CONFIDENCE

The mere fact that you are a nurse does not automatically instill confidence in those you serve. Credentials alone do little to reassure patients that they're in good hands. You have to also look and act the part of a competent, professional person. In other words, you have to inspire confidence in others by doing the following:

- Putting your clients at ease.
- Quickly developing a sense of trust and care.
- Positioning yourself as an expert in their eyes.
- Remembering and relaying that you possess a body of health-care knowledge.
- Combining the above and creating a desire within your patients to continue their relationship with you.

So how do you do it? You instill confidence with your appearance, your mannerisms, your behavior, your demeanor, your communication skills, and your ability to meet your patients' needs. From the moment you encounter your patients and their families, all the rules of first impressions come into play. I discussed some of these elements earlier in this chapter and in chapter 1.

Communicating

Consider what makes you feel comfortable when *you* first meet someone. Your first sense of people is often based simply on whether they acknowledge your presence as a human being. Would you prefer that someone make immediate eye contact with you, smile, introduce him- or herself, and give you a proper greeting? Or, would you rather a person begin talking immediately about business or your next treatment while looking down at a clipboard, without so much as giving you a "good morning"? I'll talk in a minute about the right way to introduce yourself to your patients.

Always try to appear confident and calm around your clients—even if you don't feel that way. If you appear nervous and frightened when performing a procedure, your patients and their family members will likely be ill at ease, too.

If you are asked a question that you can't answer, never simply say, "I don't know." Rather, say something such as "Let me get you an answer on that" or "Let me get someone who can answer that for you." Of course, you should then find another nurse or someone else to help out and get the answer you need.

Always talk to your clients, make sure they understand everything you

---

FROM THE FRONT LINE

A Little Help

"When I find out a patient's family member is a nurse or doctor, I first try to assess where he or she works and what his or her specialty is so we can communicate better. Each area of expertise has a different level of experience and familiarity with acute care. I also ask, 'What do you think of this place?' (referring to the facility) to assess where the family member is coming from. All this helps me to work more effectively with him or her. I also let the person talk when we first meet to show an interest in him or her. I don't hesitate to ask the family member to help me with care."

—Kevin K., new grad

---

are saying, and *listen*. Communication goes both ways. Keep your patients informed to the greatest extent possible, and be your patients' advocate. Let them know you are on their side and are there to help them.

Introducing Yourself to Patients and Families

When entering a room or an exam area, make eye contact first with the patient and then with the family. Remember that the patient is your primary client, but keep in mind that both the patient and the family are your clients. When appropriate, shake hands as part of your introduction. Because you may be doing more intimate touching during exams and treatments of your patients, starting out with a respectful type of touching such as shaking hands is a good way to start the relationship.

Years ago, it was easy to distinguish the nurse from other staff members. *She* was the one in the white uniform and cap, and patients took comfort in that appearance. Today, health-care workers, including nurses and doctors, often work in a generic uniform of scrubs and lab coats. While some nurses believe they identify themselves by their mannerisms and demeanor, they are sadly mistaken. Because many nurses are men and many physicians are women today, confusion can result if a proper introduction does not take place.

A Proper Introduction

Remember that handshaking and certain types of contact and introductions do not have a place in every aspect of health care, such as in some emergency situations. And, of course, there are certain cultures that forbid handshaking between members of the opposite sex. Use whatever contact and introduction is appropriate based on the entire situation. It will do much to position you as a competent, credible practitioner and to put your patients and their family members at ease.

While we would like to believe that people can identify us by our behavior, that is not always the case. A few years ago, my father was hospitalized after surgery. I spent considerable time with him during the first two days postoperative. I deliberately observed the staff members who flowed in and out during the day to see if they identified themselves. If they didn't identify themselves, I tried to guess what their credentials were before asking. I tried to read their name badges, but I discovered that many staff members wore name badges that were hidden by lab coats or sweaters or were turned around so that I couldn't read them. In some cases, the print was so small that I couldn't read the names even when the badges were visible.

I observed staff members' appearance, including their dress, body language, use of eye contact—or lack thereof—and other visual cues. If they did not introduce or otherwise identify themselves, I would eventually ask them for their name and title. Sometimes, I was right in my assumptions about their position, and sometimes I was not. One woman was very sloppy in her dress and grooming and handling of equipment. She made no eye contact with anyone in the room and didn't in any way identify herself, and I guessed she was a nurse's aide or other ancillary position. When I asked her for her credentials, she informed me, much to my dismay, that she was a registered nurse. On another occasion, a very well-groomed woman entered the room, addressed my father by his surname, announced she would take his vital signs, and acknowledged both my mother and me by looking our way and saying hello. I asked if she was a nurse, and she replied cheerily, "No, I'm a nurse's aide."

Consider for a moment that you are the patient in the hospital bed and different people come for different tasks and reasons. You would want to know who the people are, what their positions are, and what they are doing there. With that in mind, whenever it is feasible, you should introduce yourself to your patients and their families using your name and credentials. Say something such as "Hi. I'm Carol Adams. I'm the registered nurse in charge of your care today." Don't remain a generic entity leaving people to guess what your credentials are. Remember that important people have names and credentials.

What's in a Name?

The question of whether you should refer to yourself as "Carol," "Carol Adams," "Nurse Adams," or "Ms. Adams" is a matter of personal preference or your facility's policy, if one exists. Years ago, nurses were addressed by their surname—Ms.

Adams, Mr. Adams—or were referred to as Nurse Adams. Somewhere along the way, that custom was dropped. For the most part, physicians are addressed as Dr. Adams, but we usually refer to nurses by their first names. Why is this an issue? Because how you address someone can imply different levels of authority—in this case, creating an unequal power structure. Shakespeare started that debate by asking, "What's in a name?" but he didn't mention anything about forms of address, which have always signified a form of respect (or disrespect) in our society. It all comes down to issues of respect, equality, and power. Ask your colleagues who have been on the job for a while what works for them. But use your discretion as to what you think is appropriate.

How to Address Your Patients

Then there's the issue of how to address your patients. Even though using first names may seem friendlier, some patients are actually more comfortable with formality in the health-care setting. Some argue that the use of surnames and titles helps to maintain the professional relationship. Formality, or what some of your patients may deem as respectful forms of address, may be more comfortable for your patients than being addressed by their first name. There are many people, especially of the older generation, who consider it disrespectful to be addressed by their first name. We have become an increasingly informal society and sometimes automatically address people by their first name when we should not do so. Be sensitive to your patients' preferences. Sometimes it is safer to start out with formal forms of address and progress from there.

Appearance

Although appearance isn't everything, it has a greater impact on credibility than we realize. When you walk into a room, before you even introduce yourself, your patients begin to create an opinion about you. If you look like you don't care about yourself, how can you expect your patients to believe you will care about them? Make sure you are clean and together and look like you are capable of taking care of another person.

FROM THE FRONT LINE

Pleased to Meet You

"When I do my admission assessment, I introduce myself to the patient and his or her family members by saying, 'My name is Agnes Harris. I'm the RN in charge of your care today.' I explain to all patients that many people will be involved in their care and then give the rundown for the day, including the names of the team members they're likely to encounter, such as 'Carol Anderson is the nurse's aide who will be doing most of your physical care. John Engells, RN, will be giving you your medication. If you need anything, ring the call bell and someone will assist you.' If they're scheduled for a procedure or test, I mention these to them, along with the anticipated time, so they know what to expect. I might say, 'You're scheduled for an x-ray at ten this morning. Someone from the x-ray department or transport team will be up thereabouts to take you downstairs. Do you have any questions?' I try to leave them with some paper and a pencil and advise them that if they have any questions during the shift, they should write them down so they won't forget when I or the doctor or another nurse comes in. This conveys that it's okay to ask questions.

"I have found that all of this puts people at ease, empowers them to be more in control of their own care, and makes them feel taken care of. If I prepare patients for what to expect, they are calmer, less demanding, and more in control. If there is a change in schedule, if their medication is changed, or any other changes occur, I make a note to let them know. Patients have a lot of time on their hands, so they spend a great deal of time thinking. They are usually very familiar with their care and routine and become unnerved when something changes that they haven't been told about or if things don't happen on schedule.

"I also let patients know that I am in charge of their care. I tell them that if they need to see a social worker or a dietician, I am the one who will arrange that. This way they get a sense that one person, their nurse, is coordinating their care and is in charge, even though they may not see me for a good part of the day."

—Agnes, nurse

A WORD (OR TWO) ABOUT DOCTORS

Nurses have a long and rich history of working side by side with doctors in health care. Doctors and nurses have always been, and still are, the major practitioners in health care. We complement and enhance each other's practice. Remember that one cannot do a job without the help of another in many health-care settings. We are collaborators of care.

The relationship between doctors and nurses has evolved considerably over the years. For instance, there was a time when nurses were taught to stand when a physician entered the nurses' station, and our dialogue consisted mostly of the doctor saying, "Nurse, get me this," and the nurse responding, "Yes, doctor." Nursing practice has evolved considerably, and societal norms have changed somewhat in relation to gender—as has the relationship between doctor and nurse. In any event, it is a complex and interesting dynamic.

You may hear some horror stories from other nurses about how difficult certain doctors can be—about how you have to stroke their egos and so forth. While there is no denying that some of this may be true, the good news is that there is more equality and respect between nurses and doctors than ever before. As new doctors (both men and women) come along, as well as new nurses (both men and women, too), we are seeing a new relationship develop.

Today, some nurses and doctors are on a first-name basis with one another when not in the presence of patients or their families. This was virtually unheard of years ago. But it is a sign of the changing times. As more and more nurses become advanced practitioners and work on a more even keel with physicians, this relationship will continue to evolve.

Lookin' Good—or Not

Years ago, I worked with an orthopedic surgeon who always looked very disheveled and unkempt. He even wore a shirt with a pocket that was torn—it was held up with a safety pin! Whenever I saw him, my motherly instincts would kick in and make me want to run down the hall after him and ask him to take his shirt off while I stitched up the pocket. Of course I never did, and neither did anyone else apparently, because I saw him in that ripped shirt all the time. I don't know if he wore the same shirt all the time or if all his shirts were torn. In any event, it left a negative impression in my mind. I heard he was a good surgeon, but I remember thinking that I wouldn't want him to operate on me because he might try to safety-pin my joints together rather than fixing them properly.

Likewise, when I had abdominal surgery years ago, there was one nurse who would occasionally come in to check my dressing and incision. She looked like she was overdue for a shower, and her lab coat was stained and unpressed. I was very uncomfortable having her touch my incision. Her appearance made me wonder how often she washed her hands. Obviously, appearance does matter. Look good, and your patients will feel comfortable in your care even before they get to know you.

I have my share of doctor-related war stories to tell, but for the most part, I always liked physicians and got along well with them. I regarded them as colleagues and found that they would then regard me as the same. A large part of your relationships with physicians has to do with your level of confidence and your assertiveness.

It's important to spend some time reflecting on your role and your place in health care, especially as it relates to physicians.

Tips on Working with Doctors

The more you get to know any individual, doctors included, the better. You must remember that doctors are people, too. They deserve to be treated with honesty and respect just like you do. Doctors have interests, families, and concerns just like everyone else. They have a lot they can teach you as well as learn from you. The better you communicate with them, the more mutually beneficial your relationship will be. And with that, the better care you will provide. The following are some tips for developing a positive rapport with physicians.

> • *Introduce yourself to doctors.* You need to take the first step. Go out of your way to introduce yourself to physicians. Approach them with a smile, make eye contact, and extend your hand to shake. Say something such as "Dr. Harris, my name is Ann Gable/Ms. Gable. I'm a recent RN graduate and will be working on the day shift here on 4 North. It's a pleasure to meet you, and I look forward to working with you." I guarantee you that this will make a positive first impression and implant you in their memory.

• *Sincere flattery never hurts.* It is always a good idea to say something such as "I have heard a lot of good things about you and look forward to learning from you." This sets the stage for physicians (and others) to want to help you. It's a good way to start a relationship.

• *Don't be intimidated.* Many new graduates feel intimidated by physicians. Perhaps it's because of their advanced education, the power they wield in the system, or the respect that society has for them in general. Whatever the reason, maintain perspective. You are both in the same business, on the same team, and have the same goals for your clients. One is not better than the other or superior to the other in any way. You each have your own job to do and are both vital links in the system. Respect the physician, but respect yourself, too.

• *Be assertive.* Don't be timid, and always be an advocate for your patient. Never call physicians and say, "I'm sorry to bother you," or, "I'm sorry to be calling you so late." You're not bothering them; that's their job, and you are doing *your* job by calling them!

• *Ask questions.* Most physicians love to teach. Ask them to explain something about a treatment or disease. Ask intelligent questions, but don't be a pest by asking them at inappropriate times.

• *Establish rapport.* Take time to develop good relationships with physicians. Talk with them and give them time to get to know you and trust you. This is the basis of any good relationship. Go out of your way to say hello to them each time they come onto your unit.

• *Be honest and direct.* If a procedure is new to you, tell the doctor that before the start of the procedure. This will obviously save problems from occurring, plus the doctor has the opportunity to walk you through the procedure so you understand it in future situations.

• *Show respect and consideration—but don't be a doormat.* Assist physicians, but don't be a servant. Give them due respect, and expect the same from them. If a physician is out of line or rude, you might say, "I don't appreciate being spoken to in that way," or, "I would appreciate being spoken to in a civil tone of voice, and I promise to do the same with you," or something similar. If a physician is rude to you in front of a patient, it is best to refrain from discussing the matter until you are in private.

- *Seek clarification.* When a physician's order is unclear or you can't read it or understand it, get clarification from the doctor. It's your license on the line here. Besides, physicians sometimes make mistakes. They are human.

Communicating with Doctors

While most physicians are decent people, all of them are busy and have a lot on their minds. They are very much "bottom line" people, which means they usually want the facts, the question, or the statement of the problem in a clear, concise format. They are often on the run and will usually lose patience, as most people would, if you beat around the bush, seem unclear on what you want to say, or fumble and stammer. With doctors especially, you need to be straight to the point, clear, and concise.

When preparing to give a physician a report on a patient, take time to compose your thoughts and make some written notes beforehand. One nurse I spoke with says she will say to a new grad, "Okay, you have two minutes. What are you going to tell them?" This time limitation forces the new grads to put the information in a concise format.

"Know what you want before you call a doctor. In a teaching hospital, you may be calling interns who may ask you what you suggest. So have some suggestions ready."

—Shannon, new grad

Keep notes so you can remember what you want to report or ask. One of my colleagues leaves a self-sticking note on the chart, pointing out things she wants to discuss with the doctor and leaving her name. The doctor then seeks her out. It also gives the appearance that she is organized—even if she doesn't feel that way.

When calling a physician on the phone, state your name and credentials. You might say, "Good evening, Dr. Franks. This is Fred Schneider / Mr. Schneider, RN, from 3 East at County General." Continue by stating the name of the patient you are calling about, what you want to discuss, or what the question is. Again, don't ever say, "I'm sorry to bother you."

If an order from a doctor seems inappropriate or incorrect, rather than saying, "This order does not seem appropriate for this patient," which would likely put the physician on the defensive and make him or her feel threatened or embarrassed, try, "Teach me something, Dr. Harris. I've never seen a dosage of Lasix that high. Can you explain the therapeutic dynamics to me?" Or, "Dr. Yim—I can't figure out why you ordered an MRI of the brain on this patient. Can you help me out here?" In this way, you pique the doctor's curiosity. I frequently used this approach as a diplomatic way of questioning an order that seemed out of whack.

FROM THE FRONT LINE

A Memorable Patient

"Very early in my career, I cared for an elderly woman whom I referred to as 'acutely, chronically ill.' That means she had both acute and chronic disease processes, was very sickly, and was very needy. I frequently was assigned to her care. I got to know her daughter, who was about my age, and we got along well. Her daughter requested that I be assigned to her mother whenever possible. I got very close to both of them.

"The woman, my patient, taught me more than she ever could have dreamed. She needed various treatments and forms of care; thus, in the course of her care, I had the opportunity to practice much of what I had learned in nursing school and do many things for the first time.

"She used to ring her call bell every five minutes, and this forced me to think about what was really going on with her, how else I could help her, and how I could make her feel more comfortable. Her condition and her situation offered many opportunities for me to learn and grow and develop as a nurse.

"When she died, it really affected me. It was the first time I had developed a real nursing bond with a patient and a family. I felt that I had really been able to help her and her family and that I had made a difference. This was something I read about in nursing textbooks but had never experienced before. I owe her a debt of gratitude, and I will never forget her."

—Kevin K., new grad

This approach usually results in the physician either reevaluating the order or changing it, or providing additional documentation. At the very least, it will open the door for discussion about the order in a non-threatening way. Often, the physician would say, "Did I write that? Let me change it," or, "You've got a point there. Let's cancel it." Tact and diplomacy work wonders. Rather than sounding like you're questioning the physician's judgment, you come across as seeking additional information. This allows the physician to save face and adjust the order or provide more information.

CHAPTER 5

STAYING CONNECTED

We've talked about developing relationships with your coworkers. While that's very important, it's not enough for a well-rounded life and career. Nurses have a tendency to get very isolated in their departments, in their places of work, and even within their own specialties. What's wrong with that? They develop tunnel vision—a very limited view of the profession and the world in general. With tunnel vision, you limit your contacts, become out of touch, and develop a limited frame of reference. How can you know if your work situation is good or bad, what your career options are, and what is possible to achieve if you don't have a network outside your place of employment?

NETWORKING

To be successful, as a nurse and in life overall, you must develop professional relationships outside your workplace, outside your specialty, and even outside nursing. How do you do that? Through regular and vigorous networking. Networking is making personal contacts and connections with people. It is talking to people, getting out and meeting people, staying in touch with them, and developing mutually beneficial relationships with them.

There is an expression, "No one succeeds alone." That means that successful people have a network of others with whom they stay connected and whom they rely on throughout their professional lives. The great thing about a network is that, regardless of where you work or whether you are working at any given time, your network is always with you.

Think of networking as building a support system, a "success team" of people on whom you can call for advice and guidance. Your network also includes colleagues with whom you can get together to let off steam and commiserate. It is other professionals with whom you can share ideas and information.

There are two types of networking: networking to stay connected and networking with a specific objective. The stay-connected type of networking makes you better at your current job. It is where you turn to get information and advice—and sometimes empathy or encouragement. This is the type you'll participate in most often.

The objective type of networking may be to find a job or to promote a business or service. Career management experts will tell you that networking is the best and most effective way to find and get a job. It is also crucial in starting and building any type of business, consulting practice, or private practice.

Regardless of your intent, networking should be part of your game. Simply stated, networking is the best way to stay connected to your profession, and it will help you in many ways. Networking provides the opportunity to do the following:

- Exchange information and ideas with peers
- Stay abreast of what's happening in your profession
- Let off steam and relieve stress
- Decrease your feelings of being alone
- Get advice and guidance
- Solve problems
- Find a job
- Make important contacts

Where to Network

Of all the many ways and places to network, the face-to-face encounter is the most effective. When people meet you in person, they interact with you on several levels. They can associate a face and a personality with the name, see how you carry yourself, and get a better feel for who you are. Some of the best arenas for networking are places where lots of professional people gather, such as the following:

- Professional association meetings
- Health-care and nursing conventions
- Career fairs
- Seminars and workshops

How to Network

Now you should be convinced that networking is important. So how do you get started?

Reach Out

There are opportunities to network virtually everywhere. Since overcoming my fear of talking to people I don't know, I have met some of the most interesting people in the most unusual places. A trip to the beauty parlor once turned into a great networking opportunity. I was sitting next to a woman and couldn't help but overhear her conversation. I suspected she was a nurse by the way she was talking and asked her if she was. She looked at me quite surprised and said, "Why, yes, I am." We talked, and I learned a lot about hospice nursing, which was her area. She gave me a unique insider's perspective. We exchanged business cards and still stay in touch. You will make amazing connections and learn a great deal if you take small risks, like I did that day, and talk to more people anywhere and everywhere.

Networking involves talking to people and staying in touch with people. So start by setting a goal to introduce yourself and talk to at least one new person at the next meeting you attend. Exchange contact information with him or her and stay in touch. Introduce yourself by saying, "Hi. I'm Susan Gardner, an RN working in cardiac care at City General Hospital. How about you?" Or try starting with an icebreaker such as "Have you ever been to this event before?" Usually the conversation will go from there. With practice, you will eventually feel comfortable introducing yourself.

While in-person networking is always best, the telephone is also an effective means of networking. Getting on the phone and staying in touch with people you already know is a great way to get started. Let people know that you've graduated from nursing school and tell them where you are working or that you're looking for a job—whatever the case may be. The telephone is an appropriate way to make new contacts, too. Call someone you wish to speak with and introduce yourself. Ask if this is a good time to talk, and if it is, state the reason for your call in a clear, straightforward way: "My name is Fred Blum. I'm a recently graduated nurse. I've heard a lot of good things about you and wonder if you have any advice for a new graduate like myself." Or, "I've heard that nurses work for the department of health in various roles. I'm thinking this might be something I'd like to do in the future and wonder if you could tell me more about these opportunities."

Writing letters or notes is another way to network. This can serve as a way to introduce yourself preceding a phone call. For example, let someone know that you will call him or her next week and why you'll be calling. A letter or note is also a great way to stay in touch with people once you have made the connection.

You'll be amazed at how total strangers will be willing to talk to you and give you advice if you approach them with respect and courtesy and show your appreciation for their time and help.

Another important component of networking is to keep yourself visible within your profession and put yourself in people's minds so they will think of you. You want them to think of you and contact you when they hear of an opportunity that might be right for you or when they have some information that they think might be helpful to you. Remember, it's not just who you know, but who knows you, that can lead to some great opportunities. Your network can present you with opportunities that you hadn't even thought of or didn't even know existed. When someone has a great job opportunity that they're looking to fill, they often put the word out to people they know rather than putting an ad in the classifieds. If you've done your job, hopefully someone will think of you and call you or recommend you. Have you ever heard someone say they got a certain job through word of mouth? That's networking.

Networking Essentials

Before you head to your first networking opportunity and dive right in, there are a few other things you need to consider, from the way you look to the way you present yourself during and after your initial encounter.

Appearance

Face-to-face contact is the most effective form of networking, and a professional appearance and demeanor go a long way in getting off on the right foot with someone. Because first impressions are often created in about three seconds, you have very little time to create a favorable and professional impression. Remember that, although they happen in a matter of seconds, first impressions, once made, are lasting and difficult to shake.

So how do you relay in such a short period of time that you are professional, competent, and confident? Start with your appearance—your clothing, accessories, grooming, posture, eye contact, facial expressions, and overall demeanor. In short, dress professionally, limit accessories, be well-groomed, stand and sit up straight, make direct eye contact, smile, and be confident but not cocky. Your overall appearance is critical in a formal networking environment such as a convention or career fair.

Handshaking

Handshaking is a very important social custom, and it is an important part of face-to-face networking. The handshake is a critical part of any professional encounter. If you want to make the right first impression with someone, properly shake his or her hand.

Share the Wealth

When looking for advice and information, don't overuse one person. Develop your network constantly.

Most people consider themselves to be shy networkers. I'm sure some of you are already thinking, "You don't understand. I can't just strike up a conversation with a stranger." That's okay. Most people feel that way at first. I was a shy net-worker way back when. But when I decided to start my own business, I knew I had to start talking to people and making connections, or I would fail. My desire to be successful was more powerful than my fear of networking. It was hard at first, but it got easier and more comfortable as time went on. How I wish I had started to do this earlier in my career!

Not just any handshake will do, mind you. People will judge you not only on whether you shake their hand, but also on the quality of your handshake. A credible handshake is a full, firm shake (right hand to right hand), accompanied by direct eye contact and a smile. A full, firm shake is one in which you lock thumb webs with the other person and exert a firm, but not bone-crushing, grip. You then give it one or two pumps, and that's it. Don't forget the accompanying eye contact and smile.

Shake hands when you first meet someone and then again when you part company. Handshaking is not just for first-time meetings, either. You should get in the habit of shaking hands with colleagues you already know, too, as part of your greeting, though of course it isn't necessary with those you see and work with every day.

If you are not accustomed to shaking hands, start today. A proper handshake will favorably impress anyone you meet and give the appearance that you are a confident, intelligent professional. It is an important part of professional relationship building.

Business Cards

Every professional should have a business card, and nurses are no exception. Some of you may be given a business card as part of your job, although that's unlikely when you're first starting out. But any print shop can print you business cards at an affordable price.

Keep your card simple and professional. It's best to stick to a white card with black lettering. I don't recommend using computer-generated cards that you make yourself. They are usually somewhat flimsy, and the pop-out perforations are sometimes detectable. This does not make a good impression.

Business Cards

Make arrangements now to have business cards printed for you. If in the meantime someone asks you for your card or you simply aren't carrying them one day, *never* say, "I don't have one, but give me one of yours and I'll write my name and number on the back of it." That's bad manners. Rather, write your contact information on a piece of paper, and resolve to carry cards from then on so you never find yourself in that situation again.

Your business card should include your name, appropriate initials (RN, BSN, etc.), address, phone and fax numbers, and e-mail address. Whether you include your home or work contact information is a matter of choice. However, if you put your home contact information, you won't have to get new cards if you change jobs. Just remember to keep it basic and professional.

Once you have your business cards made, carry them with you wherever you go. You never know whom you're going to meet or when or where. Be sure to keep them in a business card holder or somewhere in your wallet or purse where they won't get dog-eared. Appearances count here, too!

Why do you need a business card? Because this is how professional people network, and you are a professional. A business card is your calling card, and collecting other people's cards is an easy way for you to keep track of your contacts. Besides, having a business card of your own makes you feel important, and it's much more professional—and more likely to be held on to by another—than tearing off a piece of scrap paper and jotting down your name and phone number on it.

I've had a number of nurses say to me, "Why do I need a business card? I don't have a business." Think of a business card as your calling card and a way to maximize your impression. Begin by giving people a tool to remember you by.

Follow Up

Just as important as making the initial contact is following up. Stay in touch with those you have met and networked with, and nurture the relationship. Remember, you're trying to build *ongoing* relationships.

After an initial meeting, send a card, an e-mail, or a letter to everyone you met at an association meeting, career fair, convention, or other venue. Tell them how much you enjoyed meeting them and that you look forward to staying in touch. Always offer to be of service. Write something such as "Let me know if I can ever help you in any way." Remember, networking is not just you looking for what you need. It is very much a reciprocal relationship. Include your business card with the note, even if you exchanged cards at your initial meeting. Make it as easy as possible for people to stay in touch with you or reach you if they need to.

She's Halfway There

Several years ago, I was attending a nursing convention. During one of the session breaks, I struck up a conversation with another nurse, who, as it turned out, was a new graduate. In the course of our conversation, she relayed to me that she desperately wanted to get into a very prestigious nurse practitioner program in the area.

I was very impressed with this young woman, as she was very bright, ambitious, outgoing, and personable. She seemed to know where she wanted to go with her career. I asked her if she had a business card, and she looked at me and said, "Why would I need a business card?"

I told her why it's important to have a business card and that I highly recommended she get some. She was unconvinced and laughed it off, stating, "I don't need a business card." I made a final pitch by saying, "You just never know when you'll run into someone with whom you want to exchange cards. It would be a good idea to get some." She smiled again, in a patronizing way, while shaking her head.

We sat at the same lunch table, and once everyone was seated, we started to go around the table and introduce ourselves. A very distinguished-looking woman introduced herself as the dean of the nurse practitioner program at the prestigious college this young nurse longed to attend! I immediately glanced over at my new friend and saw the look of utter amazement and excitement on her face. Her jaw dropped in disbelief! (Hint: This is what happens when you get yourself out there and network.) After she composed herself, she quickly chimed in that she was very interested in applying to that program. With that, the dean said to her, "Give me your business card, and I'll be happy to send you some information and see what I can do for you."

There are three lessons to be learned from this story:

1. Networking works.
2. *Always* carry business cards.
3. Listen to what I am telling you!

Tips for Getting the Most Out of a Career Fair or Convention

By now, you know that career fairs and conventions are important networking arenas and that you should make it your business to get out to them regularly. Although each event has a slightly different focus, your networking approach for both is essentially the same.

I have often heard employed nurses say, "Oh, I can't risk being seen at a career fair. I don't want my boss to know I'm looking for another job." Keep in mind that career fairs are not just for those currently in the market for a new job. They are important gatherings of large numbers of nurses and others in health care and are a great way to stay abreast of career opportunities and trends for current and future consideration. Attendance at career fairs should be part of your ongoing career management plan. Career management is not just something you do when actively looking for a job. It is something you do on a regular basis. If you do happen to bump into someone from your place of employment, you might say something such as "Aren't the education sessions great? I'm picking up a lot of continuing education credits today." An even better idea might be to just let your supervisor know you are going and ask if you can pick anything up for him or her.

Networking Is Mutually Beneficial

Remember that networking is a give-and-take situation. When talking to your contacts, ask, "Is there any way that I can help you?"

If someone gives you some information or advice that is helpful or refers you to someone, be sure to send that person a thank-you note. You can handwrite it on a formal note card or print it on quality stationery.

Then, stay in periodic touch with your network acquaintances by occasionally calling to say hello and see how they're doing, sending them a holiday greeting card, or clipping out and sending an article that might be of interest to them. Don't just contact them when you need something.

Whether attending a convention or a career fair, you'll have an opportunity for face-to-face interaction with prospective employers, and you'll be able to get information about schools of higher learning, nursing publications and products, and professional associations. You'll have a chance to attend continuing education seminars, and you'll meet and mingle with other nursing professionals. So it pays to make some effort to maximize your time there. Here are some tips to help you get the most out of each event.

• *Dress your professional best.* You'll make some of your most important professional contacts here, and first impressions count. The best thing to wear is a business suit—if you have one. Otherwise, wear your best outfit. When you are dressed well, people assume you have your act together. It's important to have a professional image to match the professional person you are.

• *Target exhibitors you most want to talk to.* Look at the list of exhibitors you receive when you arrive at the event and circle those you most want to talk to. Approach them first to make sure you get to them. When finished, you can browse through the remainder of the exhibit hall.

• *Press some flesh.* When approaching exhibitors, don't just pick up literature from their table, grab a few giveaways, and move on. Rather, take a few moments to establish rapport by extending your hand to shake and introducing yourself while making good eye contact and smiling. You should then say something such as "I'm interested to hear what kind of opportunities are available at County General."

- *Use good body language.* Your posture, mannerisms, and how you carry yourself make a strong statement about who you are. Stand and walk tall. Keep your shoulders back and your head upright. Look like you belong there. Give the impression of being confident, regardless of how you feel. Walk and talk like a winner.
- *Bring lots of business cards.* Think of these events as *the* networking events of the year. That means you'll be making lots of new contacts, so you should be prepared with more than the usual amount of business cards. People will be asking for your card at these events, and you should be offering it as well. Don't be embarrassed by not having enough. Remember, this is the professional way to exchange contact information. Put your cards in an easily accessible spot so you're not hunting in your purse or pockets to find one.
- *Bring copies of your resume even if you're not job hunting.* You never know when an interesting opportunity may present itself. An important part of networking is planting seeds for the future. That is, you may meet someone today, and he or she may call you a year from now when an opportunity that might be right for you presents itself. Always be prepared to make the connection. Besides, some experts say that the best time to look for your next job is while you're happily employed.
- *Get business cards from new contacts.* Always ask for the business card of anyone you want to stay in touch with. After walking away from people you are interested in, make a note on the back of their card as to when and where you met them and if there is something specific you want to follow up on with them. When you get home, keep these cards in a pocketed folder designed for this purpose.
- *Follow up.* Send follow-up notes and make follow-up phone calls after the event. Then, stay in periodic touch with your new contacts.

How to Find Out About Networking Opportunities

Here are some ways to discover networking opportunities:

- When you join your professional associations, you will automatically get notification of upcoming events that they sponsor.

- Ask some experienced colleagues which are the best nursing events to attend in your area.
- Many nursing websites list these events in a special online calendar.
- Most nursing career fairs are sponsored by, and well advertised in, career-related journals for nurses. Ask your colleagues about any free regional career journals you are entitled to get now that you are an RN or LPN.

Using the Internet for Networking

The Internet is another way to stay connected to your profession. It gives you access to a broad pool of people, events, and opportunities. Not only can you contact people and stay in touch with them by e-mail and via social-media sites such as Twitter, LinkedIn, and Facebook, but you can also participate in listservs and discussion groups. Here you can network with others, find all the latest information on the nursing profession, and research virtually anything you need or want to know.

Even when you can't get out to meetings and events, you can log on to the Internet anytime and get advice and information from a real person or from a data source. The Internet is a very convenient form of networking and a source for staying up-to-date on the nursing profession. The following are a few ways to put the Internet to work for you.

- *Regularly visit general nursing websites.* There are many nursing-related websites that offer information on practice-based issues, legislative issues, and career and professional development. Some post weekly articles, have e-newsletters you can subscribe to, and offer opportunities to ask questions of an expert. Some sites even offer cyber mentoring! Signing up for e-newsletters is an excellent way to keep abreast of your profession. An e-newsletter is delivered to your e-mail account on a predetermined schedule, such as weekly or monthly.
- *To stay current on the happenings in your profession,* it is essential that you regularly visit the sites of the American Nurses Association, the National Student Nurses Association, the National Federation of Licensed Practical Nurses or the Canadian Nurses Association, the Ca-

nadian Nursing Students' Association, and the Canadian Practical Nurses Association, as well as your state or province nursing association. Refer to the Resources section for numerous valuable websites.

• *Join a listserv.* A listserv is a group of people with a similar interest or background who post messages about various subjects. These posts are delivered to your e-mail account on a regular basis. Those who subscribe to the list can respond to those posts, submit their own question or comment, or just read what others are talking about. The great thing about a listserv of peers is that you can post a question or concern and get some feedback or advice from others on the list. Many nursing-related listservs exist on the Internet. Some are general in nature and others are very specific (for example, there are listservs for psychiatric nurses). Anyone can join these lists: students, nurses, and even non-nurses. Some people only "eavesdrop," while others actively participate. Subscriptions to most listservs are free.

I have been a subscriber to NURSENET, a general interest listserv for nurses, for quite a few years. Although the majority of subscribers are nurses from the United States and Canada, there are others from every corner of the world. Most of the participants are nurses, both RNs and LPNs, but there are always a few students and even a few non-nurses who participate. There are nurses from every imaginable background and level of experience on the list. And just as diverse as the subscribers are the opinions expressed by members on a variety of subjects. I first heard about the list while attending an American Nurses Association convention several years ago (networking in action!). I subscribed when I got home and can't imagine what I'd do without this vital link. It is a very active list, and I receive numerous invaluable e-mails every day. The discussion topics range from the serious to the silly, depending on the mood of the group that day or week. There are usually several topics of discussion, or "threads," going on at any given time.

In the beginning, I was just a lurker—someone who reads and observes without ever posting. However, once I became a little more comfortable with the list, I began to occasionally put my two cents in on certain discussions, ask a question, and offer advice and information when I could. In fact, there have been many occasions when I have needed some information about a disease process, treatment, or other nursing-related topic (and even some non-nursing topics). I post my question on the list and always get an answer—sometimes within minutes!

While nothing can take the place of face-to-face networking, belonging to this listserv provides me with a lot of the benefits of networking. It keeps me connected. It keeps me informed about my profession. It offers an opportunity to let off some steam (we do get silly sometimes and even make fun of ourselves). I get advice, information, and feedback from my peers, and I see what nurses are talking about. We are a virtual community of nurses—a cyber support team.

• *Use social media.* Create a LinkedIn profile and open Twitter and Facebook accounts if you haven't already. Once there, seek out other nurses and health-care professionals as well as related groups, lists, and chats on each. If this medium is new to you, ask an experienced user to show you the ropes and help you get started. It is a fast-growing form of communication.

• *Participate in discussion forums.* Many nursing and health-care websites and social media sites offer bulletin boards, message boards, or discussion forums. A bulletin board or discussion forum is similar to a listserv, except you generally don't have to subscribe to them, and the posts are not sent to your e-mail account. The bulletin board or forum simply exists in cyberspace, and you can tune in any time you are so inclined. Just like a listserv, you can read what others have posted, including responses, and selectively respond if you care to. Some bulletin boards and discussion forums have moderators who will occasionally offer expert advice and information as part of a discussion.

• *Connect to your specialty association.* Fortunately, today most specialty associations have their own websites. You should regularly visit the website of your specialty association, whether you belong to the association or not. Here you will find updates on your specialty, learn about educational events and conventions, find links to related resources, and sometimes find focused discussion forums or specialty listservs. You can also follow these associations on Twitter and become a fan on Facebook.

• *Chat live.* Some sites have regularly scheduled live chats, usually with a focus. A live chat is one in which you are conversing online in real time. Often, an expert on a specific nursing topic hosts the chat. Anyone can join in and simply observe or participate. The chats sometimes get quite lively!

Other Ways the Internet Can Help You

There are innumerable ways that the Internet can help you better yourself professionally and personally. Be creative, explore what's out there, and spend some of your time using this global library as a self-improvement tool. Here are a few ways that the Internet can improve your career:

- *Get a formal education.* No time to attend classes? No problem. You can take courses online. You can earn a college degree and get continuing education credits without ever leaving your home. It doesn't get any easier than that. You'll even find some free continuing education offerings online.
- *Find a job.* There are a host of job-related sites on the Internet that list openings for nurses. Most allow you to post your resume and give general career advice.
- *Research almost anything.* You can find out almost anything you want to know on the Internet. Whether you need more information about a disease or a medication or you want to find out more about a particular nursing specialty, the Internet is where it's at. Learn to search effectively for what you are looking for on the Internet. This is an invaluable skill.

Join and Participate in Professional Associations

An important way to stay connected to your peers and to your profession is by joining and becoming active in professional associations. Definitely join your specialty organization, such as the Emergency Nurses Association, but you should also join your state and national nurses associations.

While historically many nurses belonged to their specialty association but not always to their state or national nurses association, this is no longer sufficient. Membership to your state or national nurses association may be optional in terms of your license, but it is mandatory to your success in this profession. Don't join out of a sense of loyalty or obligation; rather, do so because of what's in it for you.

Belonging to professional associations has many benefits. Here are just a few ways that memberships can help you.

- *They make you feel part of a greater whole.* When you join and start receiving a group's publications, you will get a sense of being one of many. There is great comfort in knowing that you are not alone and that, in fact, you are part of a profession with a rich history and a bright future. Be an insider, not an outsider, in your own profession.
- *They keep you current with what's happening in your profession.* Belonging to professional associations is one of the best ways to stay on top of what's happening in your profession. Through newsletters, magazines, meetings, and conventions, you will stay aware of trends and issues. Get the whole picture, not just a small piece.
- *They offer educational opportunities.* Professional nurses associations offer local, regional, and national continuing education offerings. These offerings are often at minimal cost. I once attended a full-day seminar on managed care through my state nurses association at a cost of $15, complete with continuing education credits and a hot lunch!
- *They provide great networking venues through conventions, meetings, and special events.* Because networking is so important to your professional life, you will be notified of upcoming events in your area and will be able to attend at discounted member rates.
- *They offer support.* Once you join, you are immediately tapped into a network of peers. You have access to nurses in all specialties and levels of experience. Meetings and other events offer opportunities to let off steam, compare notes, exchange information, and commiserate.
- *They make you more marketable.* Belonging to professional associations shows that you are an informed and active member of your

"At the very least, join your state and national nurses associations because there is strength in numbers."

—Barry, new grad

profession. I have heard of employers using professional association membership as a criterion to hire and promote.

• *They create unity.* Joining your professional association helps to unite all nurses. There is strength in numbers, and this unity will allow us to speak in one loud voice for the betterment of the profession and of health care. Be a part of the solution, not part of the problem.

• *They can help you find a mentor.* Many nursing organizations have formal mentoring programs for new graduates and others. All have informal channels to pair you with a more-experienced nurse. Call your state nurses association and see what's available. You need all the help you can get. Once you gain some experience, you can do the same for others.

FROM THE FRONT LINE

Get Involved

"As soon as I graduated, I joined my state nurses association. This step made me feel like I had finally arrived. It was very validating for me.

"I had been very active in my student nurses association and kept up those ties, but this was the big time. Even if I couldn't get out to meetings regularly, I found comfort in just belonging. I started to receive the mailings and journals, which helped me keep up with the trends of nursing and my field.

"As soon as I became a member of my state and national nurses association, I got involved immediately. I attended local chapter meetings, went to the state convention, and joined the political action committee. I think it's very important to develop a social and professional base in nursing. Joining my state nurses association helped me to do that."

—Kevin K., new grad

• *They offer opportunities for personal and professional development.* Once you join, you will have opportunities to get involved in committees and special projects and programs where you can further develop.

• *They give you a competitive edge.* Those who are well-connected, have cutting-edge knowledge, and are always advancing their careers are the ones who get ahead. You put yourself at a disadvantage if you don't belong.

How to Get the Most Out of Your Memberships

While joining the appropriate organizations is certainly a step in the right direction, what you make of your time as a member is largely up to you. The following are some excellent ideas for getting the most out of your organizations.

• *Attend meetings.* Make an effort to get out to your local chapter meetings whenever possible. Everyone is pressed for time, but these meetings will energize you. They will give you a chance to let off some steam, compare notes with others in your same geographic area, and even give you a chance to laugh about your work. They will remind you that you are not alone and are part of a greater whole. They will also give you a chance to develop and maintain your networking skills. Networking skills get rusty when you don't use them regularly. At the very least, attend a few local chapter meetings per year to stay connected.

• *Attend your state nurses association convention.* Because you'll know the date of the convention in advance, ask for the day off from work. Some employers will reimburse you for the registration fee for attending an industry convention. Some will not. Let your supervisor know that you plan to attend—whether you are reimbursed or not. If your supervisor does not go to the convention, bring back some materials for him or her. This will be appreciated.

• *Keep your boss informed.* Whether a member or not, if your boss does not get to the same meetings as you, keep him or her informed of issues that were discussed. This is one way of making yourself valuable.

• *Share the information with your coworkers.* Share association publications, flyers, and information about upcoming events. Invite your coworkers, especially those who are not members, to attend a meeting with you. Become a resource and the person to whom people come when they need information.

• *Join committees.* Admittedly, you will have your hands full during your first year in practice learning the ropes and developing your skills. But being active in your professional association has many benefits. You will get to know more people in the association, and they will get to know you. You have the opportunity to develop leadership skills and learn or polish other skills, such as speaking, writing, and policy development. Find out what committees are available, choose

---

FROM THE FRONT LINE

Sign Up!

"It's important to join both *your specialty and your national nursing associations*. There's no two ways about it. Your national association supports you in ways your specialty organization cannot. You can't neglect to be a part of the big picture in nursing and expect to be successful.

"I joined the American Nurses Association (ANA) and my specialty organization as soon as I passed my nursing boards. I became active a few months later by joining the political action committee for my state association and the Nurses Strategic Action Team (N-STAT) for ANA.

"It doesn't interfere with my job at all. It actually helps me. I find lots of support through my committee activities. I regularly meet with other members, so I have them to answer questions, bounce things off of, or just to talk to. I use them as a sounding board. I'm probably the youngest nurse on these committees and the only staff nurse. So I feel I am also bringing the staff nurse perspective to the table. There are a lot of people who like to moan and complain all the time about what's wrong, but you have to get out there and do something about it.

"What's most important to me about my membership is the information aspect. If you don't belong, you don't know what's going on. I love having those resources. Otherwise, you just have your head in the sand."

—Shannon, new grad

one that interests you, and get involved, even if only to a small degree initially. With any professional association, you get out of it what you put into it—and more. Be sure to let your boss know of your involvement, too.

• *Go to a national convention.* Sure, it costs a little money for registration, travel, and lodging, but it is an investment in yourself and your professional life. Besides, the costs may be tax deductible. Check with an accountant.

I attended my first American Nurses Association convention years ago, when it was being held a few states away. It was close enough that I could drive and incur minimal expense. I went by myself and didn't know another soul who was going. What I should have done, in retrospect, was to find out who from the state or my local chapter was attending and then traveled with them and possibly even shared a room. But I didn't think of that at the time, so I was a solo traveler. Was I nervous about attending a convention by myself? Sure I was. But I kept reminding myself that these were my colleagues, and because the attendees would be mostly nurses, I would have something in common with most of them.

During lunch, I picked up a sandwich and found a seat at a table with other nurses. Usually everyone at the table was from a different part of the country. We would go around the table and introduce ourselves. It was exhilarating to meet nurses from all over the country! This was the first time I had ever seen so many nurses in one place. I felt empowered—"I am NURSE, hear me roar"—and all that. As my lunchmates and I talked, we soon discovered that all of us, whether from Montana, Mississippi, California, or New York, had the same challenges, issues, frustrations, and so on. It was both comforting and exhilarating. It really brought home the fact that I was part of a large, powerful national group.

As it turned out, I saw a few people whom I knew from my home state. But I met many others, too, while riding on the shuttle bus from the hotel to the convention center, during meals, and during special networking events. I am still in touch with a few of the people I met there.

"I get everything out of my professional associations. In addition to networking and great meetings, I learn etiquette, management, finances, and how to work with others."

—Sanna, new grad

I have worked with thousands of nurses over the years, and I have seen many successful ones and many unsuccessful ones. One common thread among those who are thriving in this glorious profession is that they all belong to and are active in their state, national, and specialty nurses association. That says something, doesn't it? It is not just a coincidence. There are many challenges involved in nursing. This is something you do to support yourself and your profession.

GETTING STARTED

Because you are reading this book, I know that you are committed to being the best nurse possible—one of the successful ones. So don't just think about networking, don't discuss it, just do it. Join and become active in your state, national, and specialty nurses association before you do anything else. Networking will pay off in big dividends in the long run.

Here are some networking goals to get you started:

- *Get business cards made.*
- *Call your state nurses association and find out when the next meeting is being held in your area.* If you're not a member yet, tell them you'd like to attend as a guest. I guarantee they will welcome you.

• *Ask your state nurses association if they have an annual convention, and, if so, when and where it is.* Plan to attend.

• *Ask some of your colleagues if they belong to any professional associations and if you can come to a meeting with them as a guest.* A word of warning, though: If you attend an event with a friend, the tendency is to just talk to that friend and no one else. Set a goal to talk to at least one new person and exchange business cards with him or her.

• *Invite someone you admire to lunch.* Ask the person what he or she attributes his or her success to.

• *Stay in touch with your college professors and instructors.* Send them a periodic note to update them on your progress.

• *If you meet someone in the course of your work who is doing something interesting or different, ask what it is all about.* A transplant nurse or pharmaceutical company representative can open your eyes to a new world. If the opportunity doesn't present itself at that time, get his or her card and ask if you can call him or her at a later date. Get the person's card in any event and give him or her yours.

• *The next time you're at a social function, talk to at least one new person.* Just because someone isn't in health care doesn't mean that you can't learn something from her or him. Besides, people know people who know people. That's the power of networking.

• *Have lunch with a coworker* to find out more about him or her.

• *If you're job hunting, get on the phone and call everyone you know.* Tell them that you are available and what you are looking for. Ask for referrals.

• *When attending a meeting or an event where there is a speaker, approach the speaker after the event or get his or her card and make contact afterward.*

• *If you read an article that interests or inspires you, contact the author directly or through the publication.* Authors love to hear from interested readers (hint, hint).

• *Join a listserv.*

• *Join and become active in your nursing associations.*

• *Use Twitter, LinkedIn, and other social media sites to create community and stay in touch.*

Develop good networking habits early in your career, and you will be ahead of the game. Networking energizes you. It keeps you connected. It is your lifeline. Don't get isolated. Get out and mix and mingle with people. Rather than thinking of it as a chore, think of it as a way to stay sane and increase your effectiveness. Network your way to success.

CHAPTER 6

CHALLENGES

The information in this chapter may be some of the most important you will read. Why? Because anticipating the challenges of being a new graduate and knowing how to overcome those challenges can, in some cases, make or break your career. You're very vulnerable during your first year in practice, especially during your first three to six months. That's why it's especially important to know what to expect and be prepared to overcome obstacles.

You've worked hard during your school years. You've studied, you've researched, and you've practiced. You've been quizzed, tested, and observed. You have the student thing down pat. So you should be ready when you get out there, right? Wrong. Nothing can really prepare you for getting out there on your own after graduation. Does that mean your education and student experience was inadequate? Not at all. It simply means that being a licensed, independent practitioner is far different from being a student.

Every phase of your career presents new challenges. Remember the first time you did clinicals as a student? Remember the first time you gave an injection? You were probably terrified, as most of us were. But you hung in there, you overcame your fears, you gained experience, and you advanced to meet the next challenge. You cleared those hurdles and have come a long way since.

If you're not challenged, you're not growing. Some challenges can seem insurmountable, but they are simply areas that require your immediate attention and energy to master. Some people, when they encounter challenges, become frozen with fear. The challenges become an impenetrable wall. Unfortunately, a few new graduates have dropped out of nursing during their first few months of practice because they did not anticipate these challenges and therefore were not prepared to cope with them. They thought, "I must have chosen the wrong career," or "I'm not cut out for nursing," or "I don't have what it takes," or "This is too scary." They were experiencing what every new grad experiences, but they didn't know they should have expected this or what they could do about it.

There is tremendous personal and professional growth, not to mention personal satisfaction, that comes from facing challenges head on and overcoming them. There are many challenges you will face as a new grad, some of which may seem insurmountable. But just as you did many times while you were a student, hang in there, overcome your fear, gain experience, and move forward. You won't regret it. Here are some of the more common challenges you will face, along with ways to deal with them.

THE TRANSITION: FROM NURSING STUDENT TO PROFESSIONAL NURSE

Making this transition is scary for many reasons. Some nurses initially experience a separation anxiety, leaving behind school, classmates, instructors, and a certain way of life. School rules your life for so long and becomes such a part of your routine that it can feel strange when it stops. "My life was broken down into semesters for so long," commented one new graduate.

FROM THE FRONT LINE

Limbo

"I felt tremendous grief and loss after graduating. I missed school and my colleagues. I had been very involved in school, and in a way it had become my job. Things weren't going well for me after graduation, either. My father got sick and I was having financial and other difficulties. My personal and social lives were in a shambles.

"When I took boards, I knew I shouldn't be studying all night the night before the test, but I was so stressed and anxious that I studied until 8 P.M. After the test was over, I felt lighter on a certain level, yet I wanted to cry. I didn't know if I was feeling sorrow or joy. I began aimlessly driving around and found myself back at school. I went in to see one of my former instructors, and she gave me a big hug. One week later, I found out I had passed my boards and was thrilled."

—Kevin K., new grad

"I thought of different times of the year not as seasons but as semesters; spring semester, fall semester, and summer."

The period of time between graduation and finding out if you passed your boards can put you in limbo. You may not be sure where you fit in. You're no longer a student, but you're not a licensed practitioner yet, either. You start asking yourself, "What do I do now? Where do I go from here? What if I don't pass my boards?" Making the transition from new grad to professional nurse is going to happen anyway, so you may as well take steps to ease the shock.

• *Stay in touch with school contacts.* Stay in touch with your former instructors and fellow students. Get together for lunch if you can, stop in for a quick visit, or stay in touch by phone or e-mail. Reach out to people, and they will do the same with you. There is no need to cut those ties.

• *Get involved in your school's alumni association.* In some cases, you will automatically be enrolled in your school's alumni association. However, some schools may require that you pay annual dues to belong to your alumni association and receive the mailings. Whatever it

---

FROM THE FRONT LINE

We've Only Just Begun

"I had a wonderful class in nursing school. We were unusually close. Some of us worked in the same hospital after graduation, but many others moved away or went in different directions. We have always made an effort to stay in touch with one another. Our school has an annual alumni dinner, and we try to get as many people there as possible. We also organize our own events to celebrate milestones like our fifth and tenth reunions. What do we do when we get together? Aside from catching up on everyone's life, we do a lot of reminiscing. We tell the same stories from nursing school over and over again, and we laugh about them as if they just happened yesterday. Even though we're all getting older, somehow those reunions keep us young because when we get together, we act just like we did when we were in school. It's also nice to see what everyone is doing professionally and how all of us are contributing. It makes me feel so proud. I realize how far we've come."

—Carolyn, nurse

takes, stay active so you'll be advised of upcoming reunions, get news on your former classmates, and stay otherwise connected. You may even want to get on a committee or offer to be an alumni representative for your class.

• *Take positive steps toward the transition.* Immediately join your state and national nurses associations. Get nursing malpractice insurance and work toward your CPR certification if necessary. Make it as "official" as possible.

• *Actively network to make new contacts.* Get out to some professional association meetings, whether you belong or not and whether you are working or not. Immerse yourself in your new profession. Rub elbows with other nurses.

CONQUERING YOUR FEAR AND APPREHENSION

Every new graduate experiences this. When you suddenly find yourself out there in the real world of nursing and health care, the reality can be terrifying. There is nothing that can fully prepare you for this. You find yourself surrounded by more-experienced people who may make you feel inadequate by comparison. The good news is that there are some things you can do to ease your fears and move toward becoming a more-experienced nurse.

• *Be realistic.* Remind yourself you are just starting out. Remember how I quipped in chapter 1 that I never learned anything until I got out of nursing school? This is just a reminder that you are entering phase two of your learning cycle. Every nurse starts out in the same place. Remember, too, that with each day you get through, you will be more experienced than the day before. At the end of a week, you will be more experienced than the previous week.

• *Immerse yourself in learning.* Study, observe, and just do. Accumulate experiences. At the end of each day, ask yourself, "What did I learn today?" Do some additional reading and research when you can. Attend in-services and seminars related to your area. Keep moving forward.

FROM THE FRONT LINE

Hard Times Made Better

"My greatest challenge as a new graduate was not having confidence. It's the realization that you're on your own and don't have your instructor there to help. I was nervous that I would do something wrong or miss something. I just plowed ahead, doing the best I could.

"What helped was I decided to work at a hospital where I had done most of my clinicals during school. I worked on a unit where I had done an entire semester as a student. I already knew a lot of the nurses. They were very helpful to me. It made a world of difference."

—Kevin H., new grad

• *Do your homework.* At the end of your shift, make efforts to further research a disease, a procedure, or a medication that you encountered that day. Even if the particular patient has been discharged or transferred, learn all you can so that next time you will be all the more familiar with it.

• *Seek help and support.* Speak up for yourself and get help when you need it. Rely on others for support. Ask questions. Use all the resources that are available to you. Don't ever pretend to know something when you don't. You can't bluff your way through nursing, so don't even try.

• *Deal with mistakes.* Mistakes happen. Doctors make them, experienced nurses make them, and you are likely to make them occasionally, too. You are only human. If you make a mistake, report it and rectify it immediately. Don't ever try to sweep it under the rug. Learn from it and move on. You'll sleep better at night, too, by being up front about your mistakes.

New grad Cathy advised, "Don't ever give a medication you don't know. Look it up in your pocket drug guide, call the pharmacist, or use resources available on your unit. Double-check, and triple-check if necessary in the beginning, so you get it right."

Knowledge Is King

Get to know the medical librarian in your facility. Find out what reference resources are available in print and online. Librarians are generally friendly, helpful people. They are there to help you find what you need. Even if a particular publication is not available in your hospital library, the librarian can often get it for you.

If you don't work in a hospital, you may be able to use a local hospital library anyway. Call and ask to speak to the librarian in a local facility. Tell him or her that you are a nurse who lives in the community, and find out if you can come in and use the hospital's library. I have done this myself and have always found the facility librarian to be very accommodating.

"I know a new nurse who never asks questions because she is afraid to. As a result, she is constantly making mistakes. I don't know how long she's going to last."

—Kevin H., new grad

• *Celebrate small accomplishments.* Think of something to be proud of every day. Pat yourself on the back for having had the courage to get through another day. Every new thing you do for the first time is a step in the right direction.

• *Use positive self-talk.* Tell yourself that you have studied long and hard to get to this point and you do know the basics. Remind yourself that you have passed a rigorous state board exam demonstrating that you are competent for entry-level practice.

• *Trust your instincts.* You're probably better prepared than you realize.

Stick to the basics, use common sense, and listen to your gut. Recent graduate Rich said, "I've found that 90 percent of nursing is common sense."

Bob, an experienced nurse practitioner, said, "Most new graduates come out of school with very low self-esteem. I advise them to rely on their basic instincts and good common sense. That will always get you through."

Experienced nurse Michele said, "Lots of new grads are afraid and don't trust their own judgment. Trust your instincts. Nine times out of ten you'll be right."

Carol, an experienced nurse, said, "Work on your assessments. Look at people's eyes, touch their skin, talk to them, and check things out. Turn them over, if applicable, and see what is happening under them, too. Use your intuitive skills and your gut feelings about what's going on with your patients. If they say they're feeling fine but you sense something is wrong, you are probably right. If someone says, 'I feel a little funny,' your antennae should immediately go up."

FROM THE FRONT LINE

Intensive Challenges

"I started in the intensive care unit. My biggest challenge was being overwhelmed by the acuity of the patients. I didn't feel at all prepared for that, but I had to get over it so I could function. I would remind myself that I didn't know everything and everyone would support me. I knew that building experience would get me through. I came to heavily rely on the support of others. I asked a million questions. I even got tired of asking questions, but I kept asking.

"My advice is, don't be hard on yourself. If you get criticism or you make a mistake, learn from it and move on. Let it go. Remind yourself that you are new and have a lot to learn. In the beginning, with important things, double-check them and triple-check them if necessary. Get validation from someone more experienced."

—*Pennie, new grad*

BECOMING AND STAYING ORGANIZED

One of the greatest challenges faced by new grads is the ability to organize care in a fast-paced, high-volume patient care environment. Staffing ratios are not always ideal, and most patients are fairly sick. The result is a challenging workload for the nurse—not to mention the inevitable crises that arise during the day.

Remember, in the beginning, it's going to take you a little longer to do everything than your experienced cohorts. You are a new nurse in a new environment. Be patient with yourself. You will be learning many new things, one of which is how to organize your time and your care. Of course, there are many proven ways that will help you organize yourself and stay on the ball.

• *Arrive to work early.* This gives you a chance to put your belongings away and not be rushed at the beginning of your shift. Don't waste time while waiting for report. If possible, find out what your assignment is for the day and start to look at the cardex or patient profiles. Check to see if the meds you need are there. Try to look up any meds you are not familiar with. If time permits, do a quick patient assessment before report, especially if a particular patient is new to you. This will make report more meaningful, and you will be better prepared to ask relevant questions.

• *Develop a plan—and a contingency.* Based on report and the current activities of the unit, plan and prioritize what needs to be done. Once you *think* you

---

FROM THE FRONT LINE

Clinically Challenged

"My greatest challenge upon entering the real world was getting my clinical skills up to speed to be safe and effective. That isn't an easy thing to do. There's nothing that can prepare you for that. You'll likely feel swamped for the first year of nursing. But I must say, my manager has been totally supportive. After four or five months, I was able to hold my own.

"My advice is, be cooperative to stay sane. Be available to help others so others will help you. People will start to come to you."

—Bill, new grad

FROM THE FRONT LINE

Organization and Prioritization

"Organization and prioritization are the key. That can't be stressed enough. If you're not organized, you get stressed out. The first thing I do is check my med administration sheets. When I get report, I write down all the facts, and then I ask, 'What's really going on with this patient?' In other words, is he or she having any pain, other difficulties, or is he or she hitting the call bell every five minutes? I'm looking for a sense of what other nurses have picked up. I obtain as much info as possible, and this gives me a lot of insight. Then I do a walk-around of all my patients. This way I know what I'm walking into each shift. It gives me a little bit of an edge."

—Rich, new grad

are set for the day and you have a great plan in place for your patients, team, and so on, don't be surprised when your plan falls apart a half hour or even ten minutes into your shift! Remember you are dealing with very sick people. So be ready with plan B if plan A doesn't fly.

• *Check in on each patient.* After report, go in and see each patient. Do at least a quick assessment and see who needs the most urgent care and who will probably need the most time and attention. Introduce yourself if a patient is new to you. Experienced nurse Agnes says, "I find that I have more time first thing in the morning than later in the day. So I'd rather spend a few quality minutes with each patient early because I never know how the rest of the day will go."

• *Prioritize.* Always do what is most urgent first. Minor, routine tasks can be done later or delegated if necessary. Be realistic about what you can get done in a day. New grad Rich said, "I usually have several patients to take care of plus admissions and discharges, so prioritizing is key. If one of my patients is being discharged in one hour, I know I have to get right in there and do an assessment."

• *Make notes.* Keep a notepad in your pocket and start writing things down: things you want to tell the doctor, things you want to ask about, things you want to do, things you want to document, and things you want to look up later. If you try to rely solely on your memory, you'll soon start to sink.

Remember my colleague in chapter 4 who left self-sticking notes on charts for doctors? You might carry a pad of self-sticking notes with you so you can write notes to the doctors over the course of the day. This will save you the trouble (and time) of rewriting your notes when you get back to the desk.

Quick Steps to Organization

Learn what resources are available to you. For example, is there a transport team or a volunteer office you can call if you need someone brought down to x-ray or something run to the lab?

Also, learn the fine art of delegation. It is something you'll get better at with practice. Part of being successful is learning to delegate.

Finally, get copies of everyone's job description on your unit. You can obtain these from your supervisor or manager. Take them home, read them, and learn them. This will make everyone's role clearer to you.

• *Delegate.* Don't feel you have to do everything yourself. In fact, you can't. Learn to delegate. Observe others in that role. Familiarize yourself with the job descriptions of those you will be delegating to. Use ancillary personnel, such as aides, techs, and the unit secretary. You *can't* do it all yourself.

• *Learn to roll with the punches.* The unexpected is bound to happen. You get a new admission, there is a computer failure, someone goes into crisis, or you have a very needy patient. This is an inevitable part of the job. Don't let it throw you. When this happens, you need to reprioritize and do what can be done in the allotted time with the available resources.

> ## FROM THE FRONT LINE
>
> ### Time Is of the Essence
>
> *"When I first got out of school, I found that I didn't have the time to spend with patients that I thought I would. It all comes back to organizational skills. It's frustrating at first, but you can do it. Sometimes I take my patients' vital signs rather than have the tech do it so I can spend a few extra minutes with them."*
>
> —Barry, new grad

• *Take time to reflect.* At the end of the day, think about how you did with your time and organizational skills. What could you have done better or differently? What will you do the next time? At the end of each day, make a list of what you want to do the next day.

• *Plan for discharge.* Find out what the expected length of stay is for each patient so you can start to plan ahead. This will help you organize and direct your plan of care, including a continuum of care after discharge. You need to be thinking about discharge from day one.

Get to know the case manager. Align yourself with this person. He or she can teach you many things about length of stay and discharge planning and can even help you effectively organize your patient care.

• *Set time limits.* Time management is a big problem for new grads. It would be nice if you could spend as much time as you wanted with each patient, but that's a fantasy. So when you go in to do some teaching, for example, allow yourself a realistic amount of time to do so and stick to it. Otherwise, your day will get progressively out of control.

• *Work on your problem-solving skills.* Take time to think and figure things out. Don't get frantic. Get logical. Think of a way to do what needs to be done. There is usually more than one way to get things done.

• *Do that which you dread first.* After doing that which is most urgent, do those things you least want to do next. Get them over with, and the day will be lighter and less stressful.

• *Ask for help.* Ask your preceptor or other competent nurses how they organize their day. Ask for their help when you need it. Asking for help is not a sign of weakness or failure. It shows that you care about your work and are motivated to learn.

Back on Track

New graduate Helen went to her supervisor after two weeks on her new job. She was in tears and said, "There is too much I don't know. I shouldn't have gotten into nursing. I can't do this." Helen's supervisor was concerned but knew that Helen really cared about what she was doing. So she spent some extra time with Helen to help her get organized so she felt more in control. Helen's supervisor also suggested ways for her to have time to do some research. Helen was able to get on track and move forward with her career.

• *Develop a system that works for you.* Everyone has a different way of doing things. Get tips and advice from others and then do what works best for you.

Bill, a recent graduate, discussed organization. "You'll learn through practice and evolve a system that works for you."

Pennie, a new grad, added, "To help myself stay organized, I have a patient worksheet that I use. I organize hour to hour because the day can be very unpredictable. I give patient care a priority over paperwork. That can wait until the end of the day."

> *"I advise students and new graduates to think of one positive thing from the day— something they accomplished. Then write it down to make it more tangible. Look at it, think about it, and fall asleep on that thought."*
>
> —Carol, nursing instructor

EFFECTIVELY DEALING WITH ADVERSITY

When you are starting out, you will have to work hard to stay positive and motivated. You will have some bad days or weeks when your patience is tried or things are not going as you would like them to. You may be exposed to the negative influences of those around you and will be dealing with the frustrations and challenges of being a novice in a high-tech, fast-paced environment. I'll talk a lot more about staying positive and motivated in chapter 7, but here are a few things you can do to get you through the tough days.

- *Focus on the positive.* Negative influences exist everywhere in our lives and work. Each of us chooses where to focus. You can dwell on all the negatives and get depressed, or you can look for the positives. If

---

FROM THE FRONT LINE

Get It Together!

"When you get out of nursing school, you discover you don't have the time to see patients that you thought you would have. I felt like a pill pusher at first. I heard another nurse refer to it as 'putting out fires' all day. Sometimes that's what it felt like in the beginning. In the beginning, you just have time for the basics. My advice on how to organize is to first of all abandon the idea of a clipboard. I know most nurses carry them, but I find them to be a bad idea. Instead, I carry a pocket-size notebook with all my important report information written in it. That way, it is always with me in my pocket, and I never worry about losing it. Then I prioritize my day from most important to least.

"Take things step by step and focus on the basics. For example, in emergency situations, I focus on the ABCs (airway, breathing, and circulation). I also save time by keeping some small common supplies (IV end caps, tape, and alcohol swabs) in my pockets and a small pocket organizer that contains my clamps, scissors, and penlight. In addition, I write down patient requests that can wait a bit. I write them down along with other things I need to do and I check them off when they are completed.

"Try not to get overwhelmed and do rely on other people to help you. You should accept all the help you can get."

—*Shannon, new grad*

---

someone is less than cordial to you, you can focus on that and make generalizations about the whole profession or you can remember the people who have been good to you and concentrate on that. If you make a mistake or feel you did a less-than-ideal job that day, you can mentally berate yourself or you can focus on what you did well over the last week. Staying positive is healthier, and you will be happier and more satisfied in your career. The choice is yours.

• *Find the bright spot in your day.* Each day, think of one thing that you did that was positive or made a difference. Focus on that. I got in the habit, years ago, of asking myself at the end of each day, "Who did I help today?" I figured if I helped someone, or made a positive difference in one person's life, then the day was worthwhile.

• *Stay focused on your goal.* There may be times that you question whether you did the right thing by becoming a nurse. You may encounter other nurses who are disgruntled and unhappy and who do nothing but bad-mouth the profession. Some of what they say may be true, but you chose this profession for good reasons. You have to stay focused on your goal and create your own positive reality. Remind yourself of the bigger picture.

• *Start a positive workbook.* This is a little different than journaling. Get a spiral notebook or a similar book. Write down why you became a nurse. Make a note of special things that happened with patients that made a difference. Write down any positive comments a patient, a coworker, a family member, or an instructor said about you that made you feel good and positive about who you are and what you are doing. Keep any positive letters or notes that you receive from patients and their families in this workbook. If a complimentary note is sent to the unit from one of your patients or from his or her family about the nursing staff, make a copy and keep it in your workbook. Take time to add to this book on a regular basis. Refer to it often, especially after a bad day or when you are questioning yourself and your chosen career.

"To stay positive, I always think of the people I've had a positive influence on and how I've made a difference. I just focus on the positive, not on the negative."

—Sanna, new grad

Managing Difficult Situations

Some new grads find themselves in a bad situation that is unlikely to get better. This is typically an environment where you are consistently given responsibility beyond what you can reasonably handle as a new grad. In this type of situation, one in which there is no support and no means to get support, you are truly putting your license on the line.

Such a difficult and dangerous situation is bad for anyone, but it is particularly bad for a new graduate because you need help and support. You are building a foundation for your future practice. Sometimes it can be difficult to differentiate between the normal anxiety you will experience as a new graduate and a truly bad situation. So before jumping ship, take measures to assess the situation and look for solutions.

• *Try to resolve the problem.* Talk to your supervisor (if appropriate), staff educator, or preceptor about your concerns. See if anything can be done to improve the situation.

• *Compare experiences with peers.* Talk to other new graduates in other facilities and units and see if they are experiencing the same thing. This will help you gain perspective and determine if your situation is unique or if it is universal.

• *Talk with someone you can trust.* Talking things out with a neutral party can help to clarify your situation and your feelings. It can also help you to make a decision about what needs to be done. Call a former instructor or an experienced nurse you know.

• *Listen to your gut.* Use your basic instincts to determine whether this is a passing situation that will improve with time or experience or whether it is a bad situation, period. Listen to your gut. This is why it's so important to choose the right first job for yourself, although it may be difficult to find.

• *Make a change if necessary.* While you don't want to be moving on every time you have a problem, sometimes finding a job at a different facility is the right thing to do. I have spoken to some new grads who found themselves in a bad job situation but were reluctant to leave because they didn't want to look like quitters. Sometimes you have to cut your losses and start over in a new situation to regain your footing.

AVOIDING BURNOUT

Burnout is not just a nurse thing. It has become commonplace in our society, especially in high-stress jobs such as securities and commodities traders, police officers, air traffic controllers, and so on.

It is a condition that occurs when people consistently overextend themselves in terms of time, energy, emotional strength, and stamina. It happens when you push yourself too hard or when your output exceeds your input by way of not taking time to refresh yourself and replenish your energy. Some other causes of burnout are lack of control, excessive criticism, emotional or work overload, and unrealistic expectations and goals. It usually manifests itself as feeling tired, frustrated, depressed, and in despair. You develop a sense of wanting to be anyplace but where you are, and you may feel stripped of your ability to function. As caregivers, we are particularly susceptible to this.

The term *burnout* is often used in a derogatory way to refer to a nurse who is fed up with the profession. In other words, some nurses believe that if they no longer have enthusiasm for their job, they must be burned out on nursing and need to find another occupation entirely. In reality, all this means is that a change is in order—either a change of jobs, circumstances, personal habits, or lifestyle—but not a departure from nursing.

What we do is very emotionally charged and challenging. We are dealing with life and death and the human condition. Sometimes we get so caught up in our work that we don't recognize the symptoms of burnout—and when we do, it is often too late.

The challenge here is to fight burnout by keeping your work interesting and challenging, changing jobs or specialties if necessary, and taking care of yourself.

You can manage situations if you're aware of the signs of stress. You can avoid burnout if you know what to look for and head it off at the pass.

On Burnout

I recently had a new graduate contact me and tell me that she had been working in a cancer treatment center for six months. She was experiencing a disinterest in her life and work, looking at the gloomy side of things, and even not caring about her own life. She thought maybe this was normal because of the area she was working in. She was exhibiting some classic symptoms of depression, but she thought this just went with the territory.

I recommended that she seek professional help and consider changing specialties. She made a job change a few weeks later, and her outlook improved considerably. She was enthusiastic about her work again, had renewed energy to move forward in her career, was doing other things she enjoyed, and was no longer gloomy. She later told me,

> In retrospect, I think oncology was not the best place for me to start out. I might go back there someday to work, but for the time being, I am much better off on a general med-surg floor. I was getting a slanted perspective on health care and feeling that I couldn't help these people—that their situation was hopeless. Death became a focal point in my life and work. It got the best of me. Changing jobs was the best thing for me to do.

If you are feeling burned out, please know that you are not the only one who is dealing with this. Seek out a trusted colleague or friend and find the best solution for dealing with your situation.

• *Set boundaries.* You're only human, and there are only so many hours in the day. Pace yourself and learn to say no. Remember that you can do and learn just so much in twenty-four hours. We live in what is quickly becoming a 24/7 society—businesses and services are open at any time of the day or night all week long. Having no downtime is touted as a virtue. Likewise, many of us are operating 24/7 and burning the candle at both ends. We are juggling home, work, family, school, and everything else. Each of us needs to catch our breath and set limits on how much time we devote to work and study.

New graduate Shannon said, "You have to learn to set boundaries. At first, I was being asked all the time to work overtime, take double shifts, and work on my scheduled day off. Sometimes you're afraid to say no when you're new—you're afraid you won't be considered a team player. But you come to a point where you are too exhausted or have simply been up too many hours. If you work too much, you burn out. Learn to say no. Some of my peers can't say no, and they're headed for disaster."

• *Manage your stress.* Everyone has stress in his or her life. Even happy things create stress. Stress will take its toll on you both physically and mentally if not tended to. So it is imperative that you incorporate a stress management program into your life. The best solution is to eliminate stressors when possible by not overextending yourself and not getting involved in too many things at one time. For all the rest, there is exercise, meditation, deep breathing exercises, the use of relaxation tapes, and diversionary activities such as bowling or needlepoint. Force yourself to get involved in activities outside of work. Find things away from nursing such as art, theater, or music lessons. Stick with a hobby you enjoy. All work and no play leads to overload. You'll be surprised how these activities diminish the hold stressors have on you.

Exercise reduces stress and, of course, has many physical and emotional benefits. It creates a sense of well-being, helps you to sleep better, and keeps you healthier. It is also critical that you take care of your mind as well as your body. Make sure you find ways to unwind and let the difficulties of your days go. Anything that relaxes you and lets your mind "cleanse" itself is ideal.

• *Take care of yourself.* As caregivers, we have a tendency to take care of everyone else before ourselves. We often feel selfish taking care of

FROM THE FRONT LINE

Shape Up!

"I found my work to be very physically demanding. I wasn't prepared for that. I exercise a lot. I really need it. It acts as stress relief and helps to keep up my stamina."

—Pennie, new grad

"I take care of myself. I come home and take a bath or I exercise. I also write in my journal. I've created a personal space for myself by setting aside a spot in the basement just for me where I can go and write in my journal and be alone."

—Sanna, new grad

"I occasionally stop at a favorite spot on the way home from work and have a burger. I take some time to wind down after a rough day. I usually just sit quietly by myself and don't even talk to anyone. The waitresses know me and leave me alone. I also listen to meditation tapes and take time to relax. Any problems I have, I leave at the job."

—Rich, new grad

"I go to the public library when I just need some quiet time. I sit and look at magazines, browse the stacks in a section that interests me, or peruse the video and audiocassette titles. Sometimes there's an art exhibit at the library or a lecture that interests me. I always feel much better when I come home. It somehow feeds my soul."

—Andrea, nurse

ourselves. This contributes to burnout. Being a nurse does not make you immune to illness. Get regular health checkups and eat well. Practice what you preach. Take time for yourself. Use your vacation time, personal days, and comp time to do the things you enjoy, including doing absolutely nothing. Chores and other responsibilities will never go away, so don't wait until you're "caught up" to take time for yourself. You have to schedule yourself in or just do it. Be sure to also find some quiet time in your day to reflect, relax, and listen to your inner voices. You have to recharge your batteries as a caregiver and develop a strong center. When you take care of yourself, you have more to give others.

• *Develop support systems.* Remember that no man is an island. You need others who you can let off steam with and get feedback from. And they need you just as much. Very often, a great deal of stress is dissipated when shared with another. Mostly, knowing you are not alone will make you stronger. Have a good support group around you to replenish your emotional energy. Buddy up with someone at work, stay in touch with your nursing friends and instructors, get out to professional association meetings, or join a nursing listserv.

• *Take care of each other, too.* Nurture each other. If a colleague looks stressed, say, "How can I help you?" If one of your coworkers is having a particularly bad day, say, "Why don't you take five minutes? I'll do that for you." We have to look out for one another in this profession. A feeling of isolation is a common reaction to stress. Letting people know they aren't alone can mean a lot. Besides, no one understands better what a nurse is feeling than another nurse.

• *Use humor.* Find time to laugh. Humor heals. Don't take everything so seriously. Lighten up. Laughter releases tension. There is humor to be found in every situation—even some of life's greatest challenges. Get together with friends or co-workers and tell funny stories about your work. A situation that was embarrassing or frightening when it occurred can be

---

FROM THE FRONT LINE

Support

"Support is important. My unit, neonatal intensive care, is fairly high stress. Fortunately, I found a very close friend with whom I work and can call to vent after a bad day. Most nurses there have support systems within the unit because it is hard for people outside to really understand, especially given the confidentiality issues. I think this is one of the most important things for a new graduate to have."

—Victoria, new grad

"My fellow graduates who also work in ICU and I talk and get together for lunch if we can, but otherwise we talk by phone. We share stories, and that helps out a lot. We see that we all have the same fears, and that somehow makes it all better. We all have the same problems and fears."

—Pennie, new grad

hysterically funny when related to friends in a social situation. The laughter will stay with you long after the conversation has ended.

• *Explore your career options.* Just knowing that you have options can decrease your anxiety about the future. It can give you something to look forward to, something to work toward, and something to strive for. The great thing about the nursing profession is that it holds so many diverse opportunities. There is something for everyone. Nurses who believe they have no options are the ones who find themselves in a rut and on the road to burnout.

Surviving the Night Shift

Many new nurses start out working on the night shift or are required to rotate to the shift from time to time. And while "nights" can be a great time to learn, the hours can play havoc on your circadian rhythms and sleep patterns if you're not prepared.

Here are some tips from new grads and experienced nurses:

- Do some physical exercise before going into work. This helps to get your blood pumping, create endorphins, and boost energy.
- While caffeine can help you stay awake during the night, it can also prevent you from sleeping during the day when you get off duty. Try to minimize caffeine, especially five to six hours before your shift ends.
- If at all possible, avoid using sleeping pills.
- Try taking a short nap before going into work, but allow enough time to adequately wake up and feel alert.
- Allow for decompression or down time after work before going to sleep.
- For a good "day's" sleep, use black-out shades or curtains (if necessary), white noise machines, and similar ways of creating an environment conducive to sleep. And don't forget to turn off your phones!
- Have a hearty meal before going to work—who knows when you'll be able to eat again, and you need to give your metabolism a boost. However, avoid too many carbs and sugars, which could make you sluggish.
- If you feel drowsy during your shift, rather than becoming reliant on caffeine, try getting a little fresh air—even for a few moments. Or, you might

try doing something physical, like stretching or sprinting down the hall.

- Find ways to maintain hobbies and outside interests when off-duty.
- Take steps to maintain a social life and spend quality family time. This can be challenging when the rest of the world is on a different schedule, but with some planning, you can make it work.

"As hard as it is, stay on the 'nights' schedule on your off days (for the most part). This means you should stay up as late as you can. Also, work night shift on consecutive days when you can. Get a fabulous sleep mask with ear covers even if your room is dark. Then, if your significant other or roommate turns on lights and bangs around, you don't notice. And join a twenty-four-hour gym!"

—Mary, new grad

Entry from New Nurse Rebecca's Blog about Working the Night Shift

I have been working night shift (6:00 P.M. to 6:30 A.M.) for several months now and have found these odd hours to be the most challenging aspect of my new profession. The darkness, the insomnia, the rebound hypersomnia—these have been my greatest challenges.

It's amazing the difference between day shift and night shift at the hospital. It's like . . . night and day. The change that comes over the floor is so profound that I'm amazed that such a drastic transition can be made every single day, day after day. As though going from so busy to so quiet and back again would somehow drain the little hospital and it would simply give up and decide to stay one way or the other.

Day shift is like a circus on our med-surg floor. It's like a madhouse. It starts with the lab technicians hitting the floor around 5:00 A.M. They come with their carts and caddies and start siphoning little vials of blood off the patients. Unless, of course, a patient has a central line—a small, plastic, tubular fast track from the big bad world right into the patient's superior vena cava or maybe even right into the patient's heart. If that's the case, then it is on you, the nurse, to draw blood from the central line.

Now imagine that same floor at 10:00 or 11:00 o'clock at night. The patients have all had their evening assessments and medications and are tucked in and comfy. The hall lights are dimmed, the floor is cast in muffled shadow. The construction workers have gone home hours ago, as have the physical therapists, social workers, housekeepers, discharge planners, surgeons, dieticians, portable x-ray technicians, and all but the most essential of doctors and respiratory therapists, because apparently most people seem to think 6:00 P.M. to 6:00 A.M. are odd hours to work. The only people left moving around the floor are the five or six nurses and maybe an aide or two padding up and down the halls or quietly charting at the nurses' station.

Sure, you *can* have a crazy night. You may have the patient who is suddenly in excruciating pain in the middle of the night. Or maybe you have to administer a blood transfusion, a meticulous and time-consuming activity. But the point is, all these things are dealt with in a general atmosphere of hushed calm, of low voices and soft lighting. It makes all the difference in the world.

I like the night shift.

TAKING ON TOO MUCH, TOO FAST

It's important to remember that regardless of your prior work experience, you are still a brand-new nurse and have a lot to learn. Building a solid base in clinical practice will give you a good foundation for your future career. You need to take some time to learn the basics now before you move on to bigger and better things.

"After only two and a half months on my first job, I was offered the charge nurse position on my unit," recent graduate Barry said. "I will admit I was thrilled and flattered. I realize now that I probably wasn't ready for that much responsibility. I did fine and nothing drastic happened, but I probably should have waited. You have to know your limitations and know when to say, 'Not yet.' "

Norma was an LPN for thirteen years before she went back to school to become an RN. For those thirteen years, she worked on the same unit in the same hospital. Shortly after becoming an RN, she was made charge nurse on her unit.

> The transition from LPN to RN to charge nurse was very difficult for me. I was suddenly in charge of people I had previously worked side by side with. Also, because I was now an RN, everyone had very high expectations of me and expected me to switch roles overnight. They even wanted to shorten my orientation! I had to remind them that I was a new RN and had much to learn. I had to stand my ground and tell them that I needed time and a full orientation. I was always up front with my weaknesses.

Here are four ways to avoid biting off more than you can chew:

• *Know your limitations.* Learn the basics now. You have your whole career ahead of you. There is no need to rush ahead. You are the only one who can gauge your comfort level. Don't take on things you're not ready for. If you do, you set yourself up for failure.

• *Speak up for yourself.* Let others know what you need. Verbalize your feelings and concerns to your preceptor or your supervisor. Talking is one of the best ways to resolve problems and to prevent others from ever occurring. Don't expect others to read your mind. Communicate.

• *Learn to say no to opportunities that are not right for you at this time.* Saying no is sometimes hard for a new grad. You don't want to be perceived as difficult or uninterested. You might say something such as "I am eager to do that in the future, but I think I would be better off getting my feet more firmly planted before moving into the role."

• *Seek opportunities with good support systems in place.* Experience alone is not always the best teacher. You need support systems in place for validation, help, and supervision while you are a new grad.

USE ANY AND ALL RESOURCES TO MAKE IT THROUGH

Many of us may fall on hard times at some point in our lives or already face great challenges every day. Some nurses are single parents, some take care of elderly relatives, some have enormous student loans to pay off, some battle illness, and some must cope with a disability. Some of us even fight addiction and depression. We are all only human. All these things add to your stress level and can further complicate your budding career. However, remember all the different suggestions made in this chapter for dealing with the potential pitfalls of nursing, and never be afraid to reach out and ask for help. The following are some additional suggestions for taking care of your well-being.

- *Seek professional help if you need it.* Take care of yourself first, and then you will have more to give others. There is no shame in seeking professional help for a problem. In fact, it is a courageous and proactive thing to do. You have to be well in order to freely give of yourself.
- *See what your employer has to offer.* Many employers offer support groups, day care services, counseling, and referrals for a whole host of situations. Talk to the occupational health nurse (employee health nurse) in your facility for confidential referrals and advice.
- *Check with your professional association.* Some state nurses associations offer special programs for nurses in recovery from addictions, nurses who need financial assistance, and other situations. Check out their website or call and talk to a member benefits representative. You may be entitled to some services whether you are a member or not.
- *Seek support and help for yourself.* There are many support groups—online, by telephone, and in person—for virtually every situation you might find yourself in. Some agencies offer free counseling services and hotlines. Look in the yellow pages of your phone book under "mental health services" or "social service agencies" to find such groups and services.

CHAPTER 7

THE GOOD STUFF

Enough about the challenges and the trials and tribulations of being a new nurse. Now it's time to talk about all the good things. It's time to talk about moving forward, making progress, and getting motivated to charge ahead. It's time to talk about the rewards, the blessings, and the sacred moments that nursing offers. Here are some additional tips to help you get the most out of this glorious profession and to keep you on track throughout your career.

TRACKING YOUR PROGRESS

We have a natural tendency to think in terms of where we are right now and where we want to go. We focus on what we have to do to get there, yet we easily forget where we have been. It *is* important to look at how far you've already come and to continue to track your progress in the future.

Record Your Accomplishments

Take time to make a list of all your major accomplishments, both personal and professional, from the last ten to twenty years—go as far back as you can. List things like finishing school, getting through a tough situation, raising great kids, solving a problem, and anything else you can think of from past and current jobs that is of note. This exercise reminds you that you are moving forward, even though it sometimes seems as if you are standing still. You need to develop a tangible frame of reference in order to see how far you've come. It may take some time to compile this list because once we accomplish something, we have a tendency to put it out of our heads and move on to the next challenge.

As nurses, we are superachievers. We are accustomed to doing whatever is asked of us without a second thought. We are also generally very modest when it comes to tooting our own horns. So, naturally, we have a tendency to minimize what we do. That's why it's important to write down what you can think of now and keep adding to the list. Ask people close to you to remind you of your accomplishments. They often have a better recollection than you do!

In addition to looking at where you've already been, you must begin keeping track of your current progress. In chapter 1, I talked about keeping a list of your professional experiences and education as part of your professional portfolio. This is something you need to keep up-to-date throughout your career. You don't have to write every day, but updating it once a week is a good idea. If you wait any longer than that, you'll likely forget things. Our memories are much less perfect than we would like to believe. However, writing even occasionally will benefit you.

Each week, list what you have accomplished, what you have learned, what you did for the first time, and what you feel proud of. Remember, you are listing not only skills and tasks here, but also feelings, results, experiences, and so on. When you look back on this log, even after a few months, you will be amazed at how much you have accomplished in such a short period of time.

Memories

Years ago, when I had to put together my first professional resume, I relied on my memory to draft it. I asked my husband to look it over and give me some feedback. He said, "What about the time you opened that office for the medical weight control center you worked for? Why didn't you mention that?" Because I had completely forgotten about it! When I began to think back, I recalled that I had been asked by my employer to do a population study of several local towns, study traffic patterns, work with a commercial real estate agent, contract with plumbers and carpenters, negotiate a lease, and hire and train all the staff—from receptionists to physicians. You're probably wondering how all this could have slipped my mind. Easily, because I remembered it all as part of my job and therefore as "no big deal." However, when my husband reminded me of it and I took the time to write it down on paper, I realized what an incredible accomplishment it was. As nurses, we have a tendency to take everything in our stride. Thus, it is important to log accomplishments while they are fresh in our minds.

Keeping a record of your accomplishments will help you with resume development, too. Some nurses stay at one job for a long time, and then when it comes time to change jobs, they have to sit down and compose their resumes completely from memory. When I work with nurses to help them develop their resumes, this is often the first time they have put their accomplishments, credentials, and significant experiences in writing. They often say about their own resumes, once completed, "Wow! Even I'm impressed!"

FROM THE FRONT LINE

The Joys of Nursing

You may have heard some negatives about this profession from both experienced nurses and maybe even from some new grads. But there are plenty of beautiful, positive, uplifting, and heartwarming stories and experiences out there, too. In the process of researching this book, the great majority of comments I received from new graduates in the field, as well as from experienced nurses, were overwhelmingly positive. This section features some of these positive comments about what's right with nursing and the wonderful influence this profession can have on individuals.

"I came to nursing as a second career. As a nurse, I get the opportunity to experience certain aspects of all the careers I considered while in college. I get to be a teacher, a police officer, a lawyer, a psychologist, and a health-care professional!

(cont.)

"I have the pleasure of helping people regain their health as well as die with dignity. The feeling I get from seeing a patient's health improve is amazing. When a patient or a family member says, 'Thank you,' the feeling is indescribable.

"Finally, I have the opportunity to do a variety of jobs. I can work with patients in a hospital, in their homes, or in schools, or I can work with a group such as Doctors Without Borders. I can even work on a cruise ship. I have the opportunity to get an advanced degree and become a nurse manager, a clinical specialist, or a nurse practitioner, or I could earn my PhD and become a nurse researcher. If I ever decide to leave patient care, I can get a degree in nursing informatics and work with computers. My biggest regret is that it took me so long to realize what a great career nursing is."

—*Barry, new grad*

"I have been a nurse for twenty-four years. I have worked in pediatrics, obstetrics/gynecology, done a long stint in the neonatal intensive care unit, and then moved on to health education and public health. I have worked in administration and am now a parish nurse while I pursue my master's degree.

"Nursing is unique in its capacity for variety. I have held the hand and wiped the tears of an elderly woman who lost her husband of fifty-five years. I didn't have to say anything profound or counsel; I just had to be present and let myself be immersed in her grief and share some of her pain and the humanity of death.

"I have been caught up in the adrenaline thrill of starting arterial lines, putting in chest tubes, clearing tracheotomies, reading electroencephalograms (EEGs) and electrocardiograms (ECGs), and maneuvering my way around expensive, high-tech machinery.

"I have sung lullabies to premature babies. I have taught teenagers and incarcerated men and women human sexuality and the risk factors associated with HIV.

"I have written grants, managed budgets in excess of three million dollars, and directed entire health-care organizations. I have advocated for the homeless and disenfranchised in Washington, D.C., before legislators and county commissioners.

"I have started women's health programs in Romania that required the coordination of Romanian and U.S. governmental agencies as well as the creation of clinical protocols. I have provided health care in the squatters' villages of Trinidad on an exam table that consisted of two tree stumps, a dirty sheet of plywood, and my bed sheet.

"Where else can one find a job that offers such diversity? One minute I use my head and the next my heart. I wouldn't choose any other profession. I feel blessed."

—*Vicki, nurse*

Keep a Journal

One of the best ways to track your progress is to keep a journal. A spiral notebook will do just as well as a lovely leather-bound book. Some people keep an online journal. That's fine, too. But I like to be able to turn my journal's pages and quickly scan from, say, pages fourteen to twenty-one. Take time to start the journal before your first job as a nurse, if possible. Actually, anytime is a good time to start. Writing is a way of staying focused and helping you to work out problems and to make decisions. It helps to clarify your thoughts and transforms the abstract into the "real."

Write about your fears, your sense of joy and satisfaction, your thoughts for the future, and so on. After you've been working for six months and you go back and read your journal, you'll see how scared you were when you first started. You'll recognize that you've moved beyond that and you will appreciate how far you've come. And, who knows, maybe someday you'll want to write your own book or even a few articles about your early days in the profession. Your journal will be a record of those experiences.

When I started my own business a number of years ago, my sister suggested that I keep a journal. At that time, writing was not something I enjoyed doing, but my sister usually has good advice, so I decided to give it a try. I wrote about all the obstacles facing me, my fears, my dreams, opportunities that were coming my way, things I was doing, and things that I still wanted to do. I would write whenever I could. If some time had passed since my last entry, I would take time to reflect on what I had been up to and write it all down. This journal became a recorded history of my career as a nurse-entrepreneur. When I look back and see how afraid I was to do things that today I take for granted, I realize the great strides I have made both personally and professionally. When I read about the self-doubt I was experiencing during different parts of my early career, it reinforces for me how important it is to move forward in spite of your fears.

Look for Opportunities to Help Those Less Experienced than Yourself

Seeing yourself next to someone less experienced helps give you perspective and helps you see how far you've come. Even after you're on a new job only a short time, you are qualified to help a new hire get oriented to your unit, know who the key players are, learn certain procedures and protocols, and so on. You will certainly have something to offer student nurses because you will have already moved beyond their level of experience. After a few months as a new grad, you will have something to offer "newer" grads coming into your workplace.

It feels good to be able to help others and to teach them something, even

> *"I recently had the opportunity to work with a nursing student. Even as a new grad, I could see how far I have come. It gave me a really good feeling and validated my experiences."*
>
> —Pennie, new grad

at a beginner's level. It reinforces your progress and helps you continue to learn because as you help and teach others, you recognize what you have to offer. I've talked throughout this book about the ways you can get the help you need. You want to be able to do the same for others and then some.

STAYING POSITIVE AND MOTIVATED

How you view yourself, other people, and the world around you has a major impact on your ability to be happy and successful. As humans, we have a natural tendency to focus on the negative aspects of our lives and ourselves. We are always aware of our shortcomings and perceived obstacles. But often we don't take the time to count our blessings and see the good around us and in us. If I asked you right now to give me your five greatest weaknesses, you'd probably be able to rattle off at least five without much thought. If I asked for three of your strongest points, most of you would be at a loss for words, or you might reply, "Just give me a minute to think about that." Why? Because the negative stuff is right up front in your mind and ready to roll, while the positive stuff gets buried in the back.

Because focusing on the negative comes so naturally to us, it's actually easy to be negative and unmotivated. So it takes work to get and stay positive and motivated. But believe me, it's worth it because when you focus on the positive, that will become your reality.

Negative influences in our lives surround us. Some people will tell you that you can't do something. Sometimes we tell ourselves the same thing. We all have negative tapes playing in our head telling us that we're too old, too young, not smart enough, not experienced enough, and so on, to be able to do something. Unfortunately, there's no "off" button on these tapes, but you can turn down the volume. You have the power to create your own positive reality. Here are several ways you can do that.

Keep a Positive Workbook

I touched on this in chapter 6 in relation to getting through a bad day. In addition to keeping track of the bright moments in your day, along with notes from patients and family members, you want to develop a compilation of positive thoughts, experiences, and inspirations. A positive workbook will help you focus on the good things about yourself and your work. You should add to this workbook regularly and review it often, particularly when you are having a bad day or feeling insecure. Just as in a relationship, it is the positive things that will carry you through the negative, difficult times. Consider keeping separate sections in this workbook for the various components that follow.

> ### FROM THE FRONT LINE
>
> #### Tell Me What You Like
>
> "The main thing I like about nursing is the flexibility we have as a profession. Nurses have so many different areas that we can branch into. Our profession has such amazing diversity. I like knowing that I have that flexibility in my profession. Also, we are respected. The public likes us. In a recent Gallup poll, we were one of the most respected professions. If that doesn't make you feel great about the profession, what will?"
>
> —Shannon, new grad

Log What People Say

Take some time to remember positive things people have said about you in the past that made you feel good and positive about who you are. Again, these things can be personal or professional. Write these down on their own page. These might include a comment a nursing instructor made about what a great nurse you are going to make. Or it might be something positive a former boss or a family member said about your personality. Whenever someone gives you a compliment, write it down. It's not enough to just think about these things. You have to record them. Why? Because otherwise they will quickly fade away and get pushed into the back of your memory. Once done, review this often to remind you of all the good things about yourself. I did this when I was first starting my business years ago, and I would pull out the book and read all these positive things when self-doubt would start to creep in or when I needed a boost. It is amazingly effective at keeping yourself positive and on track.

Include Inspirational Quotes

Accumulate positive and inspirational quotes, poems, prayers, and sayings that have meaning to you. Write them in your workbook, too. You might also copy some of your favorites onto a self-sticking note or an index card and post them around the house where you'll look at them often—perhaps on your mirror, on your refrigerator's door, or in your wallet. These are the things that sustain us. You can find books of quotes in the library as well as in bookstores.

Remember Those Magic Nursing Moments

In addition to keeping track of positive thoughts and letters from patients and patients' family members, make notes about patient care situations in which you felt you made a real difference. This will help you stay focused on your mission and on all the positive aspects of your job and your profession—your life's work. Always focus on your patients and the difference you make in their lives, especially when you are feeling down. This is what it's all about. It is those interactions, those special moments, that make life worth living.

Favorite Quotes

Here are a few of my favorite quotes from notables. As you go through life, be sure to record some of your favorites and turn to them on tough days.

"Never let the fear of striking out get in your way."

—*Babe Ruth*

"When one door of happiness closes, another opens; but often we look so long at the closed door that we do not see the one which has opened for us."

—*Helen Keller*

"Just remember, if things look hopeless, maybe you're facing the wrong direction."

—*Ziggy*

As you can see, inspiration can come from those of all walks of life—even cartoon characters!

Create and Continually Develop a List of Your Strong Points

Most people never take time to do this. We can rattle off our shortcomings without hesitation if asked. But the average person is hard-pressed to enumerate his or her strong points. Also, it is uncomfortable for many of us to think of ourselves in a positive way—never mind having to write it down.

Take time to list your strengths and assets—those things you do particularly well. This is a list that will develop over time as you accumulate more experiences and become more self-aware. While this exercise may initially be difficult for you, it is something that will help you focus and give you direction. Consider asking someone close to you what he or she perceives to be your best personality trait or special talent. Everyone has something that he or she is particularly good at or that is a strong point. But because this trait is so ingrained in us, so much a part of who we are, we never think of it, like walking or breathing. And others will not necessarily bring it to your attention unless you ask because they assume you are aware of it.

Identify What You Enjoy Doing

As you begin to practice in your profession, notice what aspects of your work give you the greatest satisfaction and present the greatest challenge. Is it the actual hands-on care that you deliver? Is it the teaching aspect? Do you enjoy policy development? Maybe the computer work stimulates you.

Whenever someone asks, "Where should I go from here?" or "How can I find my niche?" the first questions I respond with are "What are you good at?" and "What do you enjoy doing?" It's amazing how many people have never stopped to consider these questions. The answers to those questions are the key to your future success and happiness. Once you've answered them, look for opportunities to expand and develop those skills and experiences.

Other Tips for Motivation and Success

There are innumerable sources to help you get through the day or your tough times. The important thing to remember is to find something that works for *you*. Also, people often will have different methods of working through adversity, depending on the specific situation—perhaps one way for handling the loss of a patient and another for working through burnout. Here are some more invaluable means for enhancing your mood and nursing experience.

Practice Positive Self-Talk

Self-talk is that inner dialogue we have with ourselves, both negative and positive. Negative self-talk is the self-berating we go through when we are down on ourselves, such as "I'm not good enough, smart enough, or deserving." Positive self-talk is a self–pep talk of sorts. You mentally tell yourself, "I can do this. I've been in tougher situations than this. I've come a long way in my life, and this is just another challenge to overcome. I *will* make it." As you would on your stereo, use your mind's volume and balance controls. Turn up the positive and tone down the negative to stay focused.

Use Motivational Materials

There are scores of books, videos, and CDs available today to get you pumped up and positive. Start by going to a library and looking up the word *motivation* in the computerized catalog. This will probably direct you to a particular section in the library. The first time I browsed in this section, I got motivated just reading the titles! Take out a few books that grab your attention and read or at least scan them. Get some motivational CDs from the library or a bookstore, too. There are many to choose from. Listen to several and find a few that grab you. Everyone responds differently to different authors, different speaking voices, and different messages. Find the ones that grab you. Listen to them on your way to work, while you're getting ready for work, when you're exercising, or when you're doing mundane chores around the house.

This may all sound very simplistic, but it is very effective in keeping you pumped up. It's like having a personal coach with you, reminding you that you can do it and that you have a lot to offer. Sometimes we need to hear these things from other people. Negative stuff comes into our heads naturally, but it takes effort to put some positive stuff in there. Have you ever heard the expression, related to computers, "G-I-G-O," which stands for "Garbage In, Garbage Out"? The concept can be applied to your outlook on life. You can operate with "G-I-G-O" or "P-I-P-O" ("Positive Input, Positive Output"). The choice is yours.

Read Inspirational Biographies

There are many wonderful books in your local library and in bookstores about people who have overcome great obstacles or who have worked against all odds to accomplish great things. When you read about someone else, it makes you realize that you can do anything to which you set your mind.

Stay Away from People Who Drag You Down

There are positive people, and there are people who just drag you down. You know the kind of people I'm talking about. They are the people in your life who drain your emotional energy, who do nothing but complain and criticize, who try to make trouble where there is none, and who goad you into doing or saying things that you may later regret. They take up your time on the telephone, they monopolize your time at social events, and they interrupt you at work.

They find fault with your friends, your relationships, and even with you. Avoid these losers. Remember that other people judge you by the company you keep. Moreover, you adopt the attitudes and habits of those you associate with. Birds of a feather flock together.

Surround Yourself with Positive, Motivated, Upbeat People

This is one of the most important things you can do for self-motivation and positive thinking. Look for role models in your place of employment and in your life—people who seem to have their act together, who enjoy their work, and who do a good job. Observe them whenever you can and learn from them. Remember, we often adopt the attitudes and habits of those we spend our time with.

Take Care of Yourself

This is fundamental, but many people simply don't do it, and they pay for it whether they realize it or not. I shouldn't have to tell you this, but your diet, how much sleep you get (or don't), and whether you exercise have a direct relation to your mood and your ability to be happy. Create balance by spending time with family and friends, paying attention to your spiritual life, and engaging in leisure activities. Keep your own energy and health in balance for optimal results in your life.

Walk Tall and Smile

We speak with more than our words. Our walk, our stance, and our voice inflection all communicate as we speak and even before we've uttered a word. The first thing you should "say" to someone is a smile. Force yourself to walk tall and smile whenever it's appropriate. It's hard to be in a bad mood when you have a smile on your face.

Visualize Yourself Succeeding

Visualization is a powerful technique used to help create an optimal situation or a desired outcome. While visualization is used in health care for the purpose of healing, you can use it to achieve results in your life. If you imagine yourself facing an interview, giving a presentation with panache, or courageously facing up to a tough situation, you are inclined to act as you imagined. Sit quietly, with your eyes closed, if possible, and actually imagine yourself succeeding in a particular situation. Play the scene out in your mind, with you as the central character, succeeding. Visualization has a long sports history and has been used by speech coaches, therapists, and motivational speakers as well.

Be a Giving, Considerate Person

When you choose to be positive, giving, loving, and kind to others, it will come back to you in spades. If you look for the good in others, you will definitely find it. If you treat others with respect and compassion, your life will be filled with reciprocal feelings of good and respect. Throughout history, humans have been asking, "Why am I here?" or "What is the meaning of life?" I have discovered my answers to these questions. We are here to help as many other people along the way as possible, to ease pain and suffering when we can, to live a good life, and to set a good example for others to follow.

Live and Work with Passion and Joy

As I've already said, it's all about attitude. You determine your approach in life. You can consider each day sacred or cursed. You can see your work as a divine mission or as a chore. You can view your profession as a means of contributing to the world in a significant way and making a difference in human life, or you can view it simply as a job at which you punch a clock and count the days to retirement. The choice is yours, and so are the consequences. The difference is felt in the quality of your life and by those in your life, including those you help. Joy and passion make life worth living.

THE IMPORTANCE OF SETTING GOALS

It's virtually impossible to pick up a book on motivation or being successful without a discussion of goals. What exactly is a goal? Motivational speaker Zig Ziglar said, "A goal is a dream with a deadline." Self-help guru Anthony Robbins said, "Setting goals is the first step in turning the invisible into the visible—the foundation for all success in life."

Many people don't understand how to set and use goals or the power and impact of goals. Think of goals as your road map to success. Your goals constitute a written plan of action for your future. Without goals, you will have little success. James Cash Penney, founder of the J. C. Penney stores, once said, "Give me a stock clerk with a goal and I'll give you a man who will change history. Give me a man without a goal and I'll give you a stock clerk." Powerful words by Mr. Penney. People with goals go places. People without goals flounder around without direction and waste precious time.

The majority of people never set goals—probably because they're afraid they won't reach them or because of what they perceive they will have to give up in pursuit of their goals. And while everything in life is a trade-off, you pay the ultimate price for *not* having goals because never following your dreams or finding out what you are capable of doing is a very high price to pay. I once heard someone say that when your life is at its end, you never regret the things you did—only the things you wish you had done but never did. Don't go through life starting your conversations with "I should have," "I could have," or "I would have."

The Purpose of Goals

Goals give you something to work toward in your life. They give you direction. They give you a reason to get out of bed in the morning. The very fact that you have written goals will actually make you more motivated and more enthusiastic. Goals help propel you toward your future. You can let the cards fall as they will and accept the results as fate, or you can take control of your life and career and make plans today to get you where you want to be tomorrow.

It has been said that if you can dream it, you can be it. Think about where you want to be five years from now and ten years from now. Begin to envision your future. Right now you may be concerned just with surviving your first year in nursing, and indeed that is a challenging goal for a new grad. But allow your mind to wander and picture yourself as you would like to be: confident, experienced, poised, revered, and admired in a gratifying and fulfilling profession. Imagine what you might be doing, where you might be working, and how you might get there.

Everyone needs to have long- and short-term goals. A long-term goal is something you want to accomplish in the next five years, and a short-term goal would include some of the steps you need to take to achieve your long-term goals. For example, if your goal is to be attending school for a master's degree five years from now, then some of your short-term goals would be to get to a public library to research various majors and schools and then call for their catalogs. You don't have to decide on your major or know exactly when you will start school in order to begin the process.

Characteristics of Goals

Goals can be characterized as follows:

• *Goals must be written.* Research has shown that if you don't write down goals, you are more inclined to forget them and less inclined to act on them. You also need to keep them somewhere that you will look at them often, like in your wallet or on your refrigerator's door.

• *Goals must have time frames.* It's not enough to say, "I want to attain my bachelor's in nursing someday—or eventually." You need to set a realistic time frame, such as, "I want to attain my BSN within the next five years." The time frame helps propel you forward and serves as motivation to "get moving."

• *Goals must be specific.* Saying, "I want to advance my education," or, "I want to be working in an interesting specialty" is not specific enough. Make a firm decision about getting your bachelor's degree, or your master's degree, working in labor and delivery, or whatever.

• *Goals must be objective and measurable.* To say, "I want to be happy" is very subjective. What does that mean? What will it take for you to be happy? How will you measure that? Generalities such as this are wisps of smoke that are blown away by the normal course of life. Get to the meat of what you want to do and develop some concrete steps to get you there.

• *Goals should challenge you.* You can't grow if you're not challenged. So you should always be setting bigger and more challenging goals as you move forward so that you will keep growing.

Map Out Your Goals

Develop goals for every aspect of your life: physical, spiritual, career, financial, personal, and family. Think of the exact thing you want to change—what you want to accomplish, a habit you want to adopt, a skill you want to master, or a place you want to be. Ask yourself where you want to be five years from now and what you want to accomplish in your first year as a nurse. If you don't know where you want to be five years from now, set short-term, action-oriented goals that will help you make decisions for your future. For example, finding admission requirements for a higher degree in two months or contacting a professional association next week are specific short-term goals that will steer you to solid five-year goals.

Develop an Action Plan

Once you've set your goals, you should develop an action plan and get to work. An action plan involves writing down those things that need to be done in pursuit of your goals, such as people to call, things to do, places to go, and information to get. Making lists, while scoffed at by some as a habit of a compulsive personality, is actually one of the best ways to stay organized and get things done. If you don't write things down, you are more inclined to forget about them and less inclined to act on them. Just like setting goals for your long-term future, making daily and weekly lists helps you prioritize your days.

Commit to Achieving Your Goals

Once you've set a goal, you need to make a commitment to achieve it. Making a commitment means you're willing to do whatever it takes to make something happen. It means making sacrifices. But instead of making commitments, some of us make excuses. We have a tendency to make excuses for why we can't move forward in our lives or why we can't do a certain thing. Remember that most obstacles are in our own minds and of our own making.

Everyone is busy, and it is easy to get so caught up in your day-to-day activities that you forget to plan for the future. We think, "I don't have time right now," or, "I'm waiting for my kids to get out of college." But the future is happening now, regardless of what you do.

MAKING DECISIONS

Learning to make good decisions is part of the foundation for success. Often, before setting a goal, you will have to make a decision. Do I want to go back to school? If so, for what degree or in what specialty? What specialty do I want to work in? Do I want to change jobs? Should I accept the management position that's being offered to me?

Get the Ball Rolling

I went to a seminar years ago on time management in which the speaker touted the value of having written goals. It was something I had never thought about or considered previously. She made each of us write down five-year goals for ourselves on an index card. I already had thoughts of becoming an educator and a speaker someday, but it was little more than a dream and a whimsy at that time. I wrote down that I wanted to be enrolled in a baccalaureate program, have some articles published, have developed some educational programs for presentation, and be working toward a speaking career.

We had to date the card five years from the day of the seminar. I carried that card around in my wallet for at least five years. Every time I cleaned out my purse or pulled out my cash to count it or organize it, I was forced to pull out that index card and look at it. Each time I did, it reminded me of where I wanted to go and that I needed to get moving. I have no doubt that the act of writing down my five-year goals is responsible for getting the ball rolling in my professional life. Without that fateful step, I might still be asking myself, "What do I want to do when I grow up?"

Many people spend their time sitting on the fence, unable to make a decision about things that are important to their lives and future. If the answer is not apparent, the process ends or freezes up. They waste a lot of time and energy on being indecisive when, in fact, not making a decision *is* a decision of sorts. They decide that they will not act. Some people are afraid to make a decision because they know they'll have to live with the consequences if they make a mistake. No one makes perfect decisions. There is an expression that there are no wrong decisions, only bigger lessons to be learned. When things don't turn out as you had hoped they would, learn from that situation and move on.

Some people survey everyone they know and ask, "What should I do?" You can ask people eternally and put off making a decision. Don't fool yourself. It's okay to get some input from others, but only you can make the decision.

Making good decisions is something you get better at with practice. The more decisions you make, the easier and more comfortable the process becomes and the more you begin to trust your decision-making ability. So start with some small decisions in your life and work your way up from there. And fortunately, there are several tips and hints that can help make the process easier.

- *Make a pros-and-cons list.* Take a piece of paper, draw a line down the middle, and title one column "Pros" and the other column "Cons." Start to list both in regard to a particular decision you are having trouble making. Write down both the advantages and the drawbacks. Making such a list helps put things in perspective. Often, there are many advantages but only a few disadvantages. Yet we dwell on the potential drawback and hesitate to move forward. When it's in our mind unwritten, it seems overpowering.

- *Write about it in your journal.* Writing is a way to clarify your thoughts and helps you work things out. Putting your dilemma on paper or on your computer screen takes your thoughts from the abstract form and makes them concrete. Often, you can work out a problem or come to a decision on your own just by writing about it.

- *Talk it over with an objective, supportive, uninvolved party.* Talking is therapeutic. That's why so many of us are willing to pay a therapist to listen to our problems. When you have an important decision to make, it's a good idea to discuss it with someone not involved in the situation whom you can trust.

The major benefit of talking things over with someone is that the person with whom you are conversing can give you some objective feedback. An objective listener can tell you what he or she hears in your words and in your emotions, serving as validation for what you may already know is the right thing for you. Talking, as with writing, helps clarify your thoughts and makes them concrete.

I have often had other nurses come to me and ask what they should do about a particular situation—perhaps whether they should leave their current job. I ask them to tell me about their dilemma, and I listen to them talk. Without fail, I can hear a very definite leaning in their voice. It is often more a fear of change than an actual inability to make a decision that is at play. We often know in our heart what the right decision is, but we need validation.

• *Gather more information.* This is one of the simplest yet most frequently overlooked steps in making an informed decision. If you are trying to make a decision about which major to pursue in college or whether to get an advanced practice degree, the most logical place to start is to get more information about what's involved in getting a degree and talk to others who are doing it.

Network with others in the field, check out the website of that particular specialty, and consider going out to a local chapter meeting of a related professional association. Talk to nurses in your current facility and ask which they consider to be the good places to work for that specialty. Ask what they like and don't like about their specialty. You can't make an informed decision without having all the facts. You only waste time and energy trying to do so.

• *Go with your gut.* When all is said and done, you should listen to your inner voice, often referred to as your "gut," because your gut is usually right. I've heard nurses say, "I am thinking I should accept this job because it will look good on my resume, but my gut is telling me to pass on it because I don't get a good feeling about the people working in that unit." Learn to trust your instincts, but don't confuse your fear of making a change or accepting a challenge with a gut feeling that things aren't right. Learn to differentiate between the two.

EXPLORE YOUR CAREER OPTIONS

Even though you're just beginning and want to focus on getting your clinical skills down pat, it is never too soon to start looking into your career options. Knowing your options serves many purposes. First of all, you will learn the full scope of what nurses are doing out there, which gives you a better understanding of your profession. Many nurses get themselves in a rut with their work. They stay in an unhappy situation too long. They don't like their work or are tired of it, but they feel they have no options. Just knowing that you have options lessens your anxiety about the future, gives you something to look forward to, and keeps you interested and excited about your future.

Options

So what are your career options? I talked earlier about options being an effective method of avoiding burnout, but recognizing your options is also a way to celebrate the diversity of nursing. Hopefully, your nursing school education provided an overview of some of the traditional specialties for nurses. Beyond that, there are virtually endless opportunities out there for nurses, and more things are opening up all the time. Why? Because there are many ways and many places to have a positive impact on patient care, and we continue to discover new ones all the time.

For example, in the last few decades, the specialty of sexual assault nurse examiner (SANE) was created within the larger specialty of forensic nursing. Forensic nursing combines nursing science with law enforcement. Sounds exciting, doesn't it? For those of you who have ever wanted a badge or a gun, this just might be your opportunity!

A SANE is a nurse who has gone through a special training course leading to certification. A SANE nurse works for a trauma center or the county prosecutor's office and is on-call and summoned when a suspected victim of sexual assault is brought in. SANE nurses perform physical exams, counsel the victim, collect forensic evidence, and possibly testify later in court. SANE nurses tell me that since they have been involved in this way, the incidence of conviction for sexual assault has been on the rise. This is a wonderful new way nurses are making a difference and contributing to the greater good of society. This is just one possible career path. Even if you choose to stay in a clinical specialty for the remainder of your career, isn't it exciting just to know that other nurses are expanding the nursing career universe?

Nurses are also working with the homeless and are running community clinics. They own and operate holistic health and wellness centers,

---

FROM THE FRONT LINE

Good Thoughts

"I get a lot out of being a nurse. I especially enjoy working with terminal/hospice patients. I find I learn so much from them. I get a great deal of satisfaction and feel honored to be a part of someone's life at such an intimately personal time. Terminal patients are a challenge as they progress through the various stages of dying. However, when a terminal patient reaches acceptance and begins to open up to you, it is an intense, personal exchange between you and that person. I wouldn't use the word patient because at this point these roles really don't exist. You are just two people sharing that moment. Some of my fondest memories in nursing are of these exchanges. It makes me feel useful to be able to sit with a dying patient and talk openly with him or her—to fulfill this need that many people cannot. A lot of my coworkers cannot handle talking about death with a patient. They want to run away as soon as the patient's prognosis worsens or to utilize every technological advance to prolong his or her life. So, I consider being able to fulfill this role and care for these people at the end point in their life to be very satisfying."

—Shannon, new grad

incorporating complementary therapies. They even work on cruise ships and in prisons.

Discovering the Right Option for You

How can you learn more about career opportunities in nursing? Read nursing journals and get out to career fairs. Use the Internet and browse career sites that offer information about all the clinical and non-clinical specialties in nursing and attend conventions and continuing education classes related to various specialties.

Talk to other nurses in your facility who work in different specialties or who do some unusual things like wound care, infection control, occupational health, education, or management. Ask them about what they do, what the pros and cons are of their specialty, and how they got started. When you encounter a nurse from an outside entity, like a transplant nurse or a research nurse, find out what his or her job is all about.

Try things that sound interesting to you. This is how you find your niche. Success is a journey. I tried on many hats before I figured out my career path. I spent the first twenty years of my career trying different things, challenging myself, accumulating experiences, and discovering what I was good at and what I enjoyed doing.

My business places me in constant touch with nurses from all over the country. Talking to nurses in various specialties is a part of what I do. Even though I have considerable expertise in career opportunities for nurses, I am constantly meeting or talking to nurses who are doing something I haven't heard of before—something interesting and innovative. It is very uplifting to hear about all the ways and places nurses are making a difference.

CHAPTER 8

TAKING YOUR CAREER
TO THE NEXT LEVEL

Nursing is a career for your lifetime. It is continuously changing and evolving, and so, too, will your own career path within the profession. Regardless of the path you take or the changes that occur, you should always be moving forward and looking for ways to take your career to the next level. Moving up doesn't necessarily mean getting into management. But it does mean advancing your experience, your knowledge, your education, and your ability to contribute to health care. Likewise, it means enhancing your sense of satisfaction and fulfillment.

Think of your profession as a fine car or horse. In this sense, with proper care, it will carry you to new and exciting places. Neglect it, and you'll be stranded.

CONTINUING YOUR EDUCATION

Unless you already have an advanced degree, school should be in your future. There is an expression that when you cease to learn, you cease to live. Do you need to have a bachelor's degree to stay competitive in nursing? Yes. Can you get by without it? Sure, if getting by is what you want to do. But you will have limited opportunities. You'll stay in a lower pay scale and likely be looked over for promotions and advancements. Do you need to have a master's degree? That depends on your career goals. But one thing is for certain: A master's degree will expand your knowledge, broaden your horizons, increase your confidence level, and give you more options.

Bettering Yourself and Your Future

Deciding on a degree in nursing as opposed to another major also depends on your career goals. A bachelor of science in nursing (BSN) and a master of science in nursing (MSN) are very desirable in the clinical setting. Currently, you can attain clinical certification with or without a BSN from the American Nurses Association (ANA). But there has been much debate about requiring a BSN as a basis for some certifications. In fact, for a time, the ANA had required a BSN for certification. In response to protests from the profession, the organization created a two-tier system of certification to accommodate nurses with and without a BSN. If teaching nursing is in your future, an undergraduate or a graduate degree in nursing will serve you well. Pursuing a degree in nursing will expand your knowledge of nursing theory and history and nursing management and practice.

> *"Nursing is a career, not a job. It needs to be fed and nurtured."*
> —Michele, nurse

On the other hand, some nurses have no desire to get a degree in nursing. If you are one of them, don't let that stop you from moving forward with your education. Consider other related degrees, such as psychology, communication, health-care management, business, health education—the list goes on and on. There is a strong argument that a nurse with a business or management degree is uniquely equipped for today's health-care environment, where the bottom line is just as important as the delivery of quality care.

Which Degree Is Best for You?

The key to choosing a major is to first examine your career goals. Even if you're not sure where you want to be five or ten years from now, think about whether you anticipate staying in a clinical or teaching environment versus an administrative, corporate, or entrepreneurial environment. Then get to a library and seek out books in the reference section that list universities and their majors. Call a few universities and request their catalogs. Look at the admission requirements, curriculum, number of credits required to graduate, total cost, and course schedule. Find a program that looks interesting and exciting to you and allows for flexibility of course choices so you can tailor the program to your needs and interests.

Finding Time for School

Most colleges today will cater to the nontraditional student—someone who is working, raising a family, or dealing with many other responsibilities and commitments while pursuing a college degree. Some colleges offer credit for life experience, including some for non-credit nursing courses, the type offered by hospital-based diploma programs. This is an important consideration. Many colleges offer independent study projects that waive class attendance. Others offer evening and weekend classes, and some offer online courses. Finding a program that will fit in with your work and life schedules is an important consideration.

Smartening Up

I chose to attend a hospital-based diploma school for my basic nursing education. It was a three-year program that incorporated some college credit courses. Though I did not earn a degree, I did have about fifteen credits toward an associate's or a bachelor's degree. At that time, I had absolutely no intention of ever returning to school. I had an RN diploma and was quite content with that. Even without a college degree, I managed to achieve considerable success in my early career.

Some years later, and many years before I actually became an entrepreneur, I began to aspire to become a speaker and an educator. It occurred to me that it probably would be a good idea to beef up my credentials in preparation for that "someday" possibility. So when my employer offered college courses on-site as well as a tuition reimbursement benefit, I jumped at the opportunity to start my college education. This particular college offered a bachelor of science in health-care management, which was right up my alley.

Initially, I regarded furthering my education as a necessary evil that would yield little more than some additional initials after my name and a coveted piece of paper suitable for framing. But an amazing thing happened when I started attending classes: I actually began to learn something. Was any of this easy for me? Hardly. But I plowed along, keeping my goal to obtain a college degree in mind, believing it might someday come in handy.

When I finally graduated, I somehow felt more whole and complete as a person. This was entirely unexpected from someone who had spent considerable time and energy convincing herself that she didn't need a college degree. I suddenly had a renewed sense of confidence and purpose in my life.

In addition to traditional classroom-based learning, there are many nontraditional educational options available known as "distance learning." This type of program allows you to study at home on your own time, with heavy use of your computer for lectures, communicating with fellow students and professors, transmission of assignments, and test taking. Degrees at the baccalaureate, master's, and even doctoral level are available through distance education. Some programs require that you spend a few weeks periodically on campus in a traditional classroom, and some require proctored, or monitored, exams. Take time to explore these alternatives to determine if one might be right for you.

The greatest advantage of distance-learning programs is that you have great flexibility. You can work at your own pace, at any time of the day or night that is convenient for you, without having to go to class. The biggest disadvantage and criticism of this type of program is that you miss out on the classroom experience. While the Internet allows for communication with professors and other students, some argue that there is no replacement for the in-person, interactive classroom experience and live dialogue that come with classroom-based education.

Are distance-education programs legitimate and perceived as credible? Yes, provided they are from an accredited college. Before starting any course of study at any college, whether traditional or nontraditional, check out its accreditation status and ask to speak to a few current and past students. Ask students and alumni what the pros and cons are of that particular program and university. Ask about support services, flexibility, and available resources.

You'll encounter the question "Where do you want to be five years from now?" many times in your life. You can sit back and let the future happen to you, or you can be poised for the future, picking your own direction and being ready for anything.

OTHER MEANS OF BETTERING YOURSELF AND YOUR FUTURE

Obtaining a degree may be the obvious example of how to improve your education and credentials. However, there are many different paths for taking your career to the next level. While you may look at earning a particular level of certification as a long, uphill climb, if you are constantly improving yourself, taking classes, and heading toward a goal, you will be there before you know it. The following are some additional ways you can boost your knowledge, credentials, and career.

Too Good to Be True

A few words of caution: Be sure to verify the accreditation status of any distance-learning program you consider. There are some "diploma mills" that will give anyone a degree in anything for the right price. Some will even make you write a paper or two to give an air of legitimacy to the program and then grant the rest of the credits for life experience. The term "earning your degree" is to be taken quite literally. So, if the program sounds too easy and quick to be true, it is probably a sham.

Never Stop Learning

Information and skills are constantly changing, so you must make learning a lifelong process. I've already talked about formal education, but there are many opportunities for informal education all around you. There is continuing education, adult education, constructive reading, educational DVDs/CDs, and many other ways to enhance your skills and knowledge. Learning keeps you young. It makes you feel alive. It gets the blood coursing through your veins. It pumps up the volume on your self-esteem. And, as I've already said, if you're not learning, you're stagnating.

- *Utilize what your employer offers.* Many employers offer tuition reimbursement, on-site college courses, continuing education seminars, and other opportunities to enhance your knowledge and experience. Take full advantage of them. It will help you in your current and future positions. I never fully appreciated my former employer's tuition reimbursement benefit until I had to pay for parts of my own education. I wished I had gone further with my education while I had the financial backing.
- *Work on your speaking and writing skills.* These are some of the skills that will help distinguish you from others in the field and will help propel you forward. The ability to speak and write well are two of the most sought-after skills in our society. Besides, nurses need more articulate spokespeople and writers to get the word out about nursing—that is, who we are and what we do.
- *Volunteer to conduct an occasional in-service, present at grand rounds, or do some community education.* Write an article for your employee newsletter, for the local chapter of your professional association, or for a regional career magazine. Start small and work your way up. Force yourself to do these things if you are reluctant. Check out some books from a library on how to be a better speaker and how to write an article. There is much you can learn from books on these subjects. In this instance, experience alone is not always the best teacher; it will perpetuate your mistakes unless you learn how to improve these skills.

Years ago, I took a job as a department director in a community hospital, working with regulatory issues and quality improvement. I was at that job only three months when my new boss told me he wanted me to make a presentation to the medical staff at their monthly meeting about health-care reimbursement issues, something I had some limited expertise in. At the time, I was a very reluctant public speaker, like most people. I viewed this as a fate worse than death! It was bad enough that I was still a new employee and trying to acclimate myself to my new surroundings. But an audience of physicians—I couldn't imagine a more intimidating group. And to make matters worse, I had to talk to them about their least-favorite subject in the world—reimbursement. I protested vehemently, reminding my boss that I was still testing the waters and had a lot to learn. I recommended putting this off to a later date. My boss listened quietly, and when I was finished with my sales pitch, he said calmly but firmly, "You *will* make a presentation at this month's medical staff meeting." I realized he was not giving me a choice.

I prepared the best I could and tried to keep my sense of terror at bay. The dreaded night arrived. I took the podium and made my presentation. I was more nervous than I had ever been in my life. In fact, I was a complete, disastrous, nervous wreck. My stomach was in a knot, and I could hear my own voice quivering as I spoke. I felt like a fool.

When I finally finished, I was absolutely mortified and believed that I had done a terrible job. I wanted to get out of there as soon as possible. I considered quitting my job that night *and* moving so I would never have to face any of those people again. But the thoughts of my family, who weren't ready to relocate, and my need for a job made me think better of it. I decided I would just skulk into work the next day (wearing dark glasses), lie low for a few weeks, and pray that with the passage of time, this ugly incident would fade out of the memories of those who mattered.

But an incredible and unexpected thing happened. Shortly after I got to my office, one of the physicians stopped by and said, "I would have expected you to be nervous and frightened last night in front of that group. But you were forceful and confident. Congratulations, Toughy!" I heard his words, yet I couldn't believe my ears. How could it be that my abject nervousness was not detected? I had learned long ago that when a compliment was presented, whether you felt worthy of it or not, you should simply say, "Thank you," which is exactly what

I did. I convinced myself that he was just trying to be nice, but two more physicians later stopped by and had similar comments about the program content and my delivery style.

Just Do It

When starting both my undergraduate and graduate programs, I wouldn't let myself think about how long it would take me to finish or how old I would be when I graduated. If I did, I never would have started. I decided to just get started and keep moving forward, knowing that eventually I would graduate. The bottom line was that at the end of five years, either I could have my bachelor's or master's degree, or I could still be thinking about it. I'm happy to report that by the time you read this book, I will have finally completed my master's program. I'm even thinking about pursuing a doctoral degreee—me, the person who once convinced herself that a degree was not necessary!

The great thing is that as my career continues to develop and bigger and better opportunities come my way, I am prepared to meet those new challenges because of my higher education. At times, I feel as if my education is the "wave" that is propelling me into the future. The expression "Education is not the filling of a pail, but the lighting of a fire" resonates with me. Higher education has certainly lit a fire under me.

I was absolutely flabbergasted. But I learned several important lessons that helped me advance in my professional career. First, most people don't notice how nervous you feel on the inside when you are speaking. Second, you don't have to be the world's authority on something to be able to impart useful information. Finally, it is important to take the time to give positive feedback to people. Positive feedback can actually change people's lives.

After this experience, several things happened. I approached future speaking engagements with renewed confidence. I didn't let my own nervousness get in the way of doing what I had to do, and I had acquired the nickname "Toughy." That was something I wrote in my positive workbook, and it still brings a smile to my face. It reminds me of the personal growth that can come from moving forward in spite of my fears. The point is that by confronting a tough situation head on, I was able to overcome something I genuinely feared.

• *Develop management and leadership skills.* No one is a born manager. And just because someone has the title "manager" doesn't mean he or she knows how to be a good one. Like everything else, management skills are learned and improved with practice. You can start by observing competent people, taking classes, and reading books on the subject. When the time is right, look for opportunities to take occasional charge or to supervise. Seek relevant experiences such as doing the schedule, working on budgets, and developing policies and procedures.

• *Look beyond your job description.* Although your first and foremost mission as a new grad is to become competent in your new role and assimilate into your new environment, let your supervisor know that you are available to work on special projects and are interested in getting on interdisciplinary or nursing department committees, like those for recruitment and retention, policy and procedures, or nursing practice. Getting on committees and working on special projects is a great way to learn as well as to contribute in a significant way. It also makes you more visible within the organization and gives you an opportunity to develop relationships with nurses and with people from other departments.

If your employer is looking for volunteers to take blood pressures at a local health screening or to attend a convention or career fair to help recruit new nurses, step up to the plate. The experience will be great for you, and it will put you in a good light with your employer. Look for opportunities and challenges as a way to learn something new and stretch yourself. Do it to be a team player, but more important, do it to expand your experience base and to expand your horizons. Don't adopt the attitude of "That's not in my job description." Advancement, new experiences, and growth aren't in there, either.

• *Be resilient.* Everyone has bad days and weeks. Learn to bounce back. Each day gives you the opportunity to start fresh. Don't hang on to yesterday's problems and bad feelings. Don't ruminate. Rather than dwelling on what went wrong yesterday, think about what you can learn and do right today. Celebrate your life and your work and be at peace.

• *Develop good communication skills.* Communication is the foundation for success. The greatest hindrance to good communication is the illusion that it has been achieved. Learn to speak in a clear, concise way. Learn how to get your point across. Become a good listener. Don't nod and say, "I see" when you don't understand. Avoid weak phrases in your speech, like saying, "I'm sorry" all the time when you've done nothing wrong. This is a bad conversational habit some people get into. It sounds like you're apologizing all the time. Don't precede a question with a qualifier like "This is probably a dumb question, but . . ." or "You probably aren't going to want to hear what I have to say, but . . ." Just get to the point.

• *Learn to "toot your own horn."* While modesty is an admirable trait, keeping quiet about your accomplishments won't help your career. You've got to get the word out, or no one will know. When you get a degree or a certification, be sure your boss and your boss's boss know. Get it in the company newsletter. The same goes for getting elected to an office in your professional association, getting on a committee, or receiving an award. If you get an article published, cut it out and tack it on the bulletin board at work after giving a copy to your supervisor. If you get a great letter from a patient or a patient's family member, give your supervisor a copy. This is not the same as bragging or boasting, which is entirely different. Successful people have learned and utilize the fine art of self-promotion.

• *Embrace change—don't fear it.* Change is a part of the world we live in. It is inevitable. And while it is human nature to resist change, those who learn to adapt and move with it are the ones who will succeed. Anticipate change rather than being surprised or overwhelmed when it comes. You can cling to the past, or you can move forward. The choice is yours.

• *Learn to take a compliment.* If someone gives you a compliment, whether it is a client or a coworker, be gracious and simply say, "Thank you." Don't downplay your contributions and abilities by saying, "It was nothing" or "Don't mention it." Likewise, don't deflect the compliment by saying, "Oh, I really didn't do that great a job" or "I really didn't do anything."

• *Develop good self-marketing skills.* Learn the art and science of interviewing. Read books, attend seminars, and get some practice. Go on interviews when you have the opportunity. It's a good way to keep your interview skills sharp, make some important contacts, and see what's available. Develop a powerful, professional resume that highlights your accomplishments and more-interesting experiences rather than presenting a resume that reads like a laundry list of routine duties. Be able to articulate your strengths and assets. Be proud of who you are and what you do.

• *Stay abreast of future trends.* See what health-care economists are predicting for the future of health care. Where are nursing jobs predicted to be in the next five to ten years? Stay ahead of the trend by preparing for it. Read nursing journals and publications. Stay active in your professional associations. Attend seminars on future trends.

• *Get a grip on the big picture.* It's not enough to understand the nursing profession. You also have to understand the bigger context of "health care." Learn all you can about reimbursement and finances, health-care management and systems, administration, and marketing. The more you know, the more you will be able to successfully navigate your way through the system. Take classes, network with others in health care, and read some general health-care magazines, such as *Modern Healthcare.* You can find these in the health sciences or medical library in your facility or a neighborhood facility and in some college libraries. Ask your manager to pass these on to you if he or she gets them. There are also Internet services you can subscribe to for all the latest in health-care news. You can also do Internet news searches for particular topics.

• *Learn to negotiate.* Whether looking for a raise or a promotion, seeking a new job, or trying to implement some changes in your workplace, the art of negotiation will serve you well. While most people think of negotiating skills only in relation to salary issues, negotiating is part of everyday life. It has many uses when you are part of a team or a committee. There are certain rules and methods that can be learned and practiced. Like everything else, negotiating is something you get better at with knowledge and experience.

MENTORING

An important factor to consider in your career growth and development is finding and establishing one or more mentoring relationships. What is a mentor? A mentor, traditionally, is an experienced person who works with a novice or protege to develop professional goals and plans and to support the protege's professional growth and development. You will discover, as you read on, that there are many different types of mentoring relationships, both formal and informal, that can help you take your career to the next level.

A traditional mentor is someone with whom you have created a formal partnership for mutual benefit. This type of mentor is someone you would be in touch with on a regular basis for sage advice, to discuss things with, to ask questions of, to use as a sounding board, and to get feedback from. A mentor will listen to your goals and dreams, give you direction, help keep your career on track, encourage you to move forward, and let you know when you are straying.

A mentor can help you by increasing your visibility and exposure in the workplace and in your profession by introducing you to influential people, vouching for you, and recommending you when certain opportunities come up. A mentor can teach you things, give you perspective, and act as a role model.

The mentoring relationship has been popular for a long time in the business community. However, it is still a relatively new concept for nurses. Mentoring is slightly more prevalent in nursing administrative ranks than on the staff level, but it is still highly underutilized in the nursing community.

Mentor Versus Preceptor

A mentor is different from a preceptor. A preceptor is someone who is assigned to work with you for a limited period of time and in a very structured format during your early clinical experience. While a preceptor may teach you many things, his or her role is primarily to see that you get the clinical skills you need when just starting out. You may or may not like your preceptor, you may have several different preceptors during your early career, and your preceptor may not always have the time to give that you need. Also, some preceptors have not chosen to be preceptors—they may have been required to participate by their employer.

A traditional mentor, on the other hand, is usually someone whom you choose, who has taken a special interest in helping you, and who has agreed to work with you. This type of relationship takes a commitment on the part of both parties and is mutually supportive.

A mentor might be someone who works for the same organization as you do. In that case, he or she can help you move up the corporate ladder in that organization and can give you good insights into the key players there. Your mentor can show you the way things are done and how decisions are made in that organization. He or she can give you inside information about a particular institution or department, the culture, how people are promoted, office politics, and who the influential people are. Whether or not you work in the same place as your mentor, he or she can give you valuable insights into your profession.

Mentor Relationships

There are several different types of mentors and mentoring relationships. Some mentoring relationships are somewhat formal, or structured. In this type of relationship, you may set up specific times each week or month to meet or speak with your mentor. You might report on your progress, discuss specific challenges you have, and develop a plan of action.

Other mentoring relationships are informal. The mentor and protege may call each other periodically to check in and discuss current challenges and accomplishments without a predetermined frequency.

Your Role as a Mentee

The mentoring relationship is a two-way street. While your mentor has a clear role in the process, you, as the mentee, also have certain responsibilities and obligations. You have to be proactive and take responsibility for the relationship's dynamics.

• *Know what you need help with.* Take some time to examine your strong points and your weaknesses. Have a concept of what your objectives and goals are. A mentor is not a parent figure or a hand holder. You have to have a notion of what you want to accomplish and what you want out of the relationship. Make sure your mentor knows this. Listen to his or her feedback.

• *Stay in touch with your mentor.* Don't just call when you need something or have a question. Keep your mentor posted on your progress, share your triumphs and accomplishments, and call to see how he or she is doing. Let your mentor know how and when you have been able to implement his or her advice. It is important for you to stay in regular touch with your mentor.

• *Say "thank you."* Show appreciation for your mentor's time and attention. Don't ever take that for granted. Even after the mentoring relationship has ended, don't forget to continue to acknowledge your mentor and the help given to you.

• *Support your mentor.* Speak highly of your mentor to his or her superiors, if applicable, and to others in the field. As appropriate, refer and recommend your mentor, provide business leads, or nominate him or her for an award. Celebrate your mentor's accomplishments. Look for ways to promote his or her career. These are some of the ways to "pay back" your mentor.

• *Be open to advice.* There is much your mentor can teach you. Listen, observe, and learn. In addition to advising you on how to proceed, your mentor will tell you if you screw up. Don't take it personally. Appreciate the valuable opportunity to get that feedback so you don't make the same mistake twice.

• *Use your mentor's time well.* Know what you want to discuss. Be prepared with what you will say and what you need help with when you call or meet with your mentor. Respect your mentor's time. Your mentor wants to help you, but he or she doesn't have unlimited time to do so.

• *Give back.* Continue the cycle. Always look for opportunities to become a mentor yourself. Do good unto others as has been done to you. Don't wait to be asked. Look for potential in others. Once you have even a little experience, there are newcomers around who can benefit from your wisdom and advice. Those who are mentored are likely to mentor others in the future. It's a powerful and positive cycle. What you sow is what you will reap.

The Power of Mentorships

A mentor can help you when you are new in a career, new in a certain level of management, or new to a certain venue, like business ownership or advanced practice. I have had several mentors during my career. One such person was a woman I worked with when I had my first administrative position in a large health-care system. Although I had previously held management positions with small companies, I was now playing in the big leagues and had a lot to learn. I was doing my own job well enough, but I was very naive regarding office politics and the ways of the corporate world. When I was invited to join other executives—all of whom were at a higher level on the corporate ladder than I was—on a yacht excursion, I panicked. I didn't know whether to accept the invitation, and if I did, I didn't know what to wear, how to act, or what to do. Out of desperation, I approached this woman and asked for her advice. She was very forthcoming, and I soon learned that I could learn a lot from her.

Our relationship further developed as we began to work on a project together that would, eventually, get passed down to me. On one occasion when we were speaking, she said to me, "You are a very talented lady." I was astounded by her words. I always felt as if I was struggling and not making much progress. Those six words, coming from someone I respected and admired, were validation for me. They stay with me, even today, after many years.

There are two lessons here. One, it goes to show how important a mentoring relationship can be, and two, it illustrates how important positive feedback is, however brief.

I had a few very informal mentoring relationships in my career, although I didn't necessarily recognize them as such at the time. In each case it was with a woman more experienced and credentialed than myself to whom I had reached out for advice and help. Early in my career, there were many times when I could have used a mentor, but I had never even heard of the concept (and I certainly had no idea how to find a mentor or develop that relationship). In fact, I used to think that asking for help was a sign of weakness and that toughing it out on my own was the way to go. In retrospect, I know that I could have made fewer mistakes, gone further sooner, and had more confidence to do more and perform better had I had mentors.

Today, I give advice to other nurses and entrepreneurs all the time, but there are certain people with whom I have a more personal, ongoing relationship. These take the form of an informal mentoring relationship. My mentees call when they need help and advice or just to stay in touch. They support me in my endeavors, and I am always looking for ways to help them grow and advance in their careers. We may occasionally get together, but more often than not, we stay in touch by phone and e-mail.

What to Look for in a Mentor

When looking for a potential mentor, keep in mind you will want a mentor to be someone

- you admire and respect.
- who has considerable expertise in his or her specialty or profession.
- who seems to have it all together.
- with high standards and who is a leader in the field.
- who communicates well.
- who is enthusiastic about his or her profession.
- who has a caring attitude.
- you feel comfortable with.
- who can help your career.
- who is well-connected.
- you can trust.

How to Find a Traditional Mentor

Think about the people you already know, work with, and come in contact with. Perhaps you have a current or former professor who fits the bill. Consider someone who is already doing and is successful at something you want to do. Don't be afraid to aim high. You often have to reach far to get the best fruit.

Mentors can be found through professional associations, such as your state or specialty nurses association, as well as through special interest groups, like the American Assembly for Men in Nursing and the National Black Nurses Association. Joining and becoming active in professional associations, by attending meetings and getting on committees, is a good way to meet and develop relationships with potential mentors.

A mentor does not have to be someone of your race or gender—nor does that person necessarily have to be older than you. I have seen cases of women mentoring men and vice versa as well as a younger, more-experienced nurse mentoring an older nurse who is new to the profession or new to management.

Could your mentor be your boss? Ideally, no. While your boss can certainly be instrumental in advancing your career, a traditional mentoring relationship requires that you be able to discuss anything with your mentor. You can't always be completely honest with your boss, and sometimes it is your boss and your relationship with him or her that needs discussing. Besides, your boss may be good at what he or she does but not necessarily good at objectively advising you on your career.

How to Establish a Mentor-Mentee Relationship

Once you have identified a potential mentor, take steps to establish a more formal relationship. If it's someone you already know, start with a phone call. Tell that person how much you admire him or her and that you aspire to have similar characteristics. You might ask for a formal mentoring relationship, or you might ask for an in-person meeting to seek advice and see how it goes. Sometimes these relationships need to develop naturally. You'll be able to tell if your prospective mentor is receptive to you and a more formalized mentoring relationship.

Mentors Can Broaden Your Horizons

When I decided to start my own business several years ago, I felt at times as if I were drowning in a sea of the unknown. There was so much to do, so much to learn, and so much at risk. I reached out to several experienced nurse entrepreneurs who mentored me through the early days. Was I nervous about calling them and asking for their help? I was indeed. But my desire to succeed helped me overcome my fear of picking up the phone and contacting them. They were all very giving and generous with their time and knowledge. Most of them told me that other nurse entrepreneurs had helped them when they got started and that they were happy to do the same for me now. Likewise, I look for every opportunity today to return the favor to other nurses coming up.

Similarly, several years ago, when I first contemplated writing a book, a colleague, whom I knew only via the Internet and who had published many books, acted as a mentor to me in the process of trying to get a book published. She gave me advice and guidance, shared her experiences with me, made introductions for me in the publishing world, recommended books for me to read, critiqued my proposal, and otherwise gave me support and encouragement. That proposal was eventually accepted by a prestigious publishing firm. I have no doubt that it was because of my mentor's advice and guidance.

If you have targeted potential mentors with whom you are not acquainted, you might start with a letter of introduction and follow it with a phone call. Tell them that you admire them and aspire to be like them. Briefly state your goals, objectives, and aspirations, and tell them that you are seeking their help and advice. Mention what you have in common with them, if applicable. For example, if you know that one of the potential mentors was originally an emergency room nurse, you might say, "Like you, I am starting my career in the emergency room."

State in your letter that you will be calling on the phone in a week as a follow-up. When you make this phone call, be clear on what you want to say. Prepare a brief introduction and ask for what you want. This might be to set up a meeting, to make a telephone appointment to talk further, or to ask some specific questions. You might want to make some notes before you call so you won't get tongue-tied or forget anything you want to say. Also, in the event this person says that he or she doesn't have time to enter into a formal mentoring relationship with you but will be happy to answer any questions you have now, you want to be ready.

While there is some benefit to being geographically close to your mentor and being able to occasionally meet face to face, you may find a mentor who is in another part of the country. In this case, regular communication by phone and e-mail can be quite effective.

What if your prospective mentor says no to your request? Don't take it personally. He or she is simply being realistic about his or her ability to give you what you want and need. At the very least, regard this person as a networking contact and follow all the rules and guidelines for staying in touch that I discussed in chapter 5. Regardless of the outcome of this initial meeting or phone call, follow up with a thank-you note.

Mentoring relationships are transitional and will eventually run their course. Some are short-lived and others may continue for several years. It all depends on your needs and the path that both of your careers take. Even though the mentoring relationship may end, the personal relationship may continue for years to come.

Other Types of Mentoring

There are other types of mentoring that could work out just as well or better for you. Below are several alternatives to, or additions to, traditional mentoring.

- *Company-sponsored mentors.* More and more hospitals are implementing mentoring programs for nurses. In this type of program, more-experienced nurses are assigned to new graduates or new hires to show them the ropes, assist them with their professional development, and help them become indoctrinated in their new profession. This type of mentoring goes beyond the preceptor role in that it is generally longer and covers more than clinical skills.

  Company-sponsored mentorship has been used in the business community for some time with great debate about its effectiveness.

FROM THE FRONT LINE

My Mentor

"The person I consider to be my mentor is Cathy, one of my nursing instructors in my diploma program. Cathy was also the adviser for the National Student Nurses Association (NSNA) chapter at my school and served as the immediate past president for one of the Sigma Theta Tau (National Honor Society for Nurses) chapters at one of the local universities. She has great leadership qualities, and I truly admire her. I can and do still call her up, meet with her, and exchange ideas. The perspective that she gives me on things helps me plan my future career goals. One of the best qualities she has, and an important quality to have in a mentor, is that she is a good listener. She listens and reflects back to me what she has heard. It helps me find my own answers. That is not to say that she doesn't give me an opinion if I ask for one. But she tries hard to help me find my own answers without imposing her viewpoint."

—Shannon, new grad

Some in business say it is not effective because it lacks the commitment and personal aspect of a traditional mentoring relationship. However, the concept is gaining momentum in the nursing profession, and some positive results are being reported. In any event, I would advise you to take whatever is offered along these lines and get everything you can out of the relationship. Remember that your attitude and interest level can impact any mentoring relationship.

• *Mentoring programs.* Some professional associations and nonprofit organizations offer mentoring programs in which volunteer mentors are paired with mentees. These individuals may be randomly paired or may be matched according to background or interest.

Several years ago, my state nurses association launched a mentoring program. The organization asked for members to volunteer to work with new graduates to establish a mentoring relationship for at least one year. I volunteered for this program and was matched up with a new graduate. We talked on the phone regularly and got together for lunch when we could. This relationship was beneficial to both of us, and we each made a new friend in the process. Our mentoring relationship ran its course and ended after about a year, but we still stay in touch. My former mentee recently told me that she has a new mentor, a nurse whom she works with who is experienced in her clinical specialty, which is exactly what she needs at this time.

• *Online mentoring.* Not surprisingly, mentoring programs for nurses are now available on the Internet. There are various sites that offer cyber mentoring to nurses. The mentors are experienced nurses who have volunteered to mentor new graduates or any nurse who needs mentoring for any reason.

CHAPTER 9

STEREOTYPES, ANNOYANCES, AND MYTHS

Every profession has its stereotypes, special challenges, and misconceptions, and nursing is no exception. You will learn, sometimes quickly, that the public perception of the nursing profession is very different from the reality. There are certain questions and comments you'll hear repeatedly that prove this to you. Sometimes they'll come from your own colleagues. Your mission is to anticipate them, understand where they come from, and, most important, use the opportunity to change perceptions and promote our profession. Find the humor in these encounters. They are a chance to enlighten someone.

WHY DIDN'T YOU BECOME A DOCTOR?

This is a question that every nurse is asked at least once in his or her professional life: "You're so intelligent. Why didn't you become a doctor?" Ouch! What is that supposed to mean? That nurses aren't intelligent? That people who are intelligent become doctors and people who are not intelligent become nurses or sales clerks? Of course, that's not what people mean when they say that, but it can really rub you the wrong way. So here's what to say the next time someone asks: "It's precisely because I am so intelligent that I chose nursing as a profession." Good one, eh? Then you can go on to say, "Nursing and medicine are two entirely different professions. It's a different career choice. One is not an elevated version of the other. I chose nursing so I can stay in close proximity to the patient, in a more personal, nurturing, hands-on environment." That one is guaranteed to give the person who asked the question food for thought!

MEN IN NURSING

Men have been a part of the nursing profession for eons. In fact, there is some evidence indicating that men were some of the first nurses. And, while men are a growing force in the profession, they remain a minority

> ### FROM THE FRONT LINE
>
> #### Why Didn't You Become a Doctor?
>
> "I have had people ask me why I would look at earning a doctoral degree in nursing when I could just become a medical doctor. They would say things like 'You're so smart and so young. You should go to medical school.' It is degrading to hear such a statement, even though I know the person who said it meant it as a compliment. One such time, I took the opportunity to educate a woman as to why I am in nursing. Nurses are different. We are holistic in our approach. In general, we look at the whole person rather than the parts of the illness. Doctors and nurses are different in many areas and aspects, but intelligence is not one of those areas. We each have a different focus."
>
> —Shannon, New Grad

and, in some cases, are viewed as an anomaly. They are often subjected to the prejudices and preconceived notions of the general public and their own profession.

If you are a man in nursing, you may as well get used to it. Many people will find it necessary to refer to you as a "male nurse" rather than simply as a "nurse." Why? For the same reasons some people still refer to physicians who are women as "female doctors" and women who are lawyers as "female attorneys." The old stereotypes die hard. Even if the nursing profession were to become more gender

"It drives me nuts when people say, 'So, you're a male nurse.' I respond by saying, 'No, I take care of females, too.'"

—Barry, new grad

balanced, as the medical profession has, you would probably still get the "male nurse" label from those who have been around for a while.

If you're a man and people don't already know you are a nurse, they will probably assume you are a doctor or, at the very least, a medical student. Why? It is another one of those deeply embedded stereotypes; men in health care are doctors and women are nurses.

Barry, a new grad, says, "People automatically assume you are a doctor, especially if you are in green scrubs. Because there is so much confusion, when I go into a patient's room with a physician, I say, 'This is the physician, and I am the nurse.' I say 'physician' instead of 'doctor' because there are many nurses who have doctoral degrees and therefore have the title 'doctor.'"

When dealing with such questions, simply establish with your patient that you are a nurse despite your gender and that you are completely qualified to take care of all of his or her health-care needs. That's what is important.

Are You Gay?

Unfortunately, one of the misguided assumptions people often make is that if you are a male working in a predominantly female profession, you must be gay.

Nurse Rob said, "One of the unspoken questions or assumptions of men in nursing is 'Is he gay?' That probably comes from the stereotypical female nurturing characteristics that are so helpful in nursing. It doesn't matter what one's orientation is as long as it doesn't interfere with the job performance. I have noticed that the men in nursing who are married and wear their wedding bands are more easily accepted than single folks like myself."

FROM THE FRONT LINE

"Male Nurse"

"Some people will ask, even though they already know the answer, 'Are you a male nurse?' When people ask me that, I am tempted to say, 'No, I am a woman trapped inside a man's body.' Of course, I keep those thoughts to myself."

—Kevin K., new grad

"I used to cringe at the term 'male nurse' and try to change everyone's thinking about it, but it was futile. I tried to say, 'Men in nursing,' 'Men who are nurses,' or some other word plays, even dropping the gender reference with 'Yes, I'm a nurse.'" But nothing seems to work."

—Rob, new grad

Special Challenges for Men in Nursing

There are many specific stereotypes and issues that all men in nursing will in-variably encounter. Let's discuss some of the more common challenges of this nature and how some men in nursing handle these situations.

Hercules Complex

It seems that when you are a man working in a predominantly female environ-ment, you are presumed to have all the attributes stereotypically associated with men. In particular, your female coworkers will begin to seek you out for your perceived brute strength to lift heavy packages and turn and lift patients. Even if there are women on the unit bigger and stronger than you, people seem to be programmed to seek a man's help for certain chores. One nurse commented, "It's interesting because I was never particularly muscular or anything. But I be-came a nurse, and all of a sudden my new coworkers need my help with lifting and turning because I am a man."

> *"Occasionally there is a patient who doesn't feel comfortable having a male nurse. Generally, I find I am well accepted."*
> —Barry, new grad

All the men I spoke with said, for the most part, that they don't mind help-ing out and do so happily. "It just goes with the territory," noted one. But one nurse notes that men in nursing sometimes get used and abused for their per-ceived physical strength. He states that there are days when he is asked so often to help lift or move that it starts to interfere with his work. He says he occasion-ally has to put a stop to it or he won't get his own work done.

Assuming

A few years ago, my husband and I went to visit my uncle in the hospital. During the course of our visit, a man in scrubs entered the room and nodded a greeting at us but never spoke. My uncle was unconscious, so there obviously was no verbal interaction between him and the man. The man, whom I knew to be a nurse by his actions, went about checking the IV and taking my uncle's vital signs. This was the only person who entered the room during our visit. Later that evening, my husband made reference to the time "when the doctor was in the room." I looked at him in utter disbelief and began to rant somewhat, saying, "That wasn't a doctor. It was a nurse! Just because he was a male you assumed he was a doctor?" I sighed as I thought, "My own husband: a man who has been married to a nurse for a good, long time. Where did I go wrong?" Hopefully, as time goes by, people will continue to develop more gender-neutral assumptions.

Gender Bias

Probably because people in general are accustomed to caregivers being women, some patients and family members resist, and on occasion outright refuse, to have nurses who are men take care of them. This seems to be particularly an issue with men giving personal care of an intimate nature to a woman, like labor and delivery, although it can occur in any situation with either gender. There are even some cultures that actually forbid intimate touching of women by men, even in a caregiving relationship. But, as with everything else, men in nursing take it all in stride and learn effective ways to cope with it or get around it.

Most men report that when the situation arises, they will say to a female counterpart, "Let's switch patients." That can work both ways, too. Another nurse said that sometimes during report, he will hear of a male patient who is acting out in an inappropriate manner (sexual remarks or gestures) with the female nurses. "I will offer to take that patient for the shift because that patient shouldn't be doing that to anyone."

The nursing profession has much to offer men, as do men to the profession. Despite all the challenges and stereotyping that exist, every man in nursing I spoke to has no regrets about his career choice. In fact, they all see nursing as a great career opportunity.

"There can be added pressure on men in nursing because everyone remembers your name. You'd better be extra caring and excellent at what you do."

—Rob, new grad

The more men who enter the profession, the better the chances of changing the image of men in nursing and increasing their acceptance. Those of you who have already chosen to become nurses can contribute in many ways, including by presenting yourself as a role model to other men and young boys who might not otherwise consider nursing as a viable career option.

PRACTICAL NURSES

Although they have varying initials after their names, practical nurses have been making valuable contributions to health care for decades. Licensed practical nurses (LPNs), licensed vocational nurses (LVNs), or registered practical nurses (RPNs) are essentially the same thing. The particular credential and accompanying initials simply depend where in North America you practice.

FROM THE FRONT LINE

The Lighter Side of Being a Man in Nursing

Maintaining a sense of humor is a survival tactic for all nurses. Humor makes things lighter, eases tension, and helps shatter stereotypes. Here are just a few of the things that men in nursing find humorous about their situation.

"I once overheard a nurse state his credentials as 'RN, NWP.' Someone asked him what NWP stood for, and he replied, 'Nurse With Prostate.' Everyone cracked up. You must have a sense of humor."

—Kevin K., new grad

"There are a few nurses who are men on my floor. Sometimes someone will say, 'Oh, this is the male floor.' I'll say, 'Yes, this is the manly floor. You have to have a certain amount of testosterone to work here.' It's all in fun."

—Rich, new grad

> "As a staff RN, more than half of the time when I answer the telephone to talk to inquiring family members, they say at the end of several minutes, 'Thank you, ma'am,' as we hang up! Because I'm a nurse, they assume I'm a woman. Either that, or I haven't gone through puberty yet with my voice!"
>
> —Rob, nurse
>
> "A video at work portrayed nurses as women, exclusively using feminine pronouns. After the program, the nurse educator said, 'What did you think?' I said, 'It's all about women. Everything is marketed to women in this profession, which makes me crazy. Everyone says "she." How about just saying "the nurse?"' The educator said, 'Oh you "Five Percenters" want everything,' referring to some estimates that men make up 5 percent of the nursing population."
>
> —Kevin K., New Grad

LPN is the most common title used in both the United States and Canada. If you are licensed in Texas or California, the title is LVN. In New Brunswick, Canada, the title is registered nursing assistant (RNA), and in the Northwest Territories of Canada, certified nursing assistant (CNA). Although the CNA and RNA designations also exist in the United States, it is a different type of designation than in parts of Canada, where it is comparable to an LPN, except in Ontario, Canada, where you are an RPN. However, this is not to be confused with a registered psychiatric nurse (also known as an RPN) found in the western territories of Canada. A registered psychiatric nurse is one who works exclusively with psychiatric patients. For our purposes here, I will refer to nurses with any of these credentials (except the registered psychiatric nurse) as practical nurses.

Practical nurses often get a bad rap. Their role has long been misunderstood and often maligned in health care. Practical nurses are sometimes referred to as "not real nurses" who "can't really do anything." These statements show

"I've only had one female patient refuse [to have me care for her], and that was a cultural thing."
—Barry, new grad

a fundamental lack of knowledge on the part of the accuser as to the practical nurse's background, capabilities, and role in health care. Because of this confusion, practical nurses sometimes get lost in the system. Some health-care providers are still not sure how or where they fit in or what their role really is. Just like men in nursing, many practical nurses express frustration at having to justify their existence and explain what it is they do.

Just like registered nurses (RNs), practical nurses have been taking on more and more responsibility over the years. They play an important part and are a vital link in the system. While conducting interviews for this book, several recent RN graduates told me about an experienced practical nurse who "taught me everything I know" or "saved my skin on more than one occasion."

Practical nurses have had their ups and downs in this profession over the years and likely will continue to in the future. In times of nursing shortages, they are sought out to fill the gap and provide necessary assistance to RNs and physicians. Yet there have been times when practical nurses were "on the outs" in acute care. For example, there was a trend in the 1980s to deliver all-RN primary care, and many practical nurses lost their jobs.

FROM THE FRONT LINE

Men in Nursing: Up Close and Personal

"In general, men in nursing have to work on self-confidence and acceptance issues. I was scared to death, as a nursing student, to even walk into a patient's room. For me, there is always an unspoken barrier of 'Who are you?' I therefore have to make an extra effort to win that patient's acceptance. I introduce myself by saying, 'Hi. I'm Rob Smith, and I'll be your registered nurse this evening.' As a male, I focus on doing noninvasive items first, like vital signs or checking IV drips, to gain some trust before doing a head-to-toe basic physical assessment.

"If patients prefer not to have me put them on the bedpan or do personal care (changing gowns, cleaning sensitive areas), they will sometimes ask politely. I'm even getting better at sensing some discomfort, so I will occasionally ask their unspoken question: 'Would you like a lady to help you with that?' When I approach staff for assistance, I simply ask, 'Can I have a female favor please?' The trade-off for helping the women nurses is that they usually come to me when they need some extra hands for lifting help, with transfers, with IVs that are stuck together, or with patients who go out of control."

—Rob, nurse

"There is a positive and negative side to everything. Sometimes I walk in, and a female patient is uncomfortable because she's not used to having a man take care of her. In that case, I just swap patients with someone else. I get a little of that, but not a lot. It's no big deal. I don't have any gender issues in this profession. I think some people make more of it than it really is."

—Bill, new grad

Practical nurses have always been a major force in long-term care, where they deliver the lion's share of care.

There is a misconception that practical nursing is a stepping-stone to becoming an RN. Some people mistakenly think that practical nurses aren't "smart enough" to get into RN school or lack the necessary motivation to get through it. Nonsense. Sometimes these misconceptions lead to animosity between RNs and practical nurses. Obviously, this is counterproductive to our goal, which is to provide the best care possible for our patients.

While some practical nurses go on to become RNs, many chose practical nursing as a career path for a reason, and they are content to stay exactly where they are. Many practical nurses prefer the close patient contact that comes with their job.

FROM THE FRONT LINE

Why Are You a Nurse?

"When people ask, 'Why are you a male nurse, and why do you want to take care of me?' I explain that this is what I want to do. I have gone through the same training and do the same things as my female counterparts. I'm proud of what I do."

—Barry, new grad

"When someone asks me, 'What made you go into nursing?' I answer, 'I was always good at biology and science, plus I like to help people.' It is interesting to hear of patients who have male relatives that are in nursing, too. In the last few years, this seems to be a little more common. In fact, I've had patients say to me, 'It's nice to see more men in nursing.' What do you say to that except, 'Thank you. I enjoy what I do.' "

—Rob, nurse

Practical and Valuable

Sanna, who was an LPN for nine years before becoming an RN, said, "As an LPN, I felt I was often lost in the system. I was often overlooked, especially in a bigger hospital. I found I had more autonomy in a nursing home. I liked that."

Linda, an LPN for many years before becoming an RN, said, "People would say, 'Oh you're not a real nurse.' I'd respond by saying, 'I *am* a real nurse. I went to school, passed a state board, and have a license.' Many people don't realize that. People would ask, 'Why aren't you an RN?' or 'Why don't you become an RN?' I would answer calmly, 'Because I like what I do, and I'm very happy.' "

Norma, who was an LPN for fourteen years before becoming an RN, said, "Sometimes patients would question my ability to do certain things, including starting an IV. They'd say, 'Are you sure you can do this?' I would have to reassure them that I was quite qualified."

Norma went on to say, "RN or LPN, you have to make your own way in the system. You have to keep learning, keep up with your specialty, and be proud of what you do. That's how you get respect." She goes on to suggest that you shouldn't hold yourself back regardless of anyone else's misconceptions of what you do. Keep moving forward.

And experienced LPN Lois added, "I worked as a nurse's aide for ten years before becoming an LPN. Choosing to remain an LPN in no way curtails my enthusiasm for career change and advancement. After working as an LPN for many more years, I created my own health-care agency. Working as an independent community health-care nurse, I find that one of the things taught to me during my first year of training still bears true: People who suffer do not seek for credentials—they seek for compassion and care. This will, to the best of my ability, continue to be my creed."

MYTHS

As with any profession, there are rumors and legends and even a few of our own stereotypes in nursing. Here are some of the more common misconceptions or myths that surround our practice.

Myth: *Nurses are still handmaidens to physicians.* You've heard about all the old stereotypes of nurses being subservient to doctors, viewed as handmaidens, and always in the background. Nurses were thought of as quietly doing their job in the shadow of the physician. Things were different years ago when all these old stereotypes were first formulated. While a few things are somewhat the same, more has changed than has not.

Truth: *Today's nurses are highly educated, are very skilled, and are making critical decisions at the bedside and in every area of health care.* We have a great deal of autonomy. We are no longer secondary caregivers, as in days gone by, but are part of the primary health-care team. We no longer work in the shadow of the physician but rather in concert with him or her, both of us vital players in the health-care system.

"The more time we spend in contention with each other, the less effective we are in attempting to reach our goals."

—Bob, nurse

You may observe some subservient behavior from nurses who have been around for a while, and you may observe some domineering doctors who still think they are lord and master. But that is now the old-fashioned model, and those who perpetuate those roles are out of touch. Remember that in order for any relationship to continue, both parties have to be willing to be in that role. Experienced nurse practitioner Bob gives the following advice to all nurses: "Break out of the subservient role." New grad Norma said, "Stand up for yourself. Respect is something you earn."

Remember, you are the next generation of nurses. While Rome wasn't built in a day, it started with some bricks and mortar and grew into a great empire. You are the bricks and mortar of the future of nursing. Start building a new foundation.

Some nurses think things will never change or can't be changed. They feel they are victims of a system that does not always respect them. Ann Landers once said, "No one can use you as a doormat without your permission." Don't accept things as they are or as you have been told they are. You can't change other people, but you can change yourself. And you can influence others by setting an example and by paving the way for others to follow.

Myth: *You must get two years of medical-surgical experience.* For decades, some nurses have been telling new graduates that they had to get at least two years of medical-surgical experience before going into any other specialty, like the intensive care unit, emergency department, or operating room. This advice is well-intended and is staunchly supported by some as necessary to develop a solid base of general practice before specializing.

Truth: *While that is good advice for many, it does not apply to all new graduates.* I have known many new graduates over the last five years who have gone directly into a specialty of their choice and have done very well. That doesn't mean that specialization right out of school is right for everyone, and I want you to under-stand that there is no one path for all nurses to follow. There are many nurses who are not cut out for medical-surgical nursing, just as some nurses are not cut out for the emergency department or intensive care unit. It is a matter of personal preference and interest.

If you have a strong desire to get into a particular specialty, I advise you to follow your heart and pursue opportunities in that specialty. That doesn't mean that everyone is ready to jump into intensive care right out of school. And much depends on the facility where you choose to have your early experiences. As we've already discussed, to be successful in any endeavor, you need a good orientation program with ongoing support systems in place.

"The public respects us. Nurses need to start respecting themselves equally as much. Refuse to lower your standards. I think it is an issue that most nurses don't realize how much power they have to make changes."

—Shannon, nurse

Positive Change

When I was in nursing school, initiation, or hazing, was quite popular. Initiation at my school consisted of upperclassmen intimidating freshmen students in various ways. We were treated like second-class citizens, were not permitted to use the elevators in the upperclassmen's dorm, and were otherwise bullied. Most of us were also just out of high school and had never been away from home. The fact that we were not being supported by the upperclassmen and in fact were being harassed did not sit well with us.

My classmates and I became change agents, although we didn't realize it at the time. We banded together and decided we weren't going to put up with any more of it. Some in the group insisted that it wasn't possible to change the system, that hazing had been going on for decades, and that we were just lowly new students with virtually no power. None of that stopped us, however, from making a collective decision that the hazing had to stop—not just for our class but for future generations of freshmen.

We rallied and refused to participate in further "meetings" and "mandatory sessions" by the upperclassmen. We stood our ground and voiced our objections to the treatment. We supported one another and came to one another's defense. The upperclassmen were incredulous, but in the end, they could not continue the hazing without our cooperation. They eventually backed off. The cycle had been broken. When future freshmen came in, we went out of our way to help them, support them, and make them feel welcomed. We remembered only too well what it felt like to be a scared, shy, and stressed-out new student. We created a change, and you can, too.

The secret to being happy in nursing is to find out what you enjoy doing and to do it. I have heard from many nurses, at every stage of their career, who are still searching for their niche. They just don't know what they want to do. If you already have an interest in or pull to one particular area, you are ahead of the game. There is no need to delay the dream.

It is important to follow your heart when making career decisions. If you have a passion for a particular specialty or really want to work in a particular facility, go for it. You have to be interested and enthusiastic about what you do in order to enjoy it. There is no one path for all nurses to follow. You've got to forge your own path. Follow your heart and carve out your own niche.

Myth: *"Real nurses" work only in hospitals.* The general public holds a deeply ingrained image of the nurse as a woman who wears a white uniform, works in a hospital (at the bedside), and assists the physician. Of course this image is stuck in the 1950s, even though nurses have come a long way since then. I've already discussed the "woman" part of the stereotype as it relates to men in nursing. So let me deal with the "hospital bedside" part.

Truth: *Nurses work in many places doing many different things.* Some of us work in a hospital, some in a business office, some on the road, and some in the halls of justice. Some of us wear uniforms, some wear business clothes, some wear scrubs, and some wear overalls. But the general public doesn't know that, even though you and I do—or do we?

I've had a largely nontraditional nursing career. After working for years in the emergency room, I worked in medical weight control, did medical exams for insurance companies, worked for a health maintenance organization (HMO) doing utilization review and quality improvement, and worked for an education company that prepared nurses to take their nursing boards, among other things. From the day I stepped out of the hospital into the world of nontraditional nursing, the questions started. One most often repeated was "Why did you leave nursing?" My own family members would introduce me to others by saying, "This is Donna. She used to be a nurse." It was maddening. Every position I've ever held was a nursing position, but I had a hard time convincing others, including some of my own colleagues. I wanted to get my nursing license out of my wallet and wear it around my neck or pin it to my shirt, like hunters and fishermen do, so everyone would know I was still a nurse.

In my youth, when the question "Why did you leave nursing?" was posed to me, I would bristle, and in an annoyed tone of voice I would explain that I was still a nurse and was working as a nurse in a nontraditional position. As I got a little older, I realized that when someone asked such a question, it was

FROM THE FRONT LINE

Follow Your Dreams

"Follow your intuition and heart when it comes to selecting an area of nursing you want to pursue. I graduated in 1976 and decided not to go into public health nursing because I felt it did not pay enough. I turned my back on my heart's desire and went for the money. Consequently, I did quite a bit of job-hopping my first year after graduation. In 1983, I decided to pursue a master's degree in public health, but still I was dancing around my dream. I thought I wanted to work in the area of international public health research. When that didn't pan out, I was once again adrift.

"Five years later, I finally woke up and began to pursue public health nursing. I found that I loved the autonomy that the job required, and I was able to truly make a difference in people's lives by introducing preventive health concepts to them. To be able to possibly prevent a serious illness or death instead of waiting until the client became incapacitated and was a burden on our health-care system was extremely gratifying to my soul.

"I stayed in public health for over ten years, and they were, by far, the finest years of my professional life. I found I was passionate about public health issues and was able to make a difference. Serving in public health, with my heart fully engaged, was a rich and stimulating experience.

"I definitely advise new nurses to search deeply in their hearts and souls to find out where they can best serve humanity. They should always reach for their dreams, even if it appears the money is not what they think it should be. It's not about money anyway. It's about fulfilling your life's purpose and being able to rest at night in peace and confidence, knowing you are living a rich and meaningful life."

—Paula, nurse

because of his or her own misconceptions about what nurses do. I saw a golden opportunity to explain, and I would say, "While many people think of nurses as only working in hospitals, at the bedside, nurses actually do many different things in many different places." They still didn't always get the point.

Around the time I was starting my business, I attended a professional association meeting of other women entrepreneurs. I struck up a conversation with a woman sitting next to me, and we both revealed what type of work we did. I mentioned that I was a nurse and that I was starting an education company to help nurses with their careers. Not surprisingly, she said to me, "So, why did you leave nursing?" By this time in my life, I was used to the question. I had fielded it so many times that I had my answer down pat. I began to explain, "While the public has a certain image of a nurse . . ." I spoke for a few minutes, covering all the important issues. The woman listened very intently. She maintained strong eye contact, nodded her head periodically, and looked genuinely fascinated by my mini-lecture about the modern nurse. When I was finally finished, I felt very satisfied, presuming I had enlightened yet another mortal to the expanded role of the nurse. She paused for a few minutes, still nodding, and then looked me directly in the eye and said, "So, why *did* you leave nursing?" Oh, well. You can't win them all.

Today, I am a nurse entrepreneur who wears a business suit and stands in front of audiences teaching and speaking. Or I'm sitting at my computer, in jeans, writing articles and books and advice columns for nurses. I still get the question "So, why did you leave nursing?" I always answer very calmly and very proudly,

> I have never left nursing. I am still every bit as much a nurse today as I was when I worked in the emergency room wearing a white uniform. Nurses are healers, teachers, and nurturers, and I still do all of those things in my professional life. There are many different types of healing. There is physical healing, emotional healing, and spiritual healing. Nurses are versatile and multitalented. There are many ways and many places to have a positive impact on health care.

I recently gave that response to someone who said, "That sounds like a politician's answer." I said, "That is because I am so accustomed to hearing that question and have had to answer it so often that my response is well-rehearsed." He nodded. He was probably thinking, "Why *did* she leave nursing?"

This stereotype does not exist only among the general public. As nurses, our own image of who we are and what we do is so tied up in working at the bedside that some of us experience an identity crisis when we change that venue. Also, when our colleagues leave the bedside for a nontraditional position, even for a management position, we often view them as "not real nurses" or "no longer in nursing." But being a nurse is about who you are, not about where you work. What makes each of us a nurse is a combination of our education and our experiences, which are enhanced by our capacity to care and to give. It is not defined by our place of employment or whether we wear scrubs or a uniform to work each day. We are vital at the bedside, but we are also vital in every other aspect of the health-care arena. We have to expand our own vision of who we are and what we are capable of doing before we can expect the rest of the world to do the same.

To underscore something I said in an earlier chapter, all nurses are equal yet different. We are each a mirror image of one another. We have the same heart, the same soul, and the same spirit. Whether we are a staff nurse at the bedside, the editor of a nursing magazine, or the owner of an adult day care center, we are all nurses. I am a nurse entrepreneur with twenty-plus years of experience, and you are a new graduate nurse. Yet we are the same. I am no different from you, and you are no different from me. Remember this always.

CHAPTER 10

PROFESSIONAL PRACTICE ISSUES

THE CARE AND FEEDING OF YOUR NURSING LICENSE

Your nursing license is a precious commodity. Once you have it, you need to take steps to keep it, protect it, and capitalize on it. Because without it, or with restrictions on it, you may not be able to practice or practice fully, and you may have trouble finding a job. All of this translates into loss of income.

For starters, it is important to understand what is required in your practice state or any state in which you hold a nursing license to maintain your license in good standing. You need to keep track of renewal dates, continuing education requirements (if any—every state is different), changes in related regulations, and more. For example, suppose you somehow miss the notification that comes in the mail that your nursing license is due to be renewed—you never see it or you misplace it and forget about it. Your license may lapse without your knowing it. This could result in your incurring additional fees to get it reinstated as well as a temporary suspension.

Even worse, you might be unknowingly practicing without a valid license— the results of which are disastrous. Working in nursing without a valid license is a violation of the law. The only person who is responsible and held accountable for that is you. You can't say, "I never got a renewal notification, so I didn't know." It's your responsibility to keep track of it. In fact, this is something to track in your professional portfolio, as discussed in chapter 1. Mark the renewal date on your calendar, and if the date is over a year away, write the date at the end of your calendar so you can carry it forward when you get a new calendar for the next year.

When you receive your initial license, you will also receive a packet of information about that license, requirements for renewal, and so on from your state board of nursing (BON). Be sure to read that information carefully and file it where you can easily find it. Then, visit the website of your state board of nursing. Read through the section on nursing licenses. Many BON websites also include valuable information about delegation, scope of practice, ethical standards, and more. Consider this required reading. The defense "I didn't know" doesn't hold up in a court of law if problems arise.

Your State BON

Each state in the United States has a regulatory body referred to as the state board of nursing (BON) that is responsible for regulating nursing practice in that state. The BONs issue nursing licenses, accredit nursing schools, certify advanced practice nurses and sometimes other health-care workers (such as home health aides), and create the scope of practice for nursing professionals, which varies slightly from state to state. Some BONs also certify sexual assault nurse examiners and massage, bodywork, and somatic therapists who may or may not be registered nurses.

Each state BON exists for the express purpose of protecting the public—the health-care consumer—and promoting safe, competent, and ethical care. BONs ensure that those who have a license to practice nursing have met certain minimum standards of education and training, are properly credentialed, and maintain some level of competency. Boards of nursing also enforce regulations and take action when violations occur and standards are not met.

In addition to licensing and practice standards, also be clear on what your state BON requires for nurses who are currently not working in nursing, are retired, or are working in non-traditional practice areas such as legal nursing consulting, case management, utilization review, and so on. Some states have an active versus an inactive status, while others require a certain number of documented practice hours for license renewal. (More on that later.) Generally speaking, it is a good idea to keep your license active, if at all possible, throughout your career even into your retirement. You'd be surprised at how many nurses have retired or temporarily left the nursing profession for personal reasons, let their licenses lapse, and then decide to continue with nursing at a later date—even if only to occasionally give flu shots. Getting your license reinstated can be a complicated and challenging matter. In some states, if your license has lapsed for more than five years, you will be required to take the licensing exam over again and/or a nursing refresher course.

Before attempting to contact your BON with questions related to your license or practice, check its website to see if the information and/or form you need is there and available for downloading. Most BONs receive a high volume of inquiries each day, so be proactive in seeking the information you need. If you can't find what you're looking for on the website, send an e-mail and/or call. It may take a board several days to get back to you, so be patient and follow up as necessary.

Because your nursing license has certain ethical and legal standards associated with it, you must conduct your private and professional life in such a way as to uphold those standards. For example, any arrests, regardless of the reason, can affect your ability to practice nursing. Unprofessional conduct, which can be anything from sexually harassing a patient or staff member to substance abuse (personal or work-related) can be cause for disciplinary action.

Some specific causes for disciplinary action, if reported or discovered, include developing an inappropriate personal relationship with a patient, striking a patient or other forms of physical or verbal abuse, committing insurance fraud, stealing of any type, practicing outside your scope of practice, tampering with documents, accessing patient medical information illegally, and misrepresenting yourself (for example, claiming to be a nurse practitioner if you're a licensed RN, or claiming to be an RN if you're an LPN).

If you are reported to a BON for any reason (any person or entity can make a report), you have certain rights, including the right to be informed of the charges, to an attorney, and to a record of the proceedings. In most cases, there is a due process involved in which you would have an opportunity to defend yourself.

Pay attention to any correspondence that comes from the board. If a response is required, respond honestly and on time. You have a duty to cooperate with any investigation and respond to any inquires. Failure to do so can cause you to be held in contempt and your license can be suspended.

I have received many questions over the years from nurses who, when reported to their state BON for something, are not aware of their rights and do not know how to defend themselves. You must be proactive in the process. Your license, your reputation, and your livelihood are at stake.

If you are ever charged with a crime, legitimate or otherwise, you should always find an attorney to advocate for you and to help you navigate your way through the system. A nurse attorney is ideal in this situation because he or she is uniquely qualified to interpret both the law and the nurse practice act. However, any competent attorney should be able to help you. Find a nurse attorney by asking for a referral from your state nurses association or specialty nursing association. You can also check with The American Association of Nurse Attorneys (www.taana.org 877-538-2262). Not every nurse attorney belongs to this association, but it is a good resource.

The Power of Attorneys

Some nurses are reluctant to seek the advice of an attorney when they are charged, fearing that legal counsel will imply guilt on their part. That is simply not the case. When dealing with any legal situation, especially those that involve allegations against you, consulting an attorney is a smart thing to do. An attorney will look out for your best interests, advocate for you, and advise you.

None of this is meant to make you paranoid—or, at least, no more paranoid than most new graduates already are. Rather, it is meant to help you understand that along with your license comes certain responsibilities and expectations that must be met. Understanding your license and scope of practice will help you to have a long, safe, and satisfying career in nursing.

For Canadian Nurses

In Canada, nursing licenses are issued and regulated by the individual provincial/territorial regulatory agencies. Just as in the United States, there are many variations and nuances from state to state and province to province. For example, in parts of Canada, you may need special permission from your regulatory agency to use the credential RN after your name if you plan to work as a self-employed nurse. The bottom line is, be sure to become thoroughly familiar with the regulations for nursing practice and license in your geographic area.

LICENSE RENEWAL

Some states require documentation of a certain number of clinical nursing hours worked in the course of a year (or renewal period) for license renewal. This documentation might include a letter or other explanatory materials from you (especially if you are self-employed, as many nurses are) attesting to how many hours you worked and in what setting.

What is considered "clinical nursing hours" may come under question and has been the subject of debate in those states that have this requirement. For example, if you work in the specialty of case management, much of your time is spent on the telephone assessing a patient's needs, creating plans of care, and making arrangements for care. You would not be providing any "hands on" care. While a board of nursing might initially not accept this experience as "clinical," you have an opportunity to defend your practice and your license by describing how your specialty, whatever it might be, is executed with nursing knowledge and expertise. Remember, your state board's responsibility is to protect the consumer, so don't take it personally if you're challenged. And because many people, even some BONs, have more narrow views of who a nurse is and what a nurse does, you may be called upon to defend your work in nursing. In these cases, good communication skills and the ability to articulate the important work you do will be invaluable.

For license renewal, other states require a certain number of documented continuing education credits within a certain time frame. You might ask, how does that ensure my practice is up to par? The presumption is simple: While the BON does not monitor the actual competency level of each individual nurse, the belief is that nurses who participate in ongoing continuing education are more informed, progressive, and actively engaged in their profession than those who do not. Ongoing professional development is vital to a healthy nursing career.

Never Stop Learning

Nursing continuing education (CE), by way of classroom-based courses, online and print materials, and CDs and DVDs, is widely available. Sources of continuing education include your employer; nursing publications and websites; nursing career fairs, conventions, and professional association meetings and websites; public seminars; private CE websites; and more.

Those states that require a certain number of continuing education credits for license renewal may also grant credit for having written a book or articles, developing or teaching certain courses, precepting new graduates and new hires, obtaining college credits, and more. Be sure to familiarize yourself with the regulations.

In some states, paying a renewal fee and filling out the appropriate paperwork is enough to renew your annual license.

Many boards of nursing now require nurses to be fingerprinted in order to obtain a nursing license. Again, don't take this personally—the proactive measure is meant to ensure that nurses don't have a criminal background. Fingerprinting helps to identify and track nurses who may attempt to change their name or change practice states when they are being investigated for, or have a history of, abuse, fraud, or other criminal activity. Unfortunately, it happens.

To find your U.S. state board of nursing or, in Canada, the regulatory authority for registered and practical nurses, see the Resources section in the back of this book.

Frequently Asked Questions About Nursing Licensure

Here are some of the most common questions nurses ask about their licenses:

Q: I currently live in New Jersey and will be graduating from a nursing program there in the next few months. I plan to work in Connecticut after graduation. Should I take my licensure exam in New Jersey and then apply for a license in Connecticut or should I just take my exam in Connecticut?
A: If you are definitely planning to move, then you may as well take your licensure exam in Connecticut—it will be the quickest way to get right to work in the state of your choice. Once you have a valid nursing license in one state, you can apply for a license "by endorsement" in another state. Read on for more about that.

Q: What if I take the exam in California and decide down the road that I want to relocate to Washington State—do I have to take my boards over again?
A: No, but you do have to apply for a license by endorsement in the state in which you wish to practice. The exceptions are the Nurse Licensure Compact (NLC) states (see the following paragraph). Applying for a license by endorsement requires that you submit the appropriate application form. This form is usually found on the website of the state BON you wish to relocate to. However, you may have to call or e-mail the board to send you an application. You will be required to pay an application fee and may be required to submit additional paperwork. This process takes between three and six weeks for approval in most states.

Q: I live in North Carolina near the border of Virginia. I heard that I can I work in Virginia with a North Carolina license. Is that true?
A: Some US states belong to what is known as the Nurse Licensure Compact (NLC). NLC states agree to allow nurses who have a license in one NLC state

and who legally reside in another NLC state to practice (physically or electronically) without applying for a license by endorsement. This is known as a multistate license. To find out which U.S. states participate in the NLC, go to https://www.ncsbn.org/nlc.htm or see the sidebar on this page. The NLC applies to both RNs and LPNs/LVNs. So in this case, because both Virginia and North Carolina participate in the NLC, you can work in Virginia with a North Carolina nursing license.

The NLC

U.S. states belonging to the Nurse Licensure Compact at the time of writing are Arizona, Arkansas, Colorado, Delaware, Idaho, Iowa, Kentucky, Maine, Maryland, Mississippi, Nebraska, New Hampshire, New Mexico, North Carolina, North Dakota, Rhode Island, South Carolina, South Dakota, Tennessee, Texas, Utah, Virginia, and Wisconsin. Be sure to check www.ncsbn.org/nlc.htm for the most up-to-date information.

Q: I received my RN license in Canada but would like to work in the United States. Can I do that?
A: Yes, once you meet the licensure requirements of the U.S. state you wish to work in and have obtained the proper authorization to work in the United States. Because every state BON has slightly different requirements for nurses educated outside of the United States, contact that state's BON (www.ncsbn.org/515.htm). Also visit the website of CGFNS International (formerly the Commission on Graduates of Foreign Nursing Schools) at www.cgfns.org and the U.S. Citizenship and Immigration Services (www.uscis.gov).

Q: I am a U.S. citizen with a U.S. RN license and wish to work in Canada. How do I go about doing that?
A: You need to contact the province you wish to work in and request an out-of-country application package. Likewise, you must apply for a work permit in Canada. Your employer (if you have one lined up) or an employment

agency can assist with that. Visit the website of Citizenship and Immigration Canada (www.cic.gc.ca).

Q: I need to relocate immediately because of family issues. I can't afford to be unemployed for the three to six weeks it would take to issue me a license by endorsement. Will any state issue me a temporary license to practice while the application is being reviewed?

A: Yes, some states will issue a temporary license to practice nursing if you have a valid license in another state and have already submitted an application for licensure by endorsement in the state you wish to work in. Usually, you must submit an additional application and fee to request a temporary license. Each state is different, so contact the BON or visit its website to find out how to request/apply for a temporary license. Temporary licenses are often presented on the spot when the applicant presents in person to the board with the required paperwork and fee.

Q: If I decide to become a travel nurse down the road, do I have to get a nursing license in every state I work in?

A: Yes, unless you have a multistate license and only work in states that are part of the NLC (see above). Otherwise, you will have to apply for licensure in any state you wish to work in. When working with a travel nurse agency, the agency will generally assist you in that process.

Q: I am a Registered Psychiatric Nurse (RPN) in Canada. Can I practice nursing in the United States?

A: Because the RPN status does not exist in the United States, you would have to complete an accredited nursing program in the United States and then take the NCLEX-RN exam. You may be able to apply some of the courses you took and credits you earned in obtaining your RPN to your educational program, but that will be up to the individual school or program that you apply for.

Q: I am an LPN in the United States. Can I practice in Canada?

A: LPN/LVN status varies from province to province, so contact the appropriate provincial agency for additional information. (See the Resources section in the back of this book.)

Q: I received my nursing education outside of the United States and Canada, but I wish to work in the United States. What do I have to do?

A: Check with the BON in the U.S. state where you wish to work, as each has differing requirements for licensure for nurses educated outside of the United States. Contact CGFNS International at www.cgfns.org for credential review and additional information.

Q: What if I do some case management or telephone triage work in which I am working with clients in various states by telephone—would I need to have a license to practice in each of those states?

A: Often you *do* need to have multiple state licenses for this type of work unless you reside in and work within those states that are part of the Nurse Licensure Compact. Your employer should advise you of what is required. If you are self-employed, check with the related professional association, such as the Case Management Society of America (www.cmsa.org), to see what is required.

Q: I have tried to contact my state board of nursing on numerous occasions, but my phone calls have not been returned. What do I do now?

A: First of all, be sure your state board of nursing is the correct agency to be addressing your question to. If it is about something other than licensure, you may be able to get the information you need from your state chapter of the American Nurses Association, nursing specialty association, state hospital association, or another regulatory/professional body.

Additionally, be sure you are contacting the correct person/division in the agency. Speak with an operator or a receptionist to verify that you have the correct contact information for the appropriate party within the agency.

Each state board operates differently, so if one does not respond to your calls, try e-mailing. Then, give the organization a few days to a week to answer. Most boards have a limited staff and can receive hundreds of inquiries each day. And while most boards are efficient and conscientious, if you have a legitimate problem contacting your board after following the above suggestions and/or if the board is not responsive to your needs, contact the National Council of State Boards of Nursing (NCSBN), which can be found online at www.ncsbn.org, to report a problem. NCSBN is an organization whose membership includes BONs in the fifty states, the District of Columbia, and four United States territories—American Samoa, Guam, Northern Mariana Islands, and the Virgin Islands.

And while NCSBN is not a regulatory body, it can be helpful in providing additional information, resources, and contacts. Before contacting NCSBN, though, you should do your best to use networking to try to get a personal contact in your state BON—someone who can resolve your issue. This is another reason why networking is such a valuable resource. In Canada, contact the Canadian Nurses Association (www.cna-nurses.ca).

STANDARDS OF CARE

Now that we've covered the licensure issue, let's look at some other important practice issues that will help you to provide the best possible care for your patients. Developing your knowledge and skills is important, but so, too, is staying abreast of established practice standards.

Standards of care are guidelines that represent the most up-to-date practice standards. These are based on the latest research, technology, and nursing science and knowledge. Therefore, they change periodically as new information comes to light. Standards are set by a particular facility, by regulatory agencies such as your state Department of Health (these would be specific to your state), The Joint Commission, nursing specialty associations, and the American Nurses Association.

Books and manuals on standards of care are available from the above listed entities. In some cases, they will be available online or in print in your department or unit, in the nursing education or quality improvement office, and/or in your facility's health sciences library. And while you do not need to read and memorize all of these standards (it would be impossible to do so), your facility should have policy and procedure (P&P) manuals that incorporate all of these. That being said, sometimes issues come up that may not be covered by P&P and standards manuals or may necessitate clarification. In such cases, consult your preceptor, unit educator, supervisor, or manager. Never be afraid to ask questions.

Every in-patient facility has a quality improvement (QI) coordinator—usually a nurse who is responsible for ensuring that standards are kept up-to-date, developed as needed, and adhered to by providers in that facility. Standards of care are important because they guarantee that patients receive the highest quality of care and the best outcomes. What's more, non-adherence to those standards can result in liability to the nurse and the facility as well as possible non-payment of services by insurance and other third-party payers.

Use the Library!

Hospitals and many health-care facilities have a Health Sciences Library, which is sometimes referred to as the Medical Library. This department exists for the use of all of the health-care staff, including nurses. It contains books, manuals, and periodicals. And wherever there is a library, there is a librarian. While some large organizations have a full-time health sciences librarian, others have a part-time librarian who is on-site for a limited number of hours per week—although the library may be accessible to the staff on an extended basis.

Be sure to acquaint yourself with your resident health sciences library and develop a relationship with the librarian. Both can be an invaluable asset to you in your professional practice. Whether looking for information about a disease or drug, needing to access a professional journal, preparing a department in-service, or requiring assistance with an in-depth online search, the library and librarian are there to support you.

Most health science libraries are vastly underused by nurses because they operate under the misconception that the libraries are the domain of the physician. Not so. They exist for the use of *all* facility employees, students, and often the community, too.

You can also use the vast resources at most college libraries, whether you are a student or not. You can't check books out if you aren't a student at a college, but you can read, take notes, make photocopies of articles, and more. Colleges and universities that offer nursing and health-care degrees usually have a very comprehensive selection of health-care and nursing books and periodicals. Don't be shy about requesting help from a research aide or librarian.

Once, after relocating to a new area, I needed access to some health-care and nursing journals for career research. I was unemployed at the time. I called the health sciences librarian in a local hospital and told her I was an RN who lived in the community. I asked if I could possibly come in to read the latest issues of a few journals. She said, "Tell me when you'll be here and I'll get them out for you." It pays to ask for what you want and need. Help is all around.

The American Nurses Association offers publications and posters on the scope and standards for various specialties in nursing. These publications, as well as those provided by nursing specialty associations, are invaluable when a nurse is going after professional certification. But they are also important forms of self-education and reference for the average nurse. Find out more at www .nursingworld.org.

ONGOING QUALITY IMPROVEMENT

Quality Improvement (QI) is the process of continually monitoring, evaluating, and improving the safety and quality of patient care provided. As mentioned above, each health-care facility has at least one person designated to oversee this activity facility-wide. Your facility QI coordinator also acts as a liaison to outside regulatory agencies, conducts ongoing QI studies to ensure proper care, and provides education for the staff. And while this coordinator often oversees QI activities for the entire facility, some facilities have one such coordinator exclusively for the nursing department and sometimes a designee on each unit.

QI activities, whether facility-wide or unit-based, encompass reviewing medical records and data, regularly evaluating outcomes and occurrences, observing and reflecting on practice, implementing changes and improvements as needed, and evaluating the effectiveness of changes to improve outcomes and reduce adverse occurrences. Examples of adverse outcomes and occurrences include, but are not limited to, deaths, complications, readmissions, patient falls, transfusion reactions, medication errors, hospital-acquired bed sores and infections, and so on.

Evidence-Based Practice

Evidence-Based Practice (EBP) is a term used to describe optimal nursing practice in which standards of care inclusive of current research, clinical expertise, and the unique needs and preferences of the patient come together. In simple terms, it is an ongoing process of looking at the way we do things through studies, research, and review. Part of the process involves making sure that there is evidence to support the continuation of practice methods—as opposed to simply doing things because they have always been done that way and without evaluating their effectiveness related to cost and quality.

As a new nurse, you certainly have your hands and your head full with trying to master basic practice and knowledge. But ongoing quality improvement is the responsibility of every nurse—in his or her own practice, on his or her unit, and at his or her place of employment. Learn about QI activities at your facility. Get to know your QI coordinator(s) and safety officer. Learn more about their role and how they do their work. Inquire about QI and safety activities and committees and consider getting involved in these when you have the opportunity. By so doing, you'll acquire knowledge that you can use in various ways in the present and future, and you'll develop a better understanding of standards of care and the process of ongoing quality improvement for nursing care and practice.

Additionally, you should engage in related self-study and reading, attend relevant seminars and classes on your own if necessary, and visit websites such as the National Quality Forum (www.nationalqualityforum.com), the Agency for Healthcare Research and Quality (www.ahrq.gov), and the Canadian Patient Safety Institute (www.patientsafetyinstitute.ca). Quality improvement is at the core of all nursing practice.

UNDERSTANDING COSTS, REIMBURSEMENT, AND UTILIZATION MANAGEMENT

Health-care costs and health-care reimbursement impact nursing practice and nursing care in multiple ways. Health-care reimbursement has become a big issue as costs continue to skyrocket. This has resulted in health-care services and facilities consolidating and downsizing, endless cutbacks, and continuous re-evaluation of programs and services. There was a time when nurses did not need to be concerned about the cost of health care. But as health-care costs started to rise at a rate faster than that of the national inflation rate, everyone involved in health care had to take fiscal responsibility. And because so much care in the United States is reimbursed by Medicare and Medicaid, both of which involve government money, increasing regulations and oversight mechanisms have been put into place.

Medicare and Medicaid

Medicare is a U.S. government insurance program, federally funded, that provides health-care coverage for those over sixty-five years of age and individuals of all ages who are on Social Security Disability.

Medicaid is a state-run assistance program that is funded partially by the state and partially by the federal government. It provides health-care services reimbursement for low-income people of all ages.

To learn more about Medicare and Medicaid, visit the website of the U.S. Department of Health & Human Services at www.hhs.gov. On this website, you'll also find great information about the Health Insurance Portability and Accountability Act (HIPAA), emergency preparedness, diseases, medication, aging, and much more.

What does this have to do with you? You will be asked questions about re-imbursement issues from patients and their family members and will eventually need to develop an understanding of how the process works. It is the responsibility of every nurse to understand how health care is paid for and what role he or she plays in ensuring that health-care resources are appropriately utilized and that his or her employer is fairly reimbursed for services rendered. And, because your salary and benefits come from this reimbursement, you have a personal stake in it.

Every hospital has at least one utilization management (UM) nurse, also known as a utilization review (UR) nurse, on staff. This nurse reviews medical records and information before, during, and after a patient's stay in the hospital. The UM nurse must first ensure that each patient meets eligibility requirements for admission, meaning that the person must either be deemed sick enough or in need of certain services or treatments that can only be rendered in a hospital. This is done to ensure that a patient's stay will be reimbursed by the insurance carrier or other payer. The UM nurse does not make subjective judgments about this. He and she follows pre-established criteria and relies primarily on documentation to make these determinations, which is one reason why clear, accurate, and timely documentation is critical for nurses, physicians, and other health-care providers. Because of this, some nurses have the title Clinical Documentation Specialists.

In addition to reviewing medical records, UM nurses have dialogue with nurses, physicians, and other health-care providers when they have questions or need clarification of something in the record. They will also remind (or request) care providers to document important information that may be missing or unclear.

Some UM nurses work for the health-care facility and others work directly for an insurance company. Some hospital nurses see all UM nurses as adversaries and an annoyance, especially those who work directly for the insurance companies. This is partly because they often come into the units and into the nurses' station, go through medical records, and ask questions—it's a territorial thing. Some staff nurses also see the UM nurses as being motivated by saving money for the insurance companies and looking to discharge patients before they're ready. On the contrary, UM nurses, including those who work for insurance companies, are advocating for good patient care and trying to keep costs down—a very delicate but necessary balance. So when a UM nurse, whether hospital employed or representing an insurance company, approaches you for some information, don't brush him or her off or get defensive. Listen and learn.

UM nurses also monitor a patient's length of stay (LOS) while in the hospital. LOS standards have been developed for commonly occurring illnesses and surgical procedures. These standards govern how much a health-care facility will get paid for services and they represent national averages. If a patient stays longer than the established LOS guidelines without documented justification, the facility may not be reimbursed for the entire stay. It is important that you start to grasp the bigger picture of health-care delivery costs—and how those costs are addressed.

You should get to know these nurses, develop a collegial relationship with them, and adopt a spirit of cooperation and support. As you get to know UM nurses, understand their work, and build relationships with them, your job will be easier and you will be a better nurse. When UM nurses, Clinical Documentation Specialists, or Discharge Planners come into the unit, ask them about their work (assuming it's a convenient time) and ask how your practice and charting can support the work they do.

The more you learn about these practices, speak with those involved in the process, and engage in self-study, the more interested and excited you will be about nursing. You will also feel more competent and confident in your practice, and you'll be better able to care for and advocate for those you serve.

Remember, nursing school was phase 1 of your education. There is much more to learn. Rather than letting that overwhelm you, let it remind you of what an amazing, broad, varied, and multidimensional profession this is, and revel in the fact that there will always be something new to learn.

A FEW WORDS ABOUT NURSING ETHICS

Because nursing is both an art and a science, it is not enough to simply master clinical techniques and develop critical thinking skills. Nurses must also uphold an ethical code of conduct, learn to make ethical decisions, and assist patients and their family members in making ethical decisions for themselves and their loved ones.

Nurses face ethical dilemmas every day—whether dealing with end of life issues, organ transplantation, privacy and confidentiality, or patient religious beliefs that may be in conflict with prescribed care. Ethical issues relate to one's own practice and professional conduct as well as to the practice and conduct of other health-care providers. Some examples of ethical issues include suspecting that a coworker is diverting drugs, considering having a personal relationship with a patient, or divulging personal information about a patient to an unauthorized source. Ethics, simply put, is doing what is right.

While most health-care facilities have a hospital-wide ethics committee, it is not solely the committee's concern; ethics is also the realm of every professional nurse. Some facilities also have a nursing ethics committee and conduct nursing ethics rounds to address issues specifically related to nursing practice. Under-stand how your facility's ethics committee(s) works and consider volunteering to be on the committee or sitting in on a session. Be sure to read manuals and policies related to nursing ethics in your facility.

If an ethical dilemma comes up related to patient care, you are fortunate to have several resources at your disposal. First, speak with your preceptor or your nurse manager. Because most health-care facilities have an ethics committee, some issues may require a subsequent consultation with that committee directly.

However, other issues may be more personal and relate to your own practice and conduct, the practice and conduct of coworkers, and broader issues in the health-care community. Consider discussing these issues confidentially with a trusted source such as a former nursing instructor, professional colleague, at-torney, family member, or friend and without identifying the patient or other involved person. Some health-care systems also have anonymous ethics hotlines from which you can get advice or direction.

You can also get anonymous online ethics advice from a nurse attorney at www.nurse.com. Of course there is no guarantee that your question will be answered, but it is worth a try. You can also use the "Article Search" feature on the nurse.com website for related articles and previously answered questions on a related subject.

For continuing education (CE) courses on ethics in nursing (available both in person and online) and articles and books related to nursing ethics, see the Resources section in the back of this book.

The American Nurses Association, the Canadian Nurses Association, and the International Council of Nurses have all written ethical standards and guidelines for nurses. Although the wording may be different in each, the fun-damental principles are the same. It is important to read this information and discuss it with your peers, supervisors, and colleagues.

Resources

The American Nurses Association's Code of Ethics for Nurses with Interpretive Statements can be found at www.nursingworld.org.

Find the Canadian Nurses Association Code of Ethics by going to www
.cna-nurses.ca and clicking on "Code of Ethics."

The International Council of Nurses (ICN) has also developed a Code of Ethics
for Nurses. You can find it at http://www.icn.ch/icncode.pdf.

ADVOCATING FOR NURSING

While nurses are patient advocates first and foremost, nurses must also constantly advocate for themselves and their profession. This includes looking for
ways to validate the vital role we play in health care, learning to articulate what
we do, standing up for ourselves, joining and getting active in professional associations, developing media savvy, having nursing representation on various
interdepartmental committees (including the board of directors) in the hospital
and other health-care settings, and being visible and active in our community.
Unless consumers, politicians, health-care administrators, regulatory agents,
and the media understand the vital role that nurses play and how they impact
care, money for nursing education, recruitment, retention, and staffing levels
will continue to be cut.

A wonderful resource on this topic is the classic book *From Silence to Voice:
What Nurses Know and Must Communicate to the Public* by Bernice Buresh and
Suzanne Gordon. It is a must read for all nurses. Another excellent resource is
The Truth About Nursing (www.truthaboutnursing.org). This non-profit organization is dedicated to promoting a positive image of nursing in the media
and beyond and increasing public awareness of the central role nurses play in
modern health care.

CHAPTER 11

CAREER CONUNDRUMS

In chapter 1 I discussed how to find your first job right out of school. But things don't always go so smoothly in those first few years. What if you don't get an opportunity to build that foundation right away? What if you can't land your dream job right away? It happens—more often than you would imagine. Here are some common questions and career challenges that new nurses face along with practical strategies for getting your career on track.

WHY CAN'T I FIND A JOB?

There has been much written about the current nursing shortage, which is predicted to be long-lasting and severe. Yet, in a few parts of the United States and Canada, new graduates are having difficulty finding work. So what's up with that? There are several factors involved.

The projected nurse shortage stems in part from the fact that the current nursing workforce is aging. The common fear is that there will be mass retirements and insufficient replacements. However, retirement is being redefined in our society, and many nurses are opting to not totally disengage from the workforce. That means that many "older" nurses are continuing to work well into their sixties and seventies, thus delaying retirement. Some do it for financial reasons, and others simply want to remain productive. Some nurses retire and then a year or more later decide to come back to nursing because they are bored or miss it.

Additionally, a large number of experienced nurses who have been out of the workforce raising families, tending to aging parents, or pursuing other interests are now returning to the workforce. There is nothing like a good nursing shortage to bring those nurses out of the woodwork and back into nursing. And, because everything seems to cost more these days, many nurses already in the workforce are picking up extra shifts and expanding their hours to boost their income. Some facilities, because of limited staffing, simply don't have the resources to take on new graduates and properly orient and precept them—they prefer to hire more-experienced nurses.

All of this has resulted in a shortage of openings for new graduate nurses in some parts of the United States and Canada. This trend is likely temporary and could reverse itself at any time, so there is no need to despair. However, those nurses in an affected geographic area may need to use different tactics to find jobs and to look in new directions for employment.

This same scenario—limited openings for new graduate nurses—happened in the 1990s for different reasons: Hospitals were downsizing and merging. The point is that, nursing shortage or not, the job market changes every few years. I've seen plenty of ups and downs in all the years I've been in the business, and the pattern will continue.

So what do you do if you can't find a job immediately upon graduation or if the job you find isn't the one you want? For starters, you may need to look beyond your local geographic area. Be sure to attend nursing career fairs in your area and in outlying areas, and attend local chapter meetings of professional associations and your state nurses association convention. Many prospective employers exhibit at these events. You'll have access to many of them in one place and can therefore maximize your chances of finding something suitable. Even if you don't find a position immediately, you'll be making valuable contacts that can turn into job leads and offers down the road.

If necessary, consider alternate care settings or specialties—even if on a temporary basis. I started out working in a psychiatric hospital because there were no openings in the emergency department (ED) I wanted to work in. I was always interested in psych, but it wasn't where I thought I'd end up. Even so,

I enjoyed the work and learned a lot in the six months I worked there until an opening came up in that ED.

If you can't find a job in your preferred area, consider long-term care, sub-acute care, rehab facilities, psych hospitals, cancer care centers, clinics, and even home care—providing they have a comprehensive new graduate program complete with extensive orientation and preceptorship for six months or more. And there is always public health nursing, assisted living, outpatient hemodialysis, and a variety of other outpatient options. There is more than one way to start your nursing career.

For example, if you're interested in pediatrics but can't find a job in an acute care hospital, look for positions in a pediatric rehabilitation facility, long-term-care facility, or other pediatric specialty facility. If you're interested in medical-surgical nursing but can't seem to land a hospital position, look for something in sub-acute or long term acute care (LTAC)—where the average patient's stay is a few weeks to several months and patients are eighteen years old and older. These patients are typically very ill and require complex care. The experience, even if it wasn't originally your first choice, could prove invaluable.

Long Term Acute Care

Long term acute care (LTAC) is a relatively new level of care designed for patients with a critical injury or illness who require intensive, twenty-four-hour attention for an extended period. LTACs differ from general acute care hospitals, which focus on stabilizing a patient's medical condition and are geared to short-term stays. And while nursing homes provide long-term care, they are not equipped to provide intensive medical care. Therefore, LTACs fill the gap by providing both critical care and therapy services to patients with medically complex conditions for long periods.

It's better to secure some work as a licensed nurse than to remain unemployed for any length of time. In any of the above-mentioned specialties and settings, you'll be learning new skills, acquiring new knowledge, building your confidence, and making great contacts.

Also keep in mind that even if jobs for new graduates are scarce in your area, recruiters and managers are willing to take a chance on someone who very favorably impresses them with their demeanor, personality, and poise. So don't stop trying to get the attention of decision-makers in a facility where you'd ideally like to work. Keep showing up at their open house and recruitment events, stop by and say hi to them at career fairs and conventions, and drop them a handwritten note every month along with your business card to stay in touch and proclaim your continued interest in working there. A monthly phone call or voice message is a good idea, too. Persistence and determination will always win out in the end.

Some Other Common Scenarios and How to Work Through Them

A. You graduate from nursing school, but for whatever reason, you never take your licensure exam. Several months or years have passed, and you want to finish what you started. But you have forgotten a great deal and some things may have even changed since you graduated.

In this case, you should seriously consider taking a licensing exam review course. Not only do these courses review basics of nursing care and the related sciences, they administer sample tests and provide feedback, teach test-taking skills, and offer many other forms of support and coaching. The course will help to assure that you are at ease and well-prepared to pass the exam.

Once you pass your licensure exam, you may also want or need to take a nursing refresher course, especially if you have been out of school for more than a year. While you can enroll in some nursing refresher courses even if you don't have a nursing license, you cannot participate in the clinical experience portion without one.

It is also advisable to start volunteering somewhere health care–related, such as an inner-city clinic, a local blood bank, and so on, until you pass your licensing exam and find paid nursing work. This is a great way to hone old skills, learn new ones, and make valuable contacts. It will also give you some recent, relevant experience to put on your resume and to discuss on an interview. Staying idle plays havoc with your psyche and chips away at your confidence. The further away you get from your profession, the larger the fear and self-doubt loom. Stay connected in some way while you get your career on track.

Because you may not be eligible to join your state nurses association until you have a nursing license, at least get out to local chapter meetings as a guest. This is a good way to get reconnected to your profession, build a support system, and find role models and mentors. Besides, networking is well known to be a great way to find and get a good job.

Tip: On an interview, you will be asked to account for the time between finishing nursing school and licensure or between finishing school and your first job search. You don't need to get into specifics, but you would do well to say something such as "I had some personal issues that required my attention. Thus the delay in my start. Those issues are resolved and I am eager to launch my nursing career and can't think of a better place to do it than [name of facility you are applying to]."

> *B. You graduated from nursing school, passed the exam, and for whatever reason never worked in nursing. More than one year has passed (maybe even several), and you want to finally start your nursing career. Where do you go from here?*

Some facilities will allow nurses to start in new graduate orientation programs if they have graduated within the last two years. Some will only consider those who have graduated within the last year. That means that you may not be viewed as a new graduate and may not be accepted into a new graduate orientation program even though you have no experience after nursing school. This also applies to scenario A (above).

In this case, a traditional nursing refresher course would be in order to get up to date with information, skills, and practice standards. Look for a comprehensive course that offers both classroom and clinical experience.

Tip: Same as scenario A.

> **Staying on Top**
>
> To locate nursing refresher courses in your area, contact your state board of nursing, state or provincial nurses association, or state hospital association. You can also do an Internet search for "RN (or LPN/LVN) refresher course in [your state]." In addition to traditional classroom-based refresher courses, there are several home study refresher programs available that include provisions for a precepted clinical experience in your local area. However, these are more appropriate for experienced nurses.

C. You have your nursing license but have job-hopped for the last year or more. Or perhaps you had one job for a short period of time and abruptly quit because you felt overwhelmed and stressed. Now you are afraid that your short work history is erratic and that you may even have burned some of your bridges. You don't see how anyone will ever hire you. You're not even sure if you should include all these short jobs on your resume.

Many new graduates get off to a rocky start in their careers for a variety of reasons. Some even take actions that they later regret, such as quitting without notice, not showing up during orientation and never returning, or quitting after a short period of employment. While these actions are not ideal and should be avoided if possible, it's not too late to get your career back on track and make a commitment to be successful.

If you recently and abruptly quit a job and regret doing so, consider contacting your former manager and apologizing for what happened. Explain that you felt overwhelmed and scared and didn't know what else to do. Admit that you should have spoken with him or her first and explained your situation, giving him or her the opportunity to help you. If it goes well, you can ask for your former manager to give you another chance with an assurance that you will commit to giving the job a real shot. It's possible that your manager will not take your call, will not be willing to talk to you, or will not be willing to rehire you. However, it's also possible that you'll repair some of the damage you did by abruptly quitting. You just may get a second chance in some cases. It can't hurt to try.

Tip: In moving forward, take steps to ensure that your next position is one you can stay with for at least one to two years and make a commitment to do so. That involves properly researching the employer and position (apply advice in chapter 1 about finding your first job), creating support systems, having realistic expectations, and taking steps to ensure your success as mentioned throughout the book. Reread earlier chapters of the book and make sure you are applying all of the principles and practices recommended.

As far as your resume is concerned, if you were at a job for a very short period of time (one to two months) or left during your orientation for any reason (this is usually considered a provisional employment period), you do not necessarily have to list the position. However, if you had a string of short jobs over the last year, you will have to show *something* on your resume or it will appear that you haven't worked at all. This situation may require the advice and guidance of a nursing career coach—both for resume development and job-seeking support.

Some colleges and schools have career centers and offer no-cost or low-cost services such as coaching and support. You can also contact your state nurses association for a referral to a nurse coach or do an Internet search for "RN Career Coach." And, because most coaches work with their clients by telephone, it is not necessary to find a coach who is geographically near you.

On an interview, when asked about your erratic work history, say something such as "I got off to a rocky start in my career. I felt overwhelmed and underprepared. I realize now that I was going through what every new grad goes through, but I didn't know it at the time. I have taken steps to build support systems for myself." If asked for examples, you can mention that you joined and are active in your state nurses association, that you are in touch with your nursing instructors and former classmates for support and perspective, and that you read this book! Conclude with, "I am now committed to staying put in my next position to allow myself to learn and grow into my new profession, and I am more determined than ever to make it work."

D. You have convinced yourself, after a short time in nursing, that this is not the profession for you. You feel overwhelmed, stressed, and disillusioned.

The truth is that most new graduates feel this way to some extent. And these feelings can be exaggerated if you are in a less than ideal work environment where you don't feel supported. Are you isolating yourself by not communicating with former instructors and classmates? Have you joined or become active in your professional associations? Have you taken steps to assimilate into your new unit and workplace?

Step back to gain some perspective. Perhaps the position itself and/or the employer are not the best place for you for a variety of reasons. Although it's not generally ideal to job-hop, sometimes a change is the right thing to do. Maybe your preceptor is stressed or indifferent and doesn't have time for you. In that case, you may need to have a heart-to-heart with your manager about finding a preceptor better-suited to you (as discussed in chapter 2).

Maybe you've started in a specialty that just doesn't resonate with you. Sometimes, a nurse knows he or she prefers working in ICU but has been told that a year or two in med-surg is the preferred way to go. Once there, you feel stifled. Or you might have accepted a position on an oncology unit because it was offered, but you find yourself getting depressed, focusing on death, and losing interest in other activities. In these situations, a change of venue might be the right thing to do.

Tip: Discuss the situation with a trusted friend, family member, former instructor, or some former classmates. Find out if the latter are experiencing something similar and what they suggest. Seek out a nursing career coach if necessary to help you keep your nursing career on track.

E. You believe you should get some hospital experience, but you are so scared and feel so insecure that you opt to work in a medical office, believing it will be less intimidating, slower paced, and an easier transition for you.

It is true that not every nurse is cut out to work in a hospital. Many nurses have happy and successful careers despite never having worked in a fast-paced hospital setting, but those nurses often choose another path because that was where their passion was from the start. For example, I recently met a new graduate nurse working in public health who told me he entered nursing school with the express intent of working in public health. That was his career path and choice, and he was doing well.

But I have also heard from many nurses who avoided working in a hospital because of fear and dread. Rather than face their fears and work through that novice phase of nursing, they went in another direction. I can't tell you how many nurses have written to me to tell me that they regret that decision. Many feel they are missing something and believe they have limited career opportunities without that hospital experience. That may or may not be true, but their perception of the situation is a strong influencer. It was also obvious that their confidence level as nurses had been adversely affected by their choice not to work at a hospital. Again, this is the case mostly with those who avoid the hospital out of fear.

Tip: Face your fears. The longer you delay working in a hospital, the more intimidated you will feel and the more difficult it will be to assimilate. Utilize all the strategies outlined in this book to get off to a good start, build support systems, and advance and grow in your new profession.

> *F. You plan to eventually work in a hospital but opt to start out in an alternate inpatient setting such as rehabilitation or sub-acute care because you believe it will be a good stepping-stone to acute care. But you are not sure that you will get good experience there, and you wonder how marketable you will be in a hospital setting in a year or more.*

A new nurse can get great experience and be very challenged in some alternate care settings, such as rehab, sub-acute care, and long term acute care. Patients in these settings generally require a great deal of specialized care and may even have tracheotomies and feeding tubes, be on respirators, and require special treatments. Taking care of these patients is by no means a walk in the park! It should also be noted that some nurses purposefully choose these specialties, remain there, and are very happy.

As previously mentioned, one concern with this route is that some alternate care facilities do not have the type of comprehensive new graduate orientation programs that most hospitals offer. However, this is improving in many places as new graduates seek out alternate work settings. And, as noted in an earlier chapter, if you are hired by a large health-care system, you may be placed in the general new graduate orientation program before starting in a specialty area.

One thing to keep in mind is that if you stay in an alternate setting for a year or more, you may no longer be eligible for new graduate orientation in the hospital if you missed out on it the first time around.

There is no hard-and-fast rule about how marketable you will be if you choose to pursue hospital employment later in your career—every employer is different. But if you demonstrate in your resume, in your cover letter, and during an interview the scope of your experience at your first place of employment and present yourself with professionalism, enthusiasm, and interest in your interviewer and his or her employer, you should be fine.

Tip: Thoroughly research each specialty and facility before accepting a job offer. Visit the employer's website, tour the facility (especially the unit you are considering), meet and speak with some of the staff if possible, and even shadow a nurse for part of a day if allowed. Visit the related professional association website to learn more about the specialty. Speak to other nurses currently working in that specialty—even those who work at other facilities. Find out what a typical day is like, what the nurses like most and least about the specialty, and what advice they can offer you about working in that specialty. If you're considering trying something new, why not rub elbows with those already experienced in that specialty?

> G. You are so fearful of taking care of multiple patients as a licensed
> nurse that you are considering working in ICU because you will "only"
> have to care for one or two patients there.

The nurse to patient ratio is much lower in ICU and other critical care areas because of the severity of the patient's illness or injury, the instability of his or her condition, the complexity of care, and the need for close and continuous monitoring. So, while it may sound "easier" to manage fewer patients, the level of acuity, the complexity of care, the speed and depth of service, and the high-level critical thinking skills involved make any critical care area a more-intense, faster-paced, and more-demanding place to work.

This does not mean that a new graduate nurse should not work in intensive care. Because while it is not right for every nurse (as discussed in a previous chapter), many new grads successfully start in critical care areas and build an entire career around that specialty. Just know and understand what you are getting into.

Tip: Same as for scenario F (above).

> *H. You have a disability that includes some limitations or restrictions. You wonder if anyone will hire you and if you need to explain your disability.*

There are more nurses who have disabilities than you might imagine. They work in every conceivable setting, traditional and non-traditional. When interviewing, or in any pre-employment situation, you are not required to mention any illness or disability unless your employer will need to make special accommodation for you. Also, there are adaptive devices available for many physical challenges. Visit the website www.exceptionalnurse.com, which is specifically for nursing students and nurses with disabilities.

Tip: Focus on your abilities and not on your disabilities. Wow any prospective employer with your personality, enthusiasm, and eagerness to work with him or her.

> *I. You have a tattoo (or tattoos) and/or piercings and wonder if either will affect your ability to get hired in health care.*

Body art is very popular these days, and many nurses and students have tattoos and piercings or are considering getting them. Here's what you need to know: Most health-care employers have dress codes that usually include a clause about tattoos and piercings. Many health-care facilities do not permit any visible tattoos. That means if you have one (or more) on your arm, you'll always have to wear long sleeves to work. If you have one on your neck, that can get a little tricky. If it's covered up, it's not a problem. One exception to these rules might be cultural tattoos such as forehead dots.

Visible piercings are also prohibited by most health-care employers, with some exceptions. For example, you may have multiple ear piercings, but you will only be allowed to wear one or two earrings in each ear. If you have lip, eyebrow, cheek, tongue, or nose piercings, you will likely be required to wear clear retainers in the piercings during work hours.

Tip: On any job interviews or while attending career fairs and recruitment events, cover up your tattoos and make visible piercings less obvious with clear retainers. Many employers find them a turn-off and do not believe they fit in with a certain image they wish to uphold for their employees and facility. When in doubt, dress conservatively.

SERIOUS CHALLENGES

In this chapter and in chapter 6, I have already listed common challenges that can hinder any aspiring nurse. However, in rare instances, a new nurse will encounter more serious hurdles that aren't quite as easy to surmount, such as paralyzing fear, work-related depression, staggering debt from student loans, and more. It's important to recognize that you are not the only one to experience these things and that there are solutions that will lead to positive outcomes. Here are some common challenges and ways to face them.

Avoiding That Which You Fear

As discussed throughout this book, a certain amount of fear comes with the territory when you're a new grad. It is always scary to do something for the first time—especially when you realize that you have people's lives and well-being in your hands. We all experience that fear, and most of us work through it with the support of others and the experience that comes with the passage of time.

But some new graduates employ avoidance as a way of coping with their fears and delaying the "experience" part of the equation—that is, avoiding doing certain procedures or treatments. And while avoidance may seem like a way to "buy some time" while you build up your nerve and your expertise, the truth is that some things can only be learned and mastered by actually doing them. Besides that, the problem with avoidance is that the longer you shy away from something, the more you begin to doubt yourself and the larger the fear looms. In my work with new graduates, I was surprised to learn that some new graduates had been practicing for one or more years in a hospital and had not attended or participated in a cardiopulmonary arrest response—not because the opportunity hadn't presented itself, but because the nurses avoided it out of fear and dread. Once you avoid something long enough, that fear can become paralyzing and require much more energy and time to confront than it would have had you confronted it early on.

"You can't be scared when you enter nursing. You have to jump in with two feet. It's not a job you can do halfway. You have to totally immerse yourself in it."

—Tom, nurse

So how can you move past this type of fear and avoidance once it has gotten out of control? Mark Twain said, "Do the thing you fear and the death of fear is certain." The sooner you actually do what you're afraid of, the sooner you'll be able to master the required skills and move forward. If your fear has gotten the better of you and you feel stuck, confide in a trusted friend, family member, or professional colleague. Talking about it helps you to face it, bring it out into the open, and commit to conquering it. Once you do something you dread doing, you'll find that it's rarely as bad as you had actually anticipated. And the more you do something, the better you get at it and the less anxious—and more comfortable—you become. The process takes time, but the only way to learn in this profession is by doing.

"You've got to work on your stress relief. I play sports and do a lot with my dog. Having a pet helps. I also spend time with family and friends when I can. But sometimes that isn't enough. Sharing common experiences with my nursing friends is the best thing."

—Justine, new nurse

Losing Your First Patient

Each of us remembers the first patient we had who died on our watch. It is always an emotional experience. But while you are a student, you are still under the watchful eye and protective wing of your instructor, who is sympathetic and helps you to cope with the experience. Once you become a nurse and lose your first patient, the experience can be particularly jarring. You are confronted with the fragility of life, the finality of death, your own mortality, and the realization that you can't save everyone—even those who are young. You must cope with the grief of the family members and your own grief.

And, while dealing with death is part of being a nurse, the first time a patient in your care dies after you become a licensed provider can cause you to feel very lonely and sad and disconcerted. You might experience guilt and self-doubt and wonder if you're really cut out for all this.

So what's a new nurse to do? Don't bury the feelings or expect them to simply go away. Cry if you need to in a private place when time and circumstances allow. Talk to a supportive friend, family member, or colleague. Write about it in your journal, and reaffirm your motives to become a great nurse and to make a difference in every phase of a patient's life and in the lives of his or her loved ones.

"As a new grad, you are so afraid of the 'what ifs': What if my patient dies? What if my patient has a cardiac arrest? What if this happens, what if that happens? But each new experience answers some of the what ifs, and it gets easier."

—Justine, new nurse

Even experienced nurses grieve and cry. When I worked in the emergency room years ago, I got very good at delaying my grief until I was home after work or when I could go to a private room on my break. There were also the occasions when I got teary eyed and even cried with a patient or family members—but in such a way that I could maintain control of the situation and keep the therapeutic relationship intact. But as you gain experience as a nurse and you begin to realize what a unique opportunity you have to help people cope with death and dying, you learn to utilize empathy and compassion for those you work with. In fact, as I get older and more experienced, I realize that helping people who are working through death and dying issues, whether caring for them physically or providing emotional and spiritual support, is one of my most important roles as a nurse.

Dealing with Lingering Financial Debt

Many nurses go into debt to finance their education. However, if you are one of those nurses, you have some options. Check out the Nursing Education Loan

"I was caring for a child who was dying. The decision was made to send the child to hospice. I felt absolutely lost. I didn't know what to say to the family. I had to keep telling myself that it wasn't my fault. I talked to my mom, who is a nurse, and she gave me some reassurance. My coworkers really supported me afterward. They made me feel better. I had a week where I didn't want to go back to work. I never wanted to go through that again. But I have learned that experience helps me to cope and makes me a better nurse."

—Justine, new nurse

Repayment Program (NELRP) at http://bhpr.hrsa.gov/nursing/loanrepay.htm. NELRP is a competitive program that repays a certain percentage of the qualifying loan balance of registered nurses selected for funding in exchange for two years of service at a critical shortage facility. Participants may be eligible to work a third year and receive an additional percentage of the qualifying loan balance. If you can be flexible with your place of residence, it is worth looking into. And who knows—there may be work opportunities not far from where you live now. This program can also be used to finance graduate school loan repayment. It is available to RNs only.

There are also some health-care facilities that will pay off part of your debt in exchange for a guaranteed number of years of service. This works well for some nurses. However, once you make such a commitment, even with the NELRP, you may have a limited choice of specialties and even facilities in a multi-facility system. And if you find that you don't like your job or your employer, you have little recourse to make a change. But it is still worth it for many nurses—just be sure to get all the facts before making a commitment.

How do you find facilities in your area that will pay off some of your debt? Start asking around. Call local health-care facilities (ask to speak with the nurse recruiter or someone in human resources) and attend career fairs and nursing conventions, where you should speak with employers. Also, check with your state nurses association and state hospital association for any special programs in your area.

For those who have not yet entered nursing school or still have a year or more to go, there is plenty of scholarship money available to finance at least part of your education. And some awards even include living expenses. Find out about nursing scholarships at www.discovernursing.com and in the reference section of your public library by asking the librarian to help you find books on available scholarships. A simple Internet search for "nursing scholarships" will also turn up many options.

To Pay or Not to Pay

When deciding whether or not to pursue higher education after completing your nursing program, keep in mind that student loan repayment starts as soon as you are no longer enrolled in school. You can defer payments by continuing your education immediately.

THE ULTIMATE CHALLENGE: TAKING, AND PASSING, YOUR LICENSURE EXAM

Every student and new graduate nurse dreads taking his or her licensure exam— the National Council Licensure Exam (NCLEX-RN and NCLEX-LPN) in the United States and the Certified Registered Nurse Exam (CRNE) in Canada. Yet it is a vital step toward becoming a professional nurse. An important thing to know is that this exam is designed to test basic nursing knowledge, so there are no trick questions. If you got through nursing school, you should have an adequate knowledge base to pass the exam.

Give Me a Break!

There is no point in trying to cram before taking the exam. You can't squeeze several years of study into a few weeks. In fact, it has been shown that the sooner you take the exam after graduation, the better your results will be. The National Council on State Boards of Nursing (NCSBN) reports that the greater the lag time between graduation and taking the exam, the lower the passing rate. So while taking a few weeks off after graduation to catch your breath, relieve stress, and celebrate your accomplishments can be good, taking too long a break can work against you.

Some new grads delay taking the exam to take a vacation after graduation, to get a few months of experience under their belt with a temporary work permit, or to go through a formal review course. Others procrastinate out of fear. But as with any fear, the longer you avoid facing it, the worse the fear becomes and the more challenging it is to overcome.

Fortunately, in the United States, computer adaptive testing allows new graduates to take the test within thirty days of graduation (after qualifying) and complete it in two hours or less rather than the old two-day paper and pencil test many of us veterans took. In Canada, the test is offered three times a year, so be sure to sign up for the next available date. The bottom line is, get to it as soon as possible.

While basic nursing education is the best preparation for passing your licensure exam, using some review materials and learning about test-taking skills can make you feel more comfortable and better prepared on the big day. These review materials or classes are available through private test prep companies, books, online material, and CD-ROMs. Your school library probably has many of these resources.

What to Do if You Have a Disability and Need Accommodation

If you have a documented disability, you can request testing accommodations from your BON. The organization may require a letter from your health-care provider and the Disability Services office at your school. Contact your BON for further details.

What to Do if You Don't Pass

There are always a certain number of candidates who do not pass on the first try (or on subsequent tries). In some cases, it is a lack of preparation and focus. In many cases, it is panic, fear, self-doubt, or lack of sleep.

It can be embarrassing and demoralizing if this happens, but there is no need to despair. You persevered through nursing school and must persevere through this. Simply set your sights on your goal of becoming a professional nurse and move forward.

Contact some former nursing instructors whom you had or have a rapport with for support and advice. Listen to motivational materials and use the strategies for positive thinking outlined in chapter 7. Reaffirm your belief in yourself and your abilities.

Use visualization to imagine yourself gliding through the next exam. Spend quiet time meditating and using positive self-talk rather than studying up to the last minute. The latter will only increase your panic and stress level. You can prepare up to a point, but eventually you have to let go, find your focus, and stay centered. Write your name on a piece of paper several times with *RN* after it. Think it, feel it, and believe it.

CHAPTER 12

TRENDS AND OPPORTUNITIES

THE NURSING WORKFORCE

One of the most interesting and dramatic changes on the horizon is the evolution of the new nursing workforce. We're seeing a changing demographic and increasing diversity. Let's look at how this evolution is changing the face of nursing.

Second Career Nurses

While new graduates were once a mostly homogenous group of twenty-something females with limited life and work experience, today's new graduate is, on average, older and more worldly. He or she often has advanced degrees obtained before entering nursing and, in some cases, has extensive and varied work experience. Many come into nursing after another career or careers, including that of a homemaker or stay at home parent. The diversity of the new nursing workforce will only serve to strengthen the profession over time.

It appears that second career nurses, because of prior work and life experience, are more motivated and more satisfied in their work. This may be partly because they are better equipped to deal with stress and conflict on the job. And because second career nurses bring a new skill set to nursing from their prior occupation, they have an opportunity to advance the profession in new ways. These skills combine with related maturity, confidence, and assertiveness to help move nursing forward.

Some are concerned that because second career nurses are entering the profession later in life, their actual nursing careers will be shorter than that of traditional younger new graduates. However, the motivation and career satisfaction of second career nurses seem to balance out their shorter nursing careers and may even keep them in the clinical setting longer than their younger counterparts.

A few examples of the varied backgrounds of second career nurses follow.

Profiles of Second Career Nurses

Barbara had worked in the banking industry for ten years. Her bank was frequently lending money to hospitals and she was always intrigued with the health-care industry. After getting married and having two kids, she realized that she needed a change and definitely needed more flexibility in her life. She was also looking for something more meaningful and something more challenging than her current career.

After completing her nursing education, she took a job in a hospital ER. Because the corporate business culture can be very different from the health-care facility culture, I asked Barbara to describe the difference. She noted that her new industry, health care, was much more welcoming and family-friendly than her previous occupation. She felt that her new employer was more understanding of family obligations and responsibilities and definitely more flexible and accommodating to her scheduling needs. She also noted that every day in hospital nursing is a new day—more exciting than the next. "At the bank," she remarked, "every day is the same."

Barbara's advice to others considering nursing as a second career is to try to work at a hospital beforehand as an aide, a tech, or in another patient care position to see if it's right for you. "I couldn't have done this type of work when I was younger, but now it is perfect for me."

Tom was an electrician for ten years before enrolling in a nursing program. "I was fed up with my career. There was no more real growth for me, and that was discouraging. I had never even considered nursing, but my mother and sister-in-law, both nurses, recommended it to me.

"I started talking to other family members who were nurses, and I looked into some schools. Once I started the program, I still wasn't convinced this was right for me until I started clinicals. Then I knew I'd found what I was looking for."

Tom talked about the adjustment he had to make when he found himself in a completely different work environment. His previous environment was an almost totally male worksite where there was a lot of screaming and cursing and where people just blurted things out when they needed something or had a problem or when something went wrong. "Let's just say I had to modify my communication style," he chuckled.

He believes that being an "older" new nurse has its advantages and makes for an easier transition. "People respect you more because you're older. Also, I was a little more confident than maybe a very young new graduate nurse would be. I was less afraid to ask questions."

Scott came to nursing after thirty years in human resources. Upon turning fifty, he was reflecting on his life and realized he hadn't left a "footprint." "I said to myself, 'Yeah, I'd done a lot, but what can I do to make a difference?'"

He saw an ad in a newspaper for a nursing program and went to an "intro" session. After hearing about the nursing shortage and the shortage of instructors, he enrolled in an MS in Nursing Education program.

"'Wow' is an understatement to describe my impression of nursing. I always thought that doctors told nurses what to do but learned otherwise. A quote I once heard pretty much sums it up for me: 'Where else can you go every day and feel like a hero?' Every day, I know that I make a difference—even a small one—in a person's life."

Honey had a degree in music business, which she never got into. She was working as a well-paid pharmaceutical sales representative and was on the road to a management position. However, she didn't feel a sense of worth at the end of the day. She loved the medical field, but she didn't want to put in the time and money to become a physician. She had an acquaintance who was a Certified

Registered Nurse Anesthetist (CRNA) and decided that was what she wanted to do.

Honey quit her job, enrolled in nursing school, lived off scholarship money, and downscaled her life big time. She notes, "I had to swallow my pride to be a student again. My professors were used to teaching eighteen-year-olds, and I sometimes felt as if I was being treated like a child. It was a humbling experience—especially getting scolded. But I had a lot of motivation."

Honey's first nursing job was less than ideal.

> I had six weeks of orientation with a preceptor, but very few classes. I didn't know how much was usual, so I accepted the position. My preceptor was so busy that she couldn't always stop to show me how to do things. I'd ask, "Can I do that?" and she'd say, "No. We don't have time. You'll have to learn next time." She was on vacation for two of the six weeks, so I was handed off to another nurse each day, and she didn't know where I was with my training.

Honey observed that the general atmosphere in this particular unit was belittling and everyone seemed to have a chip on his or her shoulder. She attributes this to the fact that the staff was completely overwhelmed. There didn't seem to be any aides or float staff available to help. She frequently was met with eye rolling when she asked a question. Her head nurse once yelled at her in front of surgeons. She had never been spoken to that way as an adult.

The good news is that, while visiting a friend out of state, Honey decided to tour a local ICU just out of curiosity. When she saw that the facility had lots of support staff, a comprehensive orientation for new grads, and staff that appeared to be friendly and supportive, she put in an application on a whim and eventually relocated! While her original goal was to work in ICU for one year and then become a CRNA, three years later she is happy to continue as an ICU staff nurse. "I'm really enjoying being a nurse. I never realized how much I would love nursing until I got into it." As it turns out, even second career nurses have trouble finding the perfect job right off the bat. Sometimes, they have to work just as hard as traditional new grads to find the right nursing environment.

An Insider's View

Second career nurses agree on the following:

- You're more readily accepted because you're "older."
- People assume you are an experienced nurse, which can be both good and bad.
- There is more of a sense of urgency to catch up with higher education and career advancement.
- The life and work experience that you bring makes you a better nurse and increases your learning curve. It gives you a little more confidence than a new graduate and makes you less afraid to ask questions. It helps you to better relate to people's problems and be a little calmer, more patient, and understanding.
- There is more teamwork in nursing than in many other professions. There is less negative competition between individual people.
- There is much more longevity in nursing than in other occupations.
- Much nursing education and training is geared toward the younger, less-experienced learner. You will likely have to swallow your pride and go with the flow.
- You may have more work experience and a higher degree but less nursing experience and knowledge than your supervisor. That can be humbling, so just concentrate on what you need to learn in nursing.

Multicultural Nurses

In addition to second career nurses of both genders, we are seeing an increasingly diverse population of multicultural nurses. Many are coming to North America to work as nurses after having received their nursing education in other parts of the world. Others migrate to North America with the desire to complete their nursing education and then work here. And some are simply part of the already ethnically diverse population in North America who choose nursing as a career path.

Ethnic diversity in any work setting is a good thing. In nursing, differing religious, cultural, and ethnic backgrounds help to bring a broader perspective to the profession and make nursing more representative of the population it serves. It also leads to providing more culturally competent care. But the very differences that strengthen the group also bring challenges. These challenges exist among nurses as well as within the larger health-care community. Racism, prejudice, and stereotyping of all kinds exist in health care just as in the larger society.

You may encounter language barriers when working with nurses for whom English is a second language. Just because everyone on your unit is speaking English doesn't mean that they are using words, phrases, and expressions in the same way or that they interpret what is said in the same way. There are also differences in overall communication style. Some cultures are more direct than others. There are issues related to eye contact, personal space, and handshaking. But it goes beyond that to values, customs, how different ethnic groups deal with conflict, level of assertiveness, how nurses are regarded in their native country, and how health-care professionals in their native country relate to patients and one another.

Nurses are often educated on how to provide care for a culturally diverse patient population but rarely on how to work with and get along with a culturally diverse workforce. The goal is to achieve mutual respect and cooperation in the workplace and to develop a broader understanding of diverse cultures.

So what can one nurse do to achieve that? In chapter 3, I discussed how to get to know and get along with your coworkers. Review and practice those strategies. Because humans have a natural tendency to migrate toward people like themselves, step out of your comfort zone and make an effort to get to know someone from a culture or an ethnic background that is different from your own. Spend time with all of your coworkers—both on and off duty—when you can. Understanding others does not come from reading a few articles or taking a related course; it is something that develops over time.

"A smile helps to bridge the cultural divide."

—Donna, nurse

Some nursing units and health-care facilities now organize intercultural events to promote understanding and harmony. I recently attended a Nurses Week celebration at an inner city hospital where part of the ceremony included ethnic performances by nurses from different cultures (including the American nurses). It was beautiful and inspiring. Not only did it give each nurse an opportunity to express himself or herself culturally and showcase hidden talents, it also was a wonderful educational opportunity for most of us in the audience. This type of program serves to validate and honor diversity, to educate and enlighten those present, and to foster dialogue.

Age Diversity

Because nurses are working longer, in many cases beyond the formerly traditional retirement age of sixty-something, we have four distinct "generations" in the workforce. Lynne C. Lancaster and David Stillman, in their book *When Generations Collide,* identify these four groups as follows:

Traditionalists (born pre-1945): They are fiercely loyal, patriotic, and hard-working.

Baby boomers (1946–1964): They are idealistic, optimistic, and competitive. Boomers are often caregivers to both their children and aging parents.

Generation Xers (1965–1980): They are highly independent, skeptical, and entrepreneurial. Members of this group are tech-savvy.

Millennials or Generation Yers (1981–1999): They are globally aware, realistic, altruistic, and practical. Millennials used computers as toddlers.

Who's Next?

Generation Z is one term being used for those born anywhere from the mid- to late-1990s or in the year 2000 and beyond—depending on the source you use. Characteristics of this group are just starting to emerge, but one thing is for sure—Zers will be well connected via social media and mobile Internet devices.

There are working nurses ranging in age from twenty to eighty or older, each with varying life experiences, priorities, values, loyalties, talents, learning preferences, and lifestyles. To further complicate matters, because people are coming into nursing at every phase of their lives and careers, a fifty-year-old is just as likely to be a new nurse as he or she is to be a seasoned veteran.

Age diversity in nursing can be a huge advantage to individual nurses, so get to know your coworkers of all age groups, look for opportunities to work closely with each, and appreciate that everyone has something unique and interesting to offer—regardless of how long they have been in nursing. Focus on commonalities rather than differences. There is something to be learned from—and shared with—everyone you encounter.

Gender Diversity

Men continue to increase in numbers in nursing, but they have a long way to go to achieve gender equality. I spoke at length in chapter 9 about some of the unique challenges and stereotypes that men face in nursing. But those stereotypes will be defeated as men become more visible and continue to make their mark in nursing. Men already in nursing have a responsibility to be visible role models and to encourage other men of all ages to enter the profession. People want and need to see others like themselves when considering career options.

Each individual, regardless of age, ethnicity, gender, or experience level, brings something of value to the table. The ever-growing diversity of the nursing workforce will strengthen the profession on every level, and every nurse has an opportunity to be both student and teacher.

TRENDS IN NURSING

Effective career management depends on your long-term goals and setting your sights on the future. Of course, the future is uncertain, but staying abreast of nursing trends will help you make key decisions and excel in your career. Here are some key factors to consider as you look ahead.

Nursing Education

There is a national trend toward mandating advanced degrees for nurses. While associate degree nursing programs will likely be around for the foreseeable future (diploma schools are rapidly disappearing), there is a movement under way in some states to require that those who graduate after a certain calendar year with an associate's degree or diploma will be required to complete their BSN within ten years after graduation for continued licensure renewal. This is something that will likely be determined state by state and will not affect those already licensed before the resolution goes into effect.

As mentioned in chapter 3, this issue has nothing to do with who is the "better nurse." However, higher education for nurses is necessary if the profession is to remain competitive and if we as nurses are to stay on-par with other health-care professionals. For more on higher education, see chapter 8.

Advanced Practice

Advanced practice nurses, or APNs (Certified Nurse Midwives, Nurse Practitioners, Clinical Nurse Specialists, and Certified Registered Nurse Anesthetists), will take on a bigger role as primary care providers in an increasingly expanded health-care market. Some examples of new roles for nurse practitioners include primary care providers in the community setting (including retail-based health centers or so-called minute clinics), care providers in wellness clinics, and NPs as hospitalists. Hospitalists provide care for hospitalized patients only and do not maintain an outside practice. Additionally, more and more community-based nursing health centers are popping up to provide for the health-care needs of communities.

This certainly does not mean that every nurse should pursue advanced practice. It *does* mean that those who aspire to advanced parctice will have more and better opportunities in the future. More and more research shows that APNs provide quality, cost-effective care. And as our health-care delivery system continues to move toward universal access to health care, APNs will become more visible and more valued, and they will provide care on a broader scale.

Nurses as Businesspeople

Today, the "business" of health care is everyone's responsibility. That means that nurses in every practice setting need to be businesspeople as much as clinicians. This might involve learning how to manage people as well as budgets, reading profit and loss statements, understanding the basics of marketing and public relations (and how they relate to good patient care and the bottom line), and committing to customer service and quality improvement. Likewise, today's nurses need to be well-versed in liability prevention as it relates to them and their employers.

Additionally, every nurse needs to develop an understanding of the health-care reimbursement system and how it works. Why? Because both your documentation and quality of care, especially when it comes to the prevention of avoidable complications (bed sores, some infections, or injuries from a fall), have a direct impact on if and how much the facility gets paid for the care of patients. And that reimbursement is directly tied to every nurse's compensation.

Nursing Residencies

Nursing has become so complex and the acute care (hospital) environment so intense that there is a movement afoot to create and implement a one-year nurse residency program (NRP) similar to those that already exist for physicians. NRPs go beyond the typical new graduate orientation program, are more comprehensive in scope, and utilize a standardized curriculum. The purpose of these programs is to increase competency while decreasing turnover within the first year of nursing. Find out more about these programs as well as where some of them are currently being offered by going to www.aacn.nche.edu/education/nurseresidency.htm. Do an Internet search to locate other NRPs in your area.

There is also a national discussion about requiring a clinical internship after graduation before receiving full licensure. Kentucky already grants a provisional license to nurses after passing NCLEX and requires that they complete a 120-hour clinical internship within six months of receiving the provisional license before receiving full licensure. This movement is gaining momentum.

Your Financial Future

As previously mentioned, we're all living and working longer. So the likelihood of staying in exactly the same specialty, same department, same position, and same place of employment for your entire career is slim. The likelihood that change will be a part of your future is a good reason to create career goals and plans! "I'm too old to go back to school" or "I'm too old to whatever" excuses don't hold water anymore.

Each nurse must take responsibility for his or her financial future. Many companies, both in and out of health care, are eliminating pension plans. That's why 401(k) and matched savings accounts are a hugely valuable employee benefit. But beyond that, personal financial planning and retirement accounts are a necessity for every nurse.

THE HEALTH-CARE INDUSTRY AS A WHOLE

Hospitals are not always an ideal setting for promoting health and wellness. While most hospitals deliver safe and effective care, there is still always the risk of infectious disease transmission, human errors of care providers, drug and blood transfusion reactions, and more. For these reasons, and the high cost of hospital care, care is continuously shifting out of the hospital and into the community, the home, and other alternative care settings.

The Aging Population

The aging population is placing increased demands on the health-care system. And although we're all living healthier, more active lives as we age, we know that the older we get, the more health-care services we require. Gerontology is now a highly specialized field for nurses and physicians and is growing in leaps and bounds. Likewise, alternative living facilities, such as assisted living and short-term rehabilitation facilities, are experiencing a surge.

The Educated Consumer

There was a time when health-care consumers put their complete faith and trust in their health-care providers and rarely asked questions. They were typically not involved in their treatment plan and knew very little about their own health condition, medications, and so on.

With the advent of the Internet, cable television, and other easily accessible sources of information, that has all dramatically changed. Consumers have become very savvy about their health, their illnesses, and their options for the most current treatment.

Health-care consumers have also become smart shoppers when it comes to choosing a health-care provider or health-care facility. For example, before planned surgery, they may contact a facility and ask how many times the procedure has been done there in the last year and how many times their surgeon has done the procedure, to ensure that both have good experience. They may also inquire as to what the death and complication rate is for the procedure and what the overall infection rate in that facility is. This information will impact their decision on where to have the procedure done and by whom.

Additionally, consumers can access online the Health Care Report Card Compendium (www.talkingquality.ahrq.gov) created by the U.S. Department of Health & Human Services (Agency for Healthcare Research and Quality), which provides comparative information on the quality of health plans, hospitals, medical groups, individual physicians, nursing homes, and other providers of care.

Emphasis on Customer Service

Because health care has become so competitive and because well-informed consumers want to be as comfortable as possible when hospitalized, many hospitals are adopting a model inspired by the hotel industry. The words *hospital* and *hospitality*, the latter a word for the hotel industry, are almost identical, and now, many hospitals have patient rooms that look more like a room at the local Marriott than a traditional hospital room.

Likewise, food service has been dramatically upgraded in some facilities to offer patients and visitors more options and better-quality food. Many hospital lobbies look like elegant hotels—with water fountains and dramatic three-story atriums. Comfortable visitor lounges, coffee kiosks, valet parking, and Internet service have become the norm. All of this creates a more tranquil and less stressful environment for patients, visitors, and staff. Some facilities even offer concierge services (errand running and personal services) for patients and staff.

A comfortable, hospitable, and attractive hospital environment can positively influence a patient's decision to be admitted there and even impacts recruitment and retention of nursing staff. More important, it can positively influence a patient's recovery and the quality of care overall.

The Technological Explosion

Technology's role in health care is expanding at an unprecedented rate. With computerized record keeping and diagnostics, bedside computer terminals, remote monitoring of patients in the home care environment, robotics, and more, nurses will be required to learn and utilize technology like never before.

One of the biggest recent developments is the push to digitalize all patient records and drug prescriptions. This new technology has the potential to improve efficiency, accuracy, and effectiveness of health care, which translates into better care at a lower cost.

Scientific Advances

Advances in medical and nursing science, research, and practice are keeping people with chronic illnesses and disabilities alive longer. This means that there is a greater need for alternative levels and locations of care, such as long-term care, sub-acute care, rehabilitation, home care, assisted living, and more, for both children and adults. This has increased the demand for health-care services overall and has expanded opportunities for nurses at the staff, management, and administrative levels.

Health and Wellness Focus

While health care in the Western world was once focused largely on treating illness and disease, the major focus today is on prevention. For those with chronic illness, much emphasis is placed on maintaining stability of their condition to keep them out of crisis and out of the hospital and improving their overall quality of life.

Western medicine has embraced holistic practice and philosophy, and practitioners now often prescribe and recommend mind, body, and spirit treatment options such as acupuncture, therapeutic massage, Reiki, meditation, and more.

Consumers want it, many insurance companies are paying for it, and a growing body of scientific research is proving its efficacy. Holistic philosophy and methodology is something every nurse should incorporate into his or her practice through self-study and more formal education and training.

Universal Access to Care

Many people believe that access to health-care services should be a right, not a privilege only for those who can afford it. Regardless of your political beliefs, it is certain that we will see expanded government-funded health-care programs and services in the United States in the coming decades, which will create expanded opportunities for all nurses.

THE FUTURE OF NURSING—WHERE ARE WE GOING?

So what does the future look like for nursing? One thing is for certain: The landscape will constantly be changing. Therefore, every nurse must stay abreast of the issues and remain open to new ways of looking at and doing things. But how can you do that?

Join and get active in your professional nursing associations. This is your support system, your network, and your information pipeline. In addition to getting out to local chapter meetings and reading the related publications, get out occasionally to state and national conventions. Here you will be exposed to the most progressive and forward thinkers of the day. You will learn about national trends; hear the latest in research, knowledge, and practice issues; and expand your network.

Attend nursing career fairs and seminars on career-related topics. Participate in continuing education and immerse yourself in self-study. Continue your formal education and make the most of opportunities at your current place of employment. Volunteer in order to gain additional experience, make additional contacts, and expand your horizons. Always look forward.

I welcome you into a profession that has been my privilege and my pleasure to be a part of for well over thirty years: nursing, the best profession on the planet.

RESOURCES

United States Resources
National Nursing Organizations

American Nurses Association (ANA)
8515 Georgia Avenue
Suite 400
Silver Spring, MD 20910-3492
Telephone: 800.274.4ANA (4262);
301.628.5000
Fax: 301.628.5001
www.nursingworld.org

Federal Nurses Association (FedNA)
8515 Georgia Avenue
Suite 400
Silver Spring, MD 20910
Telephone: 301.628.5049
Fax: 301.628.5001
www.fedna.org

This organization is open to RNs who are members of an active component of the U.S. Army, Navy, Air Force, or uniformed U.S. Public Health Service.

National Council of State Boards of Nursing
111 East Wacker Drive, Suite 2900
Chicago, Illinois 60601-4277
Telephone: 312.525.3600
Fax: 312.279.1032
Toll-free service for testing is
866.293.9600
www.ncsbn.org

National Federation of Licensed Practical Nurses
605 Poole Drive
Garner, NC 27529
Telephone: 800.948.2511 or
919.779.0046
Fax: 919.779.5642
www.nflpn.org

National League for Nursing
61 Broadway, 33rd floor
New York, NY 10006
Telephone: 800.669.1656 or
212.363.5555
Fax: 212.812.0393
www.nln.org

National Student Nurses Association
45 Main Street, Suite 606
Brooklyn, NY 11201
Telephone: 718.210.0705
Fax: 718.797.1186
www.nsna.org

Specialty Nursing Associations

Academy of Medical-Surgical Nurses
E. Holly Ave., Box 56
Pitman, NJ 08071
Telephone: 866.877.2676
www.medsurgnurse.org

American Academy of Ambulatory Care Nursing
E. Holly Ave., Box 56
Pitman, NJ 08071-0056
Telephone: 800.262.6877
www.aaacn.org

American Association of Critical-Care Nurses
101 Columbia
Aliso Viejo, CA 92656-4109
Telephone: 800.899.2226 or
949.362.2050
Fax: 949.362.2020
www.aacn.org

American Association of Neuroscience Nurses
4700 W. Lake Ave.
Glenview, IL 60025
Telephone: 888.557.2266 (U.S. only)
or 847.375.4733
Fax: 847.375.6430
Int'l Fax: 732.460.7313
www.aann.org

American Association of Occupational Health Nurses
7794 Grow Drive
Pensacola, FL 32514
Telephone: 800.241.8014 or
800.474.6963
Fax: 850.484.8762
www.aaohn.org

American Academy of Spinal Cord
Injury Professionals
801 18th St. NW
Washington, D.C. 20006
Telephone: 202.416.7704
Fax: 202.416.7641
www.ascipro.org

American Holistic Nurses Association
323 N. San Francisco St., Suite 201
Flagstaff, AZ 86001
Telephone: 800.278.2462 or
928.526.2196
Fax: 928.526.2752
www.ahna.org

American Nephrology Nurses'
Association
E. Holly Ave., Box 56
Pitman, NJ 08071-0056
Telephone: 888.600.2662 or
856.256.2320
Fax: 856.589.7463
http://anna.inurse.com

American Psychiatric Nurses
Association
1555 Wilson Blvd., Suite 530
Arlington, VA 22209
Telephone: 866.243.2443 or
703.243.2443
Fax: 703.243.3390
www.apna.org

American Public Health Association
Nursing Section
800 I St. NW
Washington, D.C. 20001-3710
Telephone: 202.777.2742
Fax: 202.777.2534
www.apha.org

American Society for Pain Management
Nursing
P.O. Box 15473
Lenexa, KS 66285-5473
Telephone: 888.34ASPMN or
913.895.4606
Fax: 913.895.4652
www.aspmn.org

American Society of Ophthalmic
Registered Nurses
P.O. Box 193030
San Francisco, CA 94119-3030
Telephone: 415.561.8513
Fax: 415.561.8531
http://webeye.ophth.uiowa.edu/asorn

American Society of PeriAnesthesia
Nurses
90 Frontage Rd.
Cherry Hill, NJ 08034-1424
Telephone: 877.737.9696 or
856.616.9600
Fax: 856.616.9601
www.aspan.org

American Society of Plastic Surgical
Nurses
7794 Grow Drive
Pensacola, FL 32514
Telephone: 800.272.0136
Fax: 850.484.8762
www.aspsn.org

Association for Professionals in
Infection Control and Epidemiology
(APIC)
1275 K St. NW, Suite 1000
Washington, D.C. 20005-4006
Telephone: 202.789.1890
Fax: 202.789.1899
www.apic.org

Association for Radiologic & Imaging
Nursing
7794 Grow Drive
Pensacola, FL 32514
Telephone: 866.486.2762
Fax: 850.484.8762
www.arinursing.org

Association of Camp Nurses
8630 Thorsonveien NE
Bemidji, MN 56601
Telephone: 218.586.2633
www.campnurse.org

Association of Nurses in AIDS Care
3538 Ridgewood Road
Akron, Ohio 44333-3122
Telephone: 800.260.6780 or
330.670.0101
Fax: 330.670.0109
www.anacnet.org

Association of Pediatric Hematology/
Oncology Nurses
4700 W. Lake Ave.
Glenview, IL 60025-1485
Telephone: 847.375.4724
Fax: 847.375.6478
www.aphon.org

Association of periOperative Registered
Nurses
2170 S. Parker Rd., Suite 400
Denver, CO 80231
Telephone: 800.755.2676 or
303.755.6304
Fax: 303.750.3212
www.aorn.org

Association of Rehabilitation Nurses
4700 W. Lake Ave.
Glenview, IL 60025-1485
Telephone: 800.229.7530 or
847.375.4710
Fax: 847.375.6481
www.rehabnurse.org

Association of Women's Health,
Obstetric and Neonatal Nurses
2000 L Street NW, Suite 740
Washington, D.C. 20036
Telephone: (U.S.) 800.673.8499
or 202.261.2400; (Canada)
800.245.0231
Fax: 202.728.0575
www.awhonn.org

Case Management Society of America
6301 Ranch Drive
Little Rock, AR 72223
Telephone: 800.216.2672
Fax: 501.221.9068
www.cmsa.org

Dermatology Nurses' Association
15000 Commerce Parkway, Suite C
Mt. Laurel, NJ 08054
Telephone: 800.454.4362
www.dnanurse.org

Developmental Disabilities Nurses
Association
P.O. Box 536489
Orlando, FL 32853-6489
Telephone: 800.888.6733 or
407.835.0642
Fax: 407.426.7440
www.ddna.org

Emergency Nurses Association
915 Lee St.
Des Plaines, IL 60016-6569
Telephone: 800.900.9659
www.ena.org

Home Healthcare Nurses Association
P.O. Box 91486
Washington, DC 20090
Telephone: 202.547.7424
Fax: 202.547.3660
www.hhna.org

Hospice and Palliative Nurses
Association
One Penn Center West, Suite 229
Pittsburgh, PA 15276
Telephone: 412.787.9301
Fax: 412.787.9305
www.hpna.org

Infusion Nurses Society
315 Norwood Park South
Norwood, MA 02062
Telephone: 781.440.9408
Fax: 781.440.9409
www.ins1.org

International Nurses Society on
Addictions
P.O. Box 14846
Lenexa, KS 66285-4846
Telephone: 877.646.8672
Fax: 913.895.4652
www.intnsa.org

National Association of Bariatric Nurses
c/o East Carolina University College
of Nursing
2111 Health Sciences Building
Greenville, NC 27858-4353
Telephone: 252.744.6379
www.bariatricnurses.org

National Association of Neonatal
Nurses
4700 West Lake Ave.
Glenview, IL 60025
Telephone: 800.451.3795
www.nann.org

National Association of Orthopaedic
Nurses
401 N. Michigan Avenue, Suite 2200
Chicago, IL 60611
Telephone: 800.289.NAON (6266)
Fax: 312.527.6658
www.orthonurse.org

National Association of School Nurses
8484 Georgia Avenue, Suite 420
Silver Spring, MD 20910
Telephone: 866.627.6767 or
240.821.1130
Fax: 301.585.1791
www.nasn.org

National Gerontological Nursing
Association
7794 Grow Drive
Pensacola, FL 32514
Telephone: 800.723.0560
Fax: 850.484.8762
www.ngna.org

Nurses Organization of Veterans Affairs
(NOVA)
47595 Watkins Island Square
Sterling, VA 20165
Telephone: 703.444.5587
Fax: 703.444.5597
www.vanurse.org

Oncology Nursing Society
125 Enterprise Drive
Pittsburgh, PA 15275
Telephone: 866.257.4ONS;
412.859.6100
Fax: 877.369.5497 or 412.859.6162
www.ons.org

Respiratory Nursing Society
309 E. Lee Avenue
Vinton, VA 24179
www.respiratorynursingsociety.org

Society for Vascular Nursing
100 Cummings Center Suite 124A
Beverly, MA 01915
Telephone: 888.536.4SVN (4786) or
978.744.5005
Fax: 978.927.7872
www.svnnet.org

Society of Gastroenterology Nurses and
Associates
401 North Michigan Ave.
Chicago, IL 60611-4267
Telephone: 800.245.7462 or
312.321.5165
Fax: 312.673.6694
www.sgna.org

Society of Otorhinolaryngology and
Head-Neck Nurses
207 Downing Street
New Smyrna Beach, FL 32168
Telephone: 386.428.1695
Fax: 386.423.7566
www.sohnnurse.com

Society of Pediatric Nurses
7794 Grow Drive
Pensacola, FL 32514
Telephone: 800.723.2902 or
850.494.9467
Fax: 850.484.8762
www.pedsnurses.org

Society of Trauma Nurses
1020 Monarch Suite 300
Lexington, KY 40513
Telephone: 859.977.7442
Fax: 859.977.7441
www.traumanurses.org

Society of Urologic Nurses and
Associates
E. Holly Ave., Box 56
Pitman, NJ 08071-0056
Telephone: 888.827.7862
Fax: 856.589.7463
www.suna.org

Wound, Ostomy and Continence Nurses
Society
15000 Commerce Parkway, Suite C
Mt. Laurel, NJ 08054
Telephone: 888.224.WOCN (9626)
www.wocn.org

State Nurses Associations

Alabama State Nurses Association
360 North Hull St.
Montgomery, AL 36104
Telephone: 334.262.8321
Fax: 334.262.8578
www.alabamanurses.org

Alaska Nurses Association
3701 East Tudor Road, Suite 208
Anchorage, AK 99507
Telephone: 907.274.0827
Fax: 907.272.0292
www.aknurse.org

Arizona Nurses Association
1850 E. Southern Ave, Suite 1
Tempe, AZ 85282
Telephone: 480.831.0404
Fax: 480.839.4780
www.aznurse.org

Arkansas Nurses Association
1123 South University, Suite 1015
Little Rock, AR 72204
Telephone: 501.244.2363
Fax: 501.244.9903
www.arna.org

American Nurses Association California
1121 L St., Suite 409
Sacramento, CA 95814
Telephone: 916.447.0225
Fax: 916.442.4394
www.anacalifornia.org

Colorado Nurses Association
1221 South Clarkson Street, Suite 205
Denver, CO 80210
Telephone: 303.757.7483
Fax: 303.757.8833
www.nurses-co.org

Connecticut Nurses' Association
377 Research Parkway, Suite 2D
Meriden, CT 06450-7160
Telephone: 203.238.1207
Fax: 203.238.3437
www.ctnurses.org

Delaware Nurses Association
5586 Kirkwood Highway
Wilmington, DE 19808
Telephone: 800.381.0939 or
302.998.3141
Fax: 302.998.3143
www.denurses.org

District of Columbia Nurses Association
5100 Wisconsin Ave, NW, Suite 306
Washington, D.C. 20016
Telephone: 202.244.2705
Fax: 202.362.8285
www.dcna.org

Florida Nurses Association
P.O. Box 536985
Orlando, FL 32853-6985
Telephone: 407.896.3261
Fax: 407.896.9042
www.floridanurse.org

Georgia Nurses Association
3032 Briarcliff Road
Atlanta, GA 30329-2655
Telephone: 404.325.5536
Fax: 404.325.0407
www.georgianurses.org

Guam Nurses Association
P.O. Box CG
Hagatna, Guam 96932
Telephone: 671.477.6877
e-mail: guamnursesassociation@
yahoo.com

Hawaii Nurses' Association
677 Ala Moana Blvd., Suite 301
Honolulu, HI 96813
Telephone: 800-486-8550;
808.531.1628
Fax: 808.524.2760
www.hawaiinurses.org

Idaho Nurses Association
3525 Piedmont Road NE
Building Five, Suite 300
Atlanta, GA 30305
Telephone: 888.721.8904 or
404.760.2803
Fax: 404.240.0998
www.idahonurses.org

Illinois Nurses Association
105 West Adams St., Suite 2101
Chicago, IL 60603
Telephone: 312.419.2900
Fax: 312.419.2920
www.illinoisnurses.com

Indiana State Nurses Association
2915 North High School Rd.
Indianapolis, IN 46224
Telephone: 317.299.4575
Fax: 317.297.3525
www.indiananurses.org

Iowa Nurses Association
1501 42nd St., Suite 471
West Des Moines, IA 50266
Telephone: 515.225.0495
Fax: 515.225.2201
www.iowanurses.org

Kansas State Nurses Association
1109 SW Topeka Blvd.
Topeka, KS 66612
Telephone: 785.233.8638
Fax: 785.233.5222
www.nursingworld.org/snas/ks

Kentucky Nurses Association
1400 South First St.
P.O. Box 2616
Louisville, KY 40201-2616
Telephone: 800.348.5411 or
502.637.2546
Fax: 502.637.8236
www.kentucky-nurses.org

Louisiana State Nurses Association
5713 Superior Drive, Suite A-6
Baton Rouge, LA 70816
Telephone: 800.457.6378 or
225.201.0993
Fax: 225.201.0971
www.lsna.org

American Nurses Association Maine
647 U.S. Route 1, Suite 14, BMP
280
York, ME 03909
Telephone: 207.877.4022
www.anamaine.org

Maryland Nurses Association
21 Governor's Court, Suite 195
Baltimore, MD 21244
Telephone: 410.944.5800
Fax: 410.944.5802
www.marylandrn.org

Massachusetts Association of
Registered Nurses
P.O. Box 285
Milton, MA 02186
Telephone: 617.990.2856
www.marnonline.org

Michigan Nurses Association
2310 Jolly Oak Rd.
Okemos, MI 48864
Telephone: 517.349.5640
Fax: 517.349.5818
www.minurses.org

Minnesota Nurses Association
345 Randolph Avenue, #200
St. Paul, MN 55102
Telephone: 800.536.4662 or
651.414.2800
Fax: 651.695.7000
www.mnnurses.org

Mississippi Nurses Association
31 Woodgreen Place
Madison, MS 39110
Telephone: 601.898.0670
Fax: 601.898.0190
www.msnurses.org

Missouri Nurses' Association
1904 Bubba Lane
P.O. Box 105228
Jefferson City, MO 65110
Telephone: 888.662.MONA or
573.636.4623
Fax: 573.636.9576
www.missourinurses.org

Montana Nurses Association
20 Old Montana State Highway
Clancy, MT 59634
Telephone: 406.442.6710
Fax: 406.442.1841
www.mtnurses.org

Nebraska Nurses Association
P.O. Box 82086
Lincoln, NE 68501
Telephone: 402.475.3859
Fax: 402.475.3961
www.nebraskanurses.org

Nevada Nurses Association
P.O. Box 34660
Reno, NV 89533
Telephone: 775.747.2333
Fax: 775.201.9002
www.nvnurses.org

New Hampshire Nurses' Association
210 N. State St., Suite 1-A
Concord, NH 03301
Telephone: 603.225.3783
Fax: 603.228.6672
www.nhnurses.org

New Jersey State Nurses Association
1479 Pennington Rd.
Trenton, NJ 08618
Telephone: 609.883.5335
Fax: 609.883.5343
www.njsna.org

New Mexico Nurses Association
P.O. Box 29658
3018 Cielo Court, Suite C
Santa Fe, NM 87592-965
Telephone: 505.471.3324
Fax: 877.350.7499
www.nmna.org

New York State Nurses Association
11 Cornell Rd.
Latham, NY 12110
Telephone: 518.782.9400
Fax: 518.782.9530
www.nysna.org

North Carolina Nurses Association
P.O. Box 12025
Raleigh, NC 27605
Telephone: 919.821.4250
Fax: 919.829.5807
www.ncnurses.org

North Dakota Nurses Association
531 Airport Road, Suite D
Bismarck, ND 58504
Telephone: 701.223.1385
Fax: 701.223.0575
www.ndna.org

Ohio Nurses Association
4000 East Main St.
Columbus, OH 43213
Telephone: 614.237.5414
Fax: 614.237.6074
www.ohnurses.org

Oklahoma Nurses Association
6414 North Santa Fe, Suite A
Oklahoma City, OK 73116
Telephone: 405.840.3476
Fax: 405.840.3013
www.oklahomanurses.org

Oregon Nurses Association
18765 SW Boones Ferry Road, Suite
200
Tualatin, OR 97062
Telephone: 503.293.0011
Fax: 503.293.0013
www.oregonrn.org

Pennsylvania State Nurses Association
2578 Interstate Drive, Suite 101
Harrisburg, PA 17110
Telephone: 888.707.7762 or
717.657.1222
Fax: 717.657.3796
www.panurses.org

Rhode Island State Nurses Association
700 Butler Drive
Providence, RI 02906
Telephone: 401.331.5644
Fax: 401.331.5646
www.risnarn.org

South Carolina Nurses Association
1821 Gadsden St.
Columbia, SC 29201
Telephone: 803.252.4781
Fax: 803.779.3870
www.scnurses.org

South Dakota Nurses Association
P.O. Box 1015
Pierre, SD 57501
Telephone: 605.945.4265
Fax: 605.945.4265
www.sdnursesassociation.org

Tennessee Nurses Association
545 Mainstream Dr., Suite 405
Nashville, TN 37228-1296
Telephone: 615.254.0350
Fax: 615.254.0303
www.tnaonline.org

Texas Nurses Association
7600 Burnet Rd., Suite 440
Austin, TX 78757
Telephone: 512.452.0645
Fax: 512.452.0648
www.texasnurses.org

Utah Nurses Association
4505 South Wasatch Blvd., Suite 135
Salt Lake City, UT 84124
Telephone: 801.272.4510
Fax: 801.272.4322
www.utahnursesassociation.com

Vermont State Nurses' Association
100 Dorset Street, #13
South Burlington, VT 05403
Telephone: 802.651.8886
Fax: 802.651.8998
www.vsna-inc.org

Virgin Islands State Nurses Association
P.O. Box 3617
Christiansted, U.S. Virgin Islands
00822
Telephone: 340.713.0293
e-mail: heylie@viaccess.net

Virginia Nurses Association
7113 Three Chopt Rd., Suite 204
Richmond, VA 23226
Telephone: 804.282.1808
Fax: 804.282.4916
www.virginianurses.com

Washington State Nurses Association
575 Andover Park West, Suite 101
Seattle, WA 98188
Telephone: 206.575.7979
Fax: 206.575.1908
www.wsna.org

West Virginia Nurses Association
405 Capitol Street, Suite 600
Charleston, WV 25301
Telephone: 800.400.1226 or
304.342.1169
Fax: 304.414.3369
www.wvnurses.org

Wisconsin Nurses Association
6117 Monona Dr. #1
Monona, WI 53716
Telephone: 608.221.0383
Fax: 608.221.2788
www.wisconsinnurses.org

Wyoming Nurses Association
PMB 101
2816 Dogwood Ave.
Gillette, WY 82718
Telephone: 800.795.6381
www.wyonurse.org

Special Interest Groups

American Assembly for Men in Nursing
AAMN
P.O. Box 130220
Birmingham, AL 35213
Telephone: 205.956.0146
www.aamn.org

Asian American/Pacific Islander Nurses
Association
www.aapina.org
e-mail: info@aapina.org

National Alaska Native American
Indian Nurses Association
www.nanainanurses.org

National American Arab Nurses
Association
P.O. Box 43
Dearborn Heights, MI 48127
Telephone: 313.680.5049
www.n-aana.org

National Association of Hispanic
Nurses
1455 Pennsylvania Ave, NW, Suite
400
Washington, D.C. 20004
Telephone: 202.387.2477
Fax: 202.483.7183
www.thehispanicnurses.org

National Black Nurses Association
8630 Fenton St., Suite 330
Silver Spring, MD 20910-3803
Telephone: 800.575.6298 or
301.589.3200
Fax: 301.589.3223
www.nbna.org

Philippine Nurses Association of
America
www.mypnaa.org

*For other clinical, advanced practice,
and nontraditional specialties, see the
ANA and state association websites and
general nursing websites for resources.*

Canadian Resources
National Nursing Organizations

Aboriginal Nurses Association of Canada
56 Sparks Street, Suite 502
Ottawa, ON K1P 5A9
Telephone: 866.724.3049 or
613.724.4677
Fax: 613.724.4718
www.anac.on.ca

Canadian Nurses Association
50 Driveway
Ottawa, ON K2P 1E2
Telephone: 800.361.8404 or
613.237.2133
Fax: 613.237.3520
www.cna-nurses.ca

Canadian Nursing Students' Association
Fifth Avenue Court
99 Fifth Avenue, Suite 15
Ottawa, ON K1S 5K4
Telephone: 613.235.3150
www.cnsa.ca

Practical Nurses Canada
55 St. Clair Avenue West, Suite 255
Toronto, ON M4V 2Y7
Telephone: 866.454.5968 or
416.922.5968
Fax: 416.967.6320
www.pncanada.ca

Registered Psychiatric Nurses of Canada
www.rpnc.ca

Provincial/Territorial Nurses Associations

Association of Registered Nurses of Newfoundland and Labrador
55 Military Road
St. John's, NL A1C 2C5
Telephone: 709.753.6040
Fax: 709.753.4940
www.arnnl.nf.ca

Association of Registered Nurses of Prince Edward Island
53 Grafton Street
Charlottetown, PE C1A 1K8
Telephone: 902.368.3764
Fax: 902.628.1430
www.arnpei.ca

College and Association of Registered
Nurses of Alberta
11620168 St.
Edmonton, AB T5M 4A6
Telephone: 800.252.9392 or
780.451.0043
Fax: 780.452.3276
www.nurses.ab.ca

College of Registered Nurses
of British Columbia
2855 Arbutus St.
Vancouver, BC V6J 3Y8
Telephone: 604.736.7331
Fax: 604.738.2272
www.crnbc.ca

College of Registered Nurses
of Manitoba
890 Pembina Highway
Winnipeg, MB R3M 2M8
Telephone: 204.774.3477
Fax: 204.775.6052
www.crnm.mb.ca

College of Registered Nurses
of Nova Scotia
4005–7071 Bayers Road
Halifax, NS B3L 2C2
Telephone: 902.491.9744
Fax: 902.491.9510
www.crnns.ca

Nurses Association of New Brunswick
165 Regent St.
Fredericton, NB E3B 7B4
Telephone: 506.458.8731
Fax: 506.459.2838
www.nanb.nb.ca

Ordre des infirmières et infirmiers
du Québec
4200, boul. Dorchester Ouest
Westmount, QC H3Z 1V4
Telephone: 800.363.6048 (Québec
only) or 514.935.2501
Fax: 514.935.1799
www.oiiq.org

Registered Nurses Association of
Northwest Territories and Nunavut
Box 2757
Yellowknife, NT X1A 2R1
Telephone: 867.873.2745
Fax: 867.873.2336
www.rnantnu.ca

Registered Nurses' Association
of Ontario
158 Pearl Street
Toronto, ON M5H-1L3
Telephone: 800.268.7199 or
416.599.1925
Fax: 416.599.1926
www.rnao.org

Saskatchewan Registered Nurses'
Association
2066 Retallack St.
Regina, SK S4T 7X5
Telephone: 306.359.4200
Fax: 306.359.0257
www.srna.org

Yukon Registered Nurses Association
204-4133 4th Ave.
Whitehorse, YT Y1A 1H8
Telephone: 867.667.4062
Fax: 867.668.5123
www.yrna.ca

Specialty Associations

Association of Women's Health,
Obstetric, and Neonatal Nurses
780 Echo Drive
Ottawa, ON K1S 5R7
Telephone: 800.561.2416 (ext. 266)
or 613.730.4192 (ext. 266)
Fax: 613.730.4314
www.awhonncanada.org

Canadian Association for
Enterostomal Therapy
1720 ch Norway
Town of Mount Royal, QC H4P 1Y2
Telephone: 888.739.5072
Fax: 514.739.3035
www.caet.ca

Canadian Association for Rural
and Remote Nursing
www.carrn.com

Canadian Association of
Critical Care Nurses
P.O. Box 25322
London, ON N6B 6B1
Telephone: 866.477.9077 or
519.649.5284
Fax: 519.649.1458
www.caccn.ca

Canadian Association of
Hepatology Nurses
www.livernurses.org

Canadian Association of Nephrology
Nurses and Technologists
336 Yonge St., Suite 322
Barrie, ON L4N 4C8
Telephone: 877.720.2819 or
705.720.2819
Fax: 705.720.1451
www.cannt.ca

Canadian Association of Neuroscience
Nurses
www.cann.ca

Canadian Association of Nurses
in AIDS Care
P.O. Box 93
Pontypool, ON L0A 1K0
www.canac.org

Canadian Association of Nurses
in Oncology
375 West 5th Ave., Suite 201
Vancouver, BC V5Y 1J6
Telephone: 604.874.4322
Fax: 604.874.4378
www.cano-acio.org

Canadian Council of Cardiovascular
Nurses
774 Promenade Echo Drive
Ottawa, ON K1S 5N8
Telephone: 613.730.2573
Fax: 613.730.1116
www.cccn.ca

Canadian Federation of Mental Health
Nurses
1 Concorde Gate, Suite 109
Toronto, ON M3C 3N6
Telephone: 416.426.7029
Fax: 416.426.7280
www.cfmhn.ca

Canadian Gerontological Nursing
Association
375 West 5th Ave, Suite 201
Vancouver, BC V5Y 1J6
Telephone: 604.484.5698
Fax: 604.874.4378
www.cgna.net

Canadian Holistic Nurses Association
www.chna.ca

Canadian Occupational Health Nurses
Association
www.cohna-aciist.ca

Canadian Orthopaedic Nurses
Association
1515 Noël Lareau
Chambly, QC J3L 5M7
Telephone: 450.447.6535
www.cona-nurse.org

Canadian Respiratory Health
Professionals
c/o The Lung Association, National
Office
1750 Courtwood Cres., Suite 300
Ottawa, ON K2C 2B5
Telephone: 888.566.LUNG (5864)
or 613.569.6411 (ext. 270)
Fax: 613.569.8860
www.lung.ca/crhp-pcsr/home
-accueil_e.php

Canadian Society of Gastroenterology
Nurses and Associates
#224, 1540 Cornwall Road
Oakville, ON L6J 7W5
Telephone: 866.544.8794
www.csgna.com

Canadian Vascular Access Association
685 McCowan Road
P.O. Box 66572
Toronto, ON M1J 3N8
Telephone: 416.696.7761
Fax: 416.696.8437
www.cvaa.info

International Society of Nurses
in Cancer Care
375 West 5th Avenue, Suite 201
Vancouver, BC V5Y 1J6
Telephone: 604.630.5516
Fax: 604.874.4378
www.isncc.org

National Emergency Nurses Affiliation
www.nena.ca

Operating Room Nurses Association
of Canada
www.ornac.ca

Urology Nurses of Canada
www.unc.org

*There are many additional associations
for other clinical, advanced practice,
and nontraditional specialties. Please
check the CNA and provincial/
territorial association websites and
general nursing websites for additional
resources.*

International Nursing Associations

International Council of Nurses
3, Place Jean Marteau
1201 Geneva
Switzerland
Telephone: 41.22.908.01.00
Fax: 41.22.908.01.01
www.icn.ch

International Nurses Society
on Addictions
P.O. Box 14846
Lenexa, KS 66285-4846
Telephone: 877.6.INTNSA
(646.8672)
Fax: 913.895.4652
www.intnsa.org

International Society of Nurses
in Cancer Care
375 West 5th Avenue, Suite 201
Vancouver, BC V5Y 1J6
Telephone: 604.630.5516
Fax: 604.874.4378
www.isncc.org

Sigma Theta Tau International
550 W. North Street
Indianapolis, IN 46202
Telephone: (U.S. and Canada)
888.634.7575; (International)
1.317.634.8171
Fax: (International) 1.317.634.8188
www.nursingsociety.org

Additional Canadian Resources

Canadian Institute for Health
Information
http://secure.cihi.ca

Canadian Institutes of Health Research
160 Elgin Street, 9th Floor
Address Locator 4809A
Ottawa, ON, K1A 0W9
Telephone: 888.603.4178 or
613.941.2672
Fax: 613.954.1800
www.cihr.ca

Health Canada
*This site offers disease and drug
information along with Canadian
health information and resources.*
www.hc-sc.gc.ca

Nursing the Future
The Voice of the New Graduate
P.O. Box 22058 RPO Wildwood
Saskatoon, SK S7H 5P1
www.nursingthefuture.ca

Heart and Stroke Foundation of Canada
222 Queen St., Suite 1402
Ottawa, ON K1P 5V9
Telephone: 613.569.4361
Fax: 613.569.3278
www.heartandstroke.ca

Recommended Reading
A Daybook for Beginning Nurses,
by Donna Cardillo
Sigma Theta Tau International
*This book offers daily inspiration and
tips in journal form.*

From Novice to Expert,
by Patricia Benner
Addison-Wesley Publishing Co. Inc.
*This one's a classic. Look for it in a
college library.*

From Silence to Voice, 2nd Edition, by
Bernice Buresh and Suzanne Gordon
ILR Press
*This is an empowering book about how
nurses communicate who we are and
what we do, how we project an image,
and how we promote ourselves and our
profession.*

*Leave No Nurse Behind: Nurses
Working with disAbilities,*
by Donna Maheady
iUniverse, Inc.
*This book offers profiles and resources
related to nurses with disabilities.*

*Legal, Ethical, and Political Issues
in Nursing,* 2nd Edition,
by Tonia Dandry Aiken
F.A. Davis Company
*This book covers issues related
to nursing employment, ethics,
documentation, liability, lobbying,
consent, harassment, discrimination,
and more.*

The Success Principles,
by Jack Canfield and Janet Switzer
Harper Paperbacks
*This motivational work offers life
advice. It is a classic self-help book.*

*The ULTIMATE Career Guide for
Nurses: Practical Advice for Thriving
at Every Stage of Your Career,*
by Donna Cardillo
Gannett Healthcare Group
*This book offers comprehensive career
advice, tips for resume writing and
interviewing, and more. Additional
information is available at www.nurse.
com/ce/7250.*

Websites
www.allnurses.com
*This site offers international nursing
resources, news, discussion forums, and
great links.*

www.discovernursing.com
*This is Johnson & Johnson's site about
nursing. It includes nursing profiles,
scholarship information, and more.*

www.minoritynurse.com
*This site caters to minority nurses and
has an educational and a career focus.
It offers great scholarship resources,
articles, discussion forums, educational
links, and information.*

www.nurse.com
*This site has a career management
focus. It features articles, webinars,
advice columns, discussion forums,
online continuing education, career
profiles, and information on career
fairs, seminars, and job postings.*

www.nurse-power.net
*This is an empowerment site for nurses
and includes books by nurse authors,
nurse entrepreneurs, nursing website
links, a newsletter, Donna's blog, and
more.*

Listservs
NURSENET
This is an international discussion list on general nursing topics. Do an Internet search for "NurseNet" to find the current home page.

To subscribe, send an e-mail to listserv@listserv.arizona.edu. Text: subscribe NURSENET yourfirstname yourlastname.

Many specialty and special interest lists and groups exist. Do an Internet search for "Nursing listservs" to locate some that might interest you.

Magazines
American Journal of Nursing
Telephone: 800.627.0484
http://journals.lww.com/ajnonline/pages

Canadian Nurse
This is the official publication of the Canadian Nurses Association. Subscription to Canadian Nurse is a benefit of CNA membership.
Telephone: 800.361.8404
www.canadian-nurse.com

Nursing
Telephone: 800.638.3030
www.lww.com

Nursing Spectrum and *NurseWeek*
www.nurse.com
These journals have a career management focus and are free to RNs in certain areas.

Clinical Databases and Information

American Heart Association
7272 Greenville Ave.
Dallas, TX 75231
Telephone: 800.AHA.USA1
www.americanheart.org

Centers for Disease Control and Prevention
www.cdc.gov
This site offers information about health, body systems, diseases and disorders, prevention, and treatments.

CINAHL Databases
www.ebscohost.com/cinahl
With a paid subscription, this site gives you access to a nursing and medical journal database. It can also be accessed in some libraries.

eMedicine
http://emedicine.medscape.com
This site offers medical information to health-care providers and consumers.

Healthfinder.gov
www.healthfinder.gov
*This site offers health and medical
information, including prevention and
self-care. It features many links and
other resources.*

Institute for Safe Medication Practices
www.ismp.org
*This nonprofit organization is dedicated
to educating the health-care community
about safe medication practices.*

MedlinePlus
www.nlm.nih.gov/medlineplus/
*This site provides free information on
drugs, conditions, and diseases. It also
offers an online medical dictionary and
other resources.*

Medscape
www.medscape.com
*This site offers free access to drug and
clinical information and articles,
continuing education modules, a
newsletter, resources, and links. A no-fee
registration is required.*

The Merck Manual Online
*This online manual is loaded with
medical information about body
systems, diseases and disorders, and
treatment.*
www.merck.com/mmpe

National Institutes of Health
http://health.nih.gov
*This site offers information, resources,
and links to health hotlines, disease
databases, and specialty organizations
such as the American Diabetes
Association, National Multiple Sclerosis
Society, and many more.*

U.S. Department of Health and Human
Services
www.hhs.gov
*This division of the U.S. federal
government is concerned with
information about health, disease, and
essential human services.*

Additional Resources
"Career Alternatives for Nurses"® on
CD or DVD
*Available at Cardillo & Associates:
www.dcardillo.com or 800.801.5796.*
"Nursing—The Career for a
Lifetime"
*Download the free video at www.nsna
.org. by clicking on "Career Center."*
"A Nurse I Am"
*This is an inspirational and educational
DVD. It is available at www.
anurseiam.com.*
"Your Future in Nursing"
*This is an educational software
program. Download it for free at www
.discovernursing.com.*

INDEX

ABOUT THE AUTHOR

Donna Wilk Cardillo, RN, is the Career Guru for Nurses. She is president of Cardillo & Associates, Professional Development Seminars.

Today Donna heals with words as a keynote speaker, author, consultant, and columnist. Her career combines more than twenty-five years of clinical, managerial, and business experience. She has gained national recognition for her **Career Alternatives for Nurses**© seminar and home-study program, which explores nontraditional career opportunities for today's nurse. Donna is the country's foremost authority on this subject.

Donna has received numerous awards, including Business Woman of the Year in New Jersey; the Athena Award, a national leadership award for women; and has been designated a Diva in Nursing by the Institute for Nursing in New Jersey for outstanding achievements and excellence in practice.

Known as "Dear Donna" at *Nursing Spectrum* and *NurseWeek* magazines, Donna writes a monthly career column and doles out daily online career advice at nurse.com. She is the former Healthcare Careers Expert at Monster.com.

As an active member of the American Nurses Association, the National Speakers Association, the National Association of Women Business Owners, the New Jersey State Nurses Association, and the New Jersey League for Nursing, she has a diploma in nursing, a bachelor's degree in health-care management, and a master's degree in corporate and public communication. Visit her website at www.dcardillo.com.

Donna wants to hear from you—about your challenges, triumphs, accomplishments, and magic moments in nursing. She welcomes your e-mails and letters. Please contact her at:

CARDILLO & ASSOCIATES
P.O. BOX 15
SEA GIRT, NJ 08750
DONNA@DCARDILLO.COM